3rd Annual Meeting of the EPSRC Network on Vision and Language and the 1st Technical Meeting of the European Network on Integrating Vision and Language

(V&L Net 2014)

Held at COLING 2014

Dublin, Ireland
23 August 2014

ISBN: 978-1-63439-222-8

Printed from e-media with permission by:

Curran Associates, Inc.
57 Morehouse Lane
Red Hook, NY 12571

Some format issues inherent in the e-media version may also appear in this print version.

Printed by Curran Associates, Inc. (2014)

Association for Computational Linguistics
209 N. Eighth Street
Stroudsburg, Pennsylvania 18360

Phone: 1-570-476-8006
Fax: 1-570-476-0860

acl@aclweb.org

Additional copies of this publication are available from:

Curran Associates, Inc.
57 Morehouse Lane
Red Hook, NY 12571 USA
Phone: 845-758-0400
Fax: 845-758-2634
Email: curran@proceedings.com
Web: www.proceedings.com

Preface

The Workshop on Vision and Language 2014 (VL'14) took place in Dublin on 23rd July 2014, as part of COLING'14. It was the joint 3rd meeting of the EPSRC Network On Vision and Language and 1st technical meeting of the new European Network on Integrating Vision and Language which is funded as a European COST Action. The VL workshops have the general aims:

1. to provide a forum for reporting and discussing planned, ongoing and completed research that involves both language and vision; and
2. to enable NLP and computer vision researchers to meet, exchange ideas, expertise and technology, and form new research partnerships.

As funding for the V&L EPSRC Network (EP/H018557) ends and funding for the iV&L Net European COST Action (IC1307) starts, the focus of the VL workshops will shift onto integration and joint modelling of language and vision. iV&L Net will take over the organisation of annual VL workshops for the next four years as the flagship workshop of this new COST Action.

The call for papers for VL'14 was issued in May 2014 and elicited a good number of high-quality submissions, each of which was peer-reviewed by three members of the programme committee. The interest in the workshop from leading NLP and computer vision researchers and the quality of submissions was high, so we aimed to be as inclusive as possible within the practical constraints of the workshop. In the end we accepted 14 submissions as long papers, and eight as short papers.

The resulting workshop programme packed a lot of exciting content into one day. We were delighted to be able to include in the programme a keynote presentation by Alex Jaimes of Yahoo! Inc., an internationally leading vision researcher. Our technical programme combined seven oral papers, seven long poster papers and seven short poster papers. Some thematic clusters emerged: combined text and image processing (Nguyen et al., Sakaki et al., Jones et al., Zhang et al., HaCohen-Kerner et al.), image description, annotation and labelling (Elliott, Liparas et al., Wang et al., Jokinen and Wilcock), data set creation (Weiland et al., Le et al., McGuinness et al.), situated dialogue (Summers-Stay et al., Schütte et al.), video analysis (Bhat and Olszewska, Shrestha et al.), aids for visually impaired people (Safi et al., Belz and Bharath), and visual analysis supported by text/speech features (Anbarjafari and Aabloo). The programme also included a discussion session on future directions for the VL community and workshops, including plans for shared task competitions.

We would like to thank all the people who have contributed to the organisation and delivery of this workshop: the authors who submitted such high quality papers; the programme committee for their prompt and effective reviewing; our keynote speaker, Alex Jaimes; the COLING 2014 organising committee, especially the workshops chairs, Jennifer Foster, Dan Gildea, and Tim Baldwin; the participants in the workshop; and future readers of these proceedings for your shared interest in this exciting new area of research.

August 2014 *Anja Belz, Marie-Francine Moens and Alan F. Smeaton*

Organising Committee

Anja Belz, University of Brighton
Darren Cosker, University of Bath
Frank Keller, University of Edinburgh
Marie-Francine Moens, University of Leuven
Alan F. Smeaton, Dublin City University
William Smith, University of York

Program Committee:

Yannis Aloimonos, University of Maryland, US
Tamara Berg, Stony Brook, US
Desmond Elliot, University of Edinburgh, UK
Erkut Erdem, Hacettepe University, Turkey
Sergio Escalera, Autonomous University of Barcelona, Spain
Claire Gardent, CNRS/LORIA, France
Jordi Gonzales, Universita Autonoma de Barcelona, Spain
Lewis Griffin, UCL, UK
Julia Hockenmaier, University of Illinois, US
John Kelleher, Dublin Institute of Technology, Ireland
Brian Mac Namee, Dublin Institute of Technology, Ireland
Dimitrios Makris, Kingston University, UK
Margaret Mitchell, University of Aberdeen, UK
Ray Mooney, University of Texas at Austin, US
Lucia Specia, University of Sheffield, UK
Chris Town, University of Cambridge, UK
Isabel Trancoso, INESC-ID, Portugal
David Windridge, University of Surrey, UK

Invited Keynote Speaker:

Alex Jaimes, Yahoo! Inc.

Table of Contents

Conference Program

Saturday, 23 August, 2014

(09.00 - 09.15) Introduction and Welcome to Workshop

(09.15 - 10.30) Interaction

The Effect of Sensor Errors in Situated Human-Computer Dialogue
Niels Schütte, John Kelleher and Brian Mac Namee

Joint Navigation in Commander/Robot Teams: Dialog & Task Performance When Vision is Bandwidth-Limited
Douglas Summers-Stay, Taylor Cassidy and Clare Voss

TUHOI: Trento Universal Human Object Interaction Dataset
Dieu-Thu Le, Jasper Uijlings and Raffaella Bernardi

(10.30 - 11.00) Morning Coffee

(11.00 - 11.40) Invited Keynote Talk - Alex Jaimes, Yahoo ! Inc.

(11.40 - 12.30) Language Descriptors

Concept-oriented labelling of patent images based on Random Forests and proximity-driven generation of synthetic data
Dimitris Liparas, Anastasia Moumtzidou, Stefanos Vrochidis and Ioannis Kompatsiaris

Exploration of functional semantics of prepositions from corpora of descriptions of visual scenes
Simon Dobnik and John Kelleher

Saturday, 23 August, 2014 (continued)

(12.30 - 13.30) Lunch

(13.30 - 14.20) Visual Indexing

A Poodle or a Dog? Evaluating Automatic Image Annotation Using Human Descriptions at Different Levels of Granularity
Josiah Wang, Fei Yan, Ahmet Aker and Robert Gaizauskas

Key Event Detection in Video using ASR and Visual Data
Niraj Shrestha, Aparna N. Venkitasubramanian and Marie-Francine Moens

(14.20 - 15.00) Poster Boasters

(15.30 - 17.00) Long Poster Papers (Parallel session)

Twitter User Gender Inference Using Combined Analysis of Text and Image Processing
Shigeyuki Sakaki, Yasuhide Miura, Xiaojun Ma, Keigo Hattori and Tomoko Ohkuma

Semantic and geometric enrichment of 3D geo-spatial models with captioned photos and labelled illustrations
Chris Jones, Paul Rosin and Jonathan Slade

Weakly supervised construction of a repository of iconic images
Lydia Weiland, Wolfgang Effelsberg and Simone Paolo Ponzetto

Cross-media Cross-genre Information Ranking based on Multi-media Information Networks
Tongtao Zhang, Haibo Li, Hongzhao Huang, Heng Ji, Min-Hsuan Tsai, Shen-Fu Tsai and Thomas Huang

Speech-accompanying gestures in Russian: functions and verbal context
Yulia Nikolaeva

DALES: Automated Tool for Detection, Annotation, Labelling, and Segmentation of Multiple Objects in Multi-Camera Video Streams
Mohammad Bhat and Joanna Isabelle Olszewska

A Hybrid Segmentation of Web Pages for Vibro-Tactile Access on Touch-Screen Devices
Waseem SAFI, Fabrice Maurel, Jean-Marc Routoure, Pierre Beust and Gaël Dias

Saturday, 23 August, 2014 (continued)

Saturday, 23 August, 2014 (continued)

(17.00 - 17.30) Discussion and Closing

The Effect of Sensor Errors in Situated Human-Computer Dialogue

Niels Schuette
Dublin Institute of Technology
niels.schutte
@student.dit.ie

John Kelleher
Dublin Institute of Technology
john.d.kelleher
@dit.ie

Brian Mac Namee
Dublin Institute of Technology
brian.macnamee
@dit.ie

Abstract

Errors in perception are a problem for computer systems that use sensors to perceive the environment. If a computer system is engaged in dialogue with a human user, these problems in perception lead to problems in the dialogue. We present two experiments, one in which participants interact through dialogue with a robot with perfect perception to fulfil a simple task, and a second one in which the robot is affected by sensor errors and compare the resulting dialogues to determine whether the sensor problems have an impact on dialogue success.

1 Introduction

Computer systems that can engage in natural language dialogue with human users are known as **dialogue systems**. A special class of dialogue systems are **situated dialogue systems**, which are dialogue systems that operate in a spatial context. Situated dialogue systems are an active research topic (e.g. (Kelleher, 2006)). Recently opportunities for more practical applications of situated dialogue systems have arisen due to advances in the robustness of speech recognition and the increasing proliferation of mobile computer systems such as mobile phones or augmented reality glasses.

When a dialogue system operates in a situated context, it needs the ability to perceive the environment. Perception, such as computer vision, always has the potential of producing errors, such as failing to notice an object or misrecognizing an object. We are interested in the effect of perception-based errors on human-computer dialogue. If the human user and the system have shared view, false perception by the system will lead to a divergence between the user's understanding of the environment and the system's understanding. Such misunderstandings are frequent in human-human dialogue and human speakers use different strategies to establish a shared understanding or common ground (Clark and Schaefer, 1989). We investigated this problem in an earlier work based on a corpus of human dialogue (Schuette et al., 2012) and are currently moving toward the same problem in human-computer dialogue.

The problem of misunderstandings in human-computer dialogue has previously mostly been addressed under the aspect of problems arising from problems in speech recognition or language understanding (e.g. (Aberdeen and Ferro, 2003; Shin et al., 2002; López-Cózar et al., 2010)). The problem of producing referring expressions when it is not certain that the other participant shares the same perception and understanding of the scene has been addressed by (Horacek, 2005). More recently (Liu et al., 2012) performed a similar experiment in the context of human-human interaction. Their work was chiefly concerned with the generation of referring expressions.

We report on a work in progress in which we investigate the effect of sensor problems on human-computer dialogue using a dialogue system for a simulated robot. We describe two experiments we performed so far. Both experiments are based on a shared experimental platform. In the first experiment participants interact with a simulated robot using a text based dialogue interface to complete a series of tasks. In the second experiment the participants again interact with the robot, except this time errors are introduced into the robots perception. The goal of the second experiment is to investigate what effect

Proceedings of the 25th International Conference on Computational Linguistics, pages 1–8,
Dublin, Ireland, August 23-29 2014.

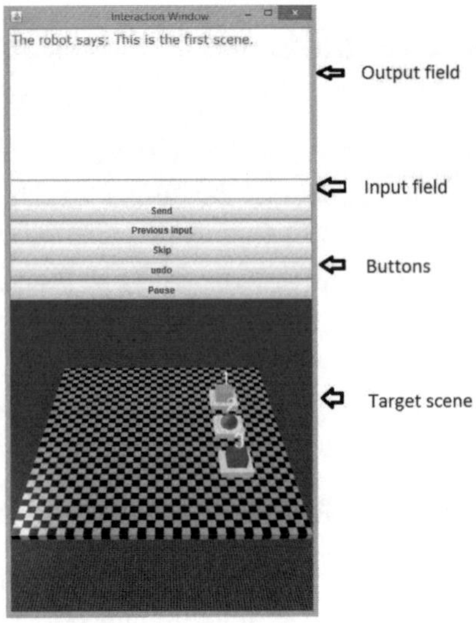

(a) The interaction window.

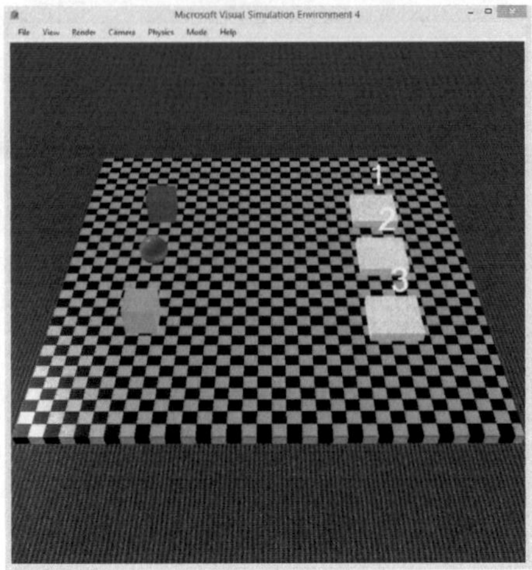

(b) The simulation view.

Figure 1: The user interface.

the presence of sensor errors has on the dialogue and the task performance and compare it to the results from the first experiment. It should be emphasized that the goal of the experiments is not to evaluate the performance of the dialogue system, but to investigate the effect of perception errors on the dialogues.

2 Experiment Methodology

The experiments were performed using an experiment system that was developed for this experiment. It consists of a simulated world and a dialogue system. The world contains a number of objects such as boxes and balls. These object can be manipulated by an abstract simulated robot arm. The dialogue system is a frame based dialogue system that uses the Stanford Parser (Klein and Manning, 2003) for parsing. The simulation environment was implement using Microsoft Robotics Studio. The system is capable of understanding and performing a range of simple to complicated spatial action instructions such as "Put the ball behind the red box" or "Pick up the red ball between the green box and the yellow box".

The participants interact with the system through the user interface shown in Figure 1. It consists of two elements. The **simulation window** shows a rendering of the simulation world that is updated in real time. The **interaction window** provides access to a text based chat interface that the participants use to interact with the simulated robot. When the participant sends a request to the system, the system analyses the input and attempts to perform it in the simulation world. If it can not perform the request, it replies through the user interface and explains its problem.

The robot's perception is provided by a simulated vision system. In general its perception is correct, but sensor errors can be introduced. For example, it can be specified that the robot perceives entire objects or some of their properties incorrectly.

Each run of the experiment consisted of a sequence of test scenes. Each scene consisted of a **start scene** and a **target scene**. The start scene determined how the objects in the simulation world were arranged at the beginning of the test scene. The target scene was presented to the participants as an image in the interaction window. The participants' task was to interact with the robot to recreate the target scene in the simulation world.

After a participant had successfully recreated the target scene, the system automatically advanced to the next scene. The participants were also offered the option to abandon a scene and go on to the next one if they thought they would not be able to complete the current scene.

All utterances by the participant and the system are transcribed and annotated with their semantic

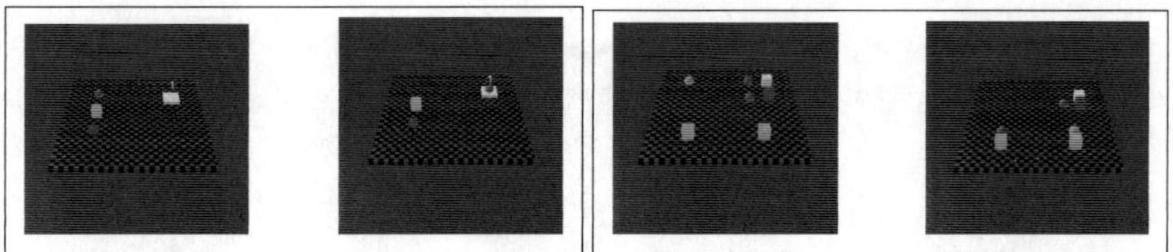

(a) Scene 1 (b) Target scene 1 (c) Scene 4 (d) Target scene 4

Figure 2: Two scenes from Experiment 1 and their target scenes.

interpretation. The system also logs metrics that are used in the evaluation of dialogue systems to describe the cost of a dialogue, such as the task completion rate, the number of utterances, the completion time and the number of errors (Walker et al., 1997).

In the following we describe two experiments we performed with this setup so far. In the first experiment participants completed a series of tasks. In the second experiment, participants also completed a series of tasks. In this iteration however, errors were introduced into the system's perception.

3 Experiment 1

The first experiment uses the basic version of the experiment system. The purpose of the experiment was to establish how difficult the basic experiment task would be and to create a set of performance measurements that could be used to compare this version of the system to later ones.

3.1 Instructions

The participants were provided with an instruction manual that described the experiment, introduced the user interface and provided example interactions. Participants were encouraged to abandon a scene if they felt that they would not be able to complete it. After reading the instructions, the participants were shown a video recording of some example interactions with the system. This was done to prime the participants towards using language and concepts that were covered by the system. No time limit was set for experiment.

3.2 Test Scenes

The set of test scenes contained 10 scenes in total. Figure 2 shows some of the start scenes together with their respective target scenes. Scene 1 (Figure 2a) is an example of a simple scene. Scene 4 (Figure 2c) is an example of a more complex scene.

The scenes were presented in fixed order. The two initial scenes contained simple tasks. Their main purpose is to allow the participants to gain practical experience with interacting with the system before approaching the actual test scenes. The remaining scenes were designed to elicit specific **referring expressions**. To transform a scene into its target scene, the participants had to move a number objects from their original location to their respective target location as specified in the target scene. To get the robot to move a target to a location, the participants had to specify which target the robot should move (e.g. "Take the red ball"), and specify where to move it (e.g. "Put it behind the green box on the left"). The complexity of the this task depends on the objects contained in the scene and their placement in relation to each other. We were particularly interested in getting the participants to use specific objects as **landmarks** in their referring expressions, and designed the scenes in such a way that participants were influenced towards specific expressions. This was done with the motive of using landmark objects as targets for perception errors in the second experiment. For each scene a set of target conditions was specified that determined when a scene was complete.

3.3 Participants

In total 11 participants participated in the experiment. Most of them were native English speakers or non-native speakers who had been speaking English for a number of years. Two of the participants were

(a) The start scene. (b) The target scene. (c) The start scene as perceived by the robot.

Figure 3: One of the scenes from Experiment 2.

female, the rest were male. The participants were between 20 and 50 years of age. All were college sciences graduates who worked with computers on a daily basis.

3.4 Results

In total 11 participants completed the experiments. This resulted in a total of 110 interactions, two of which had to be discarded due to recording problems. A summary of the recorded metrics for this experiment is given in Table 1. It shows for each scene:

- How many instructions the participants used on average to complete it.
- How long the participants needed to complete each scene on average.
- How many of the instructions the participants produced contained a reference that was either ambiguous (it could not be resolved to a unique referent) or unresolved (no referent that matched the referring expression was found).
- The final column show how often each scene was abandoned.

For the current investigation the last two columns are of primary interest. Participants had been instructed to abandon a scene if they thought that they would not be able to complete it. The fact that this only occurred three times in 108 interactions indicates that the task was not very difficult and that the dialogue system's performance was adequate for the task. The percentage of unresolved references in the second to last column is also interesting because it indicates how often participants made references that the system was not able to resolve. Since there were no errors introduced at this stage, the figures can be seen as a baseline for the system's ability to understand referring expressions.

4 Experiment 2

The main purpose of the second experiment was to investigate how the introduction of sensor errors would influence the interactions and the outcome.

4.1 Instructions

The participants were provided with an extended version of the instruction manual as well as the introduction video from the first experiment. The manual was identical to the manual from Experiment 1 except for a small section that was added to explain that errors could occur in some of the scenes. The participants were encouraged to either try to work around the errors or to abandon the scene if the thought they would not be able to finish it. Again, no time limit was set.

4.2 Test Scenes

The set of test scenes was based on the set of test scenes for Experiment 1, except that this time sensor errors were introduced. We investigated three possible error conditions. In the **missing object** condition, the perception system did not register an object at all. In the **colour misclassification**, the system did

Scene name	Average number of actions per scene	Average time per scene	Percentage of ambiguous or unresolved references	Number of times abandoned
Scene 1	2.9	00:00:56	0	0
Scene 2	2.3	00:00:54	0	0
Scene 3	8.7	00:01:45	2.1	0
Scene 4	5.9	00:01:52	10.8	0
Scene 5	2	00:00:28	0	0
Scene 6	5.2	00:01:23	5.2	1 (≈ 9%)
Scene 7	2.6	00:00:40	0	0
Scene 8	5.8	00:01:06	3.1	1 (≈ 9%)
Scene 9	5.3	00:01:12	8.4	0
Scene 10	6.8	00:01:30	6.7	1 (≈ 9%)
Average	5.1	00:01:14	6	0.3

Table 1: Summary of the cost metrics for Phase 1. Few scenes were abandoned. The percentage of unresolved references forms a baseline for the resolution performance of the system.

Scene name	Average number of actions per scene	Average time per scene	Percentage of ambiguous or unresolved references	Number of times abandoned
Scene 1	2.29	00:00:59	2.6	0 (0%)
Scene 2	3.29	00:00:56	3.6	2(≈ 11.8%)
Scene 3	9.12	00:02:13	9.7	3 (≈ 17.6%)
Scene 4	9.88	00:01:58	10.1	5 (≈ 29.4%)
Scene 5	10.35	00:01:46	9.7	2 (≈ 11.8%)
Scene 6	12.82	00:02:43	7.3	9 (≈ 52.9%)
Scene 7	4.82	00:01:08	14.6	2 (≈ 11.8%)
Scene 8	3.35	00:00:47	8.8	1 (≈ 5.9%)
Scene 9	9.88	00:01:34	9.5	4 (≈ 23.5%)
Scene 10	9.59	00:01:47	9.8	5 (≈ 29.4%)
Scene 11	10.82	00:02:08	5.4	3 (≈ 17.6%)
Scene 12	7	00:01:21	8.4	1 (≈ 5.9%)
Scene 13	6.65	00:01:29	8	2 (≈ 11.8%)
Scene 14	11.7	00:03:10	8.5	17 (100%)
Scene 15	5.18	00:01:02	15.9	1 (≈ 5.9%)
Scene 16	4.88	00:01:04	14.5	1 (≈ 5.9%)
Scene 17	6.82	00:01:01	1.7	0 (0%)
Scene 18	8.65	00:02:00	6.8	1 (≈ 5.9%)
Scene 19	9.4	00:01:45	7.8	0 (0%)
Scene 20	6	00:01:17	6.9	0 (0%)
Average	7.6	00:01:36	8.5	2.95
Average (scenes w/o errors)	6.1	00:01:20	4.9	0.5
Average (scenes w/ errors)	8.3	00:01:44	10	4

Table 2: Summary of the cost metrics for Phase 2. Scenes that contained no errors are highlighted in green. Compared to Table 1, scenes that contained errors were more often abandoned, and resolution problems were more frequent.

perceive the affected object but determined its colour incorrectly. A green ball for example, might be mistaken for a red ball. In the **type misclassification** condition, the system also perceives the object, but determines the object's type incorrectly, for example, a green ball might be mistaken for a green box. We restricted the errors so that at most one object was affected per scene. This was done to create scenes that contained errors, but would still be solvable in most cases without major communication breakdowns. The impact a sensor error has on the interaction greatly depends on which object it affects, the context the object appears in, and the role the object plays in the task. For example, if an object is affected that does not need to be moved and that is unlikely to be mentioned as a landmark, it is likely that the error will not be noticed by the participant, and have no influence on the dialogue at all. On the other hand, if an error affects an object that absolutely needs to be moved in order to complete the task in such a way that it becomes impossible to interact with the object (e.g. because the robot does not see the object at all), it becomes effectively impossible to complete the task. In less severe cases, errors may introduce problems that can be solved. For example, if the first attempt at a reference fails because a landmark is not available to the system, the participant may reformulate the expression with a different landmark. This highlights the fact that sensor errors can have different effects depending on the circumstances.

We therefore decided to design each scene and the errors for the second phase manually in order to make sure that examples for as many problem combinations as possible were presented to the participants. We based the design of the scenes on our experiences from Experiment 1. We selected suitable scenes and introduced errors such that the preferred expressions used in Experiment 1 would be affected. Each new scene created this way together with the original scene formed a **corresponding scene pairs**. Members of a pair can be compared against each other to assess the impact of errors in Experiment 2. The final set of scenes contained 14 scenes with sensor errors. We added four more scenes without errors to the test set. Their purpose was to complement the data from the first experiment, and to check if the presence of errors in other scenes would influence the behaviour of the participants in non-error scenes. We also added the two introductory scenes from the first experiment. They were always presented as the first scenes. The remaining scenes were presented in randomized order to prevent learning effects. Therefore each participant was presented with a set of 20 scenes. In total there were 22 corresponding scene pairs.

Figure 3 contains an example of a scene from the second experiment that contained a perception error. Figure 3a show the start scene as presented to the participant. Figure 3b shows the target scene that was presented to the participant. Figure 3c shows the start scene as it was perceived by the robot (it mistakes the green box for a ball).

Each scene was annotated with a set of target conditions and a set of sensor error specifications.

4.3 Participants

17 participants were recruited for the experiment from roughly the same demographic as the first experiment. About half of the participants had participated in the first experiment. A space of about 60 days was left between the first experiment and the second experiment to minimize any influence between the experiments.

4.4 Results

In total 17 participants completed the experiment. This results in a total of 340 interactions. Two interactions were lost, resulting in a set of 338 interactions. The results for this experiment are given in Table 2. The highlighted rows (Scene 1,2,17,18,19 and 20) refer to scenes in which no errors were introduced.

As in the first experiment, the two last columns are the most interesting ones. Overall it can be observed that more scenes were abandoned than in the first experiment. Every scene except for the ones without errors was abandoned at least once (Scene 14 was abandoned by all participants. This was expected because it was designed to be not completable due to the errors). This indicates that the task with the errors was more difficult than the one in the first experiment.

It also appears that unresolved or ambiguous references were more frequent than in the first experiment. At the bottom of the table we present overall averages for the different metrics. It appears that scenes with sensor errors generally show higher values than scenes without.

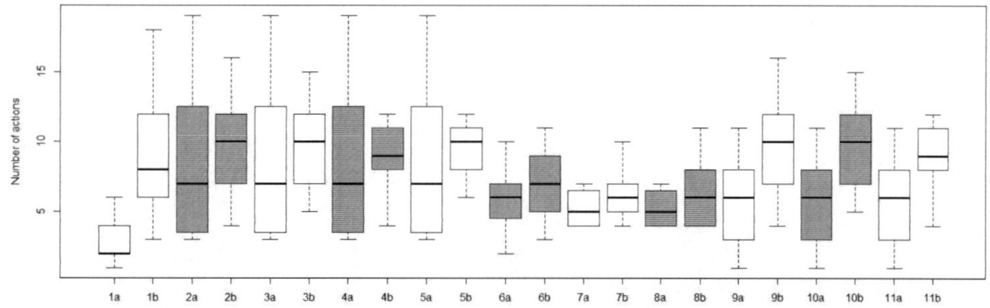

Figure 4: A boxplot comparing the number of actions between scenes from Experiment 1 and 2. Paired plots with the same colour refer to corresponding scenes (continued in Figure 5).

5 Discussion and Analysis

Overall the results indicate that the introduction of sensor errors increases the difficulty of the task. The results show that the participants had to abandon scenes with errors more often than scenes without errors. On average they used more actions to complete scenes with errors. A possible explanation can be found in the higher percentage of unresolved references. Participants attempted to refer to an object, but the system was unable to interpret it as expected due to a sensor error. This forced the participants to try a different expression to progress with the task. It should be noted that the number of unresolved and ambiguous references at the present does not account for references that were resolved to an object that was not the object intended by the speaker. We may approach this problem at a later stage.

Figure 4 and 5 visualize the distribution of the number of actions for all the corresponding scene pairs. They are numbered 1 to 22. Plots labelled with *a* correspond to scenes without errors, plots labelled with *b* to their counterparts with errors. For easier visual comprehension, we coloured pairs alternatingly in blue and white.

In general it can be observed that the median number of actions is generally higher for scenes with errors than for their non-error counterparts, and that the interquartile range also tends to be higher. The distributions appear to be fairly spread out. This suggests that there is considerable variation between participants. We performed t-tests between corresponding scenes to determine whether the differences between corresponding scenes were significant. The test shows that 12 out of 22 pairs were significantly different with a p-value below 0.05. We will investigate at a later stage how much the strength of the correspondence depends on the type of the error that was introduced.

A comparison of the distribution of the completion times was less conclusive. For some correspondence pairs, the median completion time is higher for error scenes, for other pairs it is lower. We conjecture that there is some sort of self-selection mechanism at work where participants who were less confident with the task in the first place task abandoned scenes earlier than confident participants when they encountered problems, but this will require further investigation.

To summarize: The presence of sensor errors appears to increase the difficulty of the task, although the effect appears to be small in some cases. This was in some way to be expected because the errors were designed to pose solvable problems and not lead to major communication breakdowns.

6 Future Work

The results from this experiment are still very fresh, and this paper represents the first step in their analysis. In the next step we are going to try to identify strategies the participants employed once they encountered an error and see how well they match up with the strategies we described for the human-human domain (Schuette et al., 2012). We are also interested in finding out how strategies evolved over the course of the experiment, and in how much variation there is between individual participants.

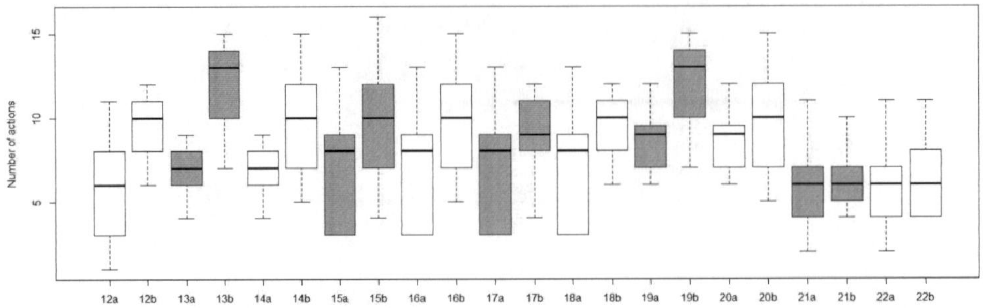

Figure 5: A boxplot comparing the number of actions between scenes from Experiment 1 and 2. Paired plots with the same colour refer to corresponding scenes (continued from Figure 5).

We are currently preparing a third experiment based on the experiment setup. In this experiment, the participants will be offered different ways of accessing the robot's understanding of what it sees to the participant. For example, in one condition, the system will be able to generate descriptions of how it perceives the scene. The results of this third experiment will be evaluated in the context of the first and second experiment.

References

John Aberdeen and Lisa Ferro. 2003. Dialogue patterns and misunderstandings. In *ISCA Tutorial and Research Workshop on Error Handling in Spoken Dialogue Systems.*

Herbert H. Clark and Edward F. Schaefer. 1989. Contributing to discourse. *Cognitive Science*, pages 259–294.

Helmut Horacek. 2005. Generating referential descriptions under conditions of uncertainty. In *Proceedings of the 10th European Workshop on Natural Language Generation (ENLG)*, pages 58–67. Citeseer.

J. D. Kelleher. 2006. Attention driven reference resolution in multimodal contexts. *Artificial Intelligence Review*, 25(1):2135.

Dan Klein and Christopher D. Manning. 2003. Accurate unlexicalized parsing. In *Proceedings of the 41st Annual Meeting on Association for Computational Linguistics-Volume 1*, page 423430. Association for Computational Linguistics.

Changsong Liu, Rui Fang, and Joyce Y. Chai. 2012. Towards mediating shared perceptual basis in situated dialogue. In *Proceedings of the 13th Annual Meeting of the Special Interest Group on Discourse and Dialogue*, page 140149. Association for Computational Linguistics.

Ramón López-Cózar, Zoraida Callejas, and David Griol. 2010. Using knowledge of misunderstandings to increase the robustness of spoken dialogue systems. *Knowledge-Based Systems*, 23(5):471–485, July.

Niels Schuette, John Kelleher, and Brian Mac Namee. 2012. A corpus based dialogue model for grounding in situated dialogue. In *Proceedings of the 1st Workshop on Machine Learning for Interactive Systems: Bridging the Gap Between Language, Motor Control and Vision (MLIS-2012).*, Montpellier, France, August.

Jongho Shin, Shrikanth S. Narayanan, Laurie Gerber, Abe Kazemzadeh, Dani Byrd, and others. 2002. Analysis of user behavior under error conditions in spoken dialogs. In *INTERSPEECH.*

Marilyn A. Walker, Diane J. Litman, Candace A. Kamm, and Alicia Abella. 1997. PARADISE: a framework for evaluating spoken dialogue agents. In *Proceedings of the eighth conference on European chapter of the Association for Computational Linguistics*, page 271280. Association for Computational Linguistics.

Joint Navigation in Commander/Robot Teams: Dialog & Task Performance When Vision is Bandwidth-Limited

Douglas Summers-Stay
Army Research Laboratory
douglas.a.summers-stay.civ

Taylor Cassidy
IBM Research
Army Research Laboratory
taylor.cassidy.ctr@mail.mil

Clare R. Voss
Army Research Laboratory
clare.r.voss.civ@mail.mil

Abstract

The prospect of human commanders teaming with mobile robots "smart enough" to undertake joint exploratory tasks—especially tasks that neither commander nor robot could perform alone—requires novel methods of preparing and testing human-robot teams for these ventures prior to real-time operations. In this paper, we report work-in-progress that maintains face validity of selected configurations of resources and people, as would be available in emergency circumstances. More specifically, from an off-site post, we ask human commanders (C) to perform an exploratory task in collaboration with a remotely located human robot-navigator (Rn) who controls the navigation of, but cannot see the physical robot (R). We impose network bandwidth restrictions in two mission scenarios comparable to real circumstances by varying the availability of sensor, image, and video signals to Rn, in effect limiting the human Rn to function as an automation stand-in. To better understand the capabilities and language required in such configurations, we constructed multi-modal corpora of time-synced dialog, video, and LIDAR files recorded during task sessions. We can now examine commander/robot dialogs while replaying what C and Rn saw, to assess their task performance under these varied conditions.

1 Introduction

Our research addresses a paradoxical situation in developing a robot capable of teaming with humans. To know what capabilities such a robot needs, we seek to determine how a human commander would interact — choice of vocabulary and sentence types, expected capabilities and world knowledge, resources used to accomplish tasks efficiently, etc. But without such a robot to interact with, we cannot know how a commander would behave. The prospect of human commanders teaming with mobile robots that are "smart enough" to undertake joint exploratory tasks requires novel methods of preparing and testing actual human-robot teams for these ventures, in advance of actual real-time operations. Furthermore, given the need for human/robot teams during emergencies (such as Japan's tsunami/Fukishima disaster), we are interested in particular in the feasibility of commander/robot shared tasks that include NL communication specifically for network contexts when bandwidth is limited by emergencies. Here we ask, how can multimodal data, as collected and processed by robots, and the robots themselves contribute real-time alerts and responses to human commanders over geographically-distributed networks?

The first phase of our approach is to introduce a human stand-in who navigates the robot, posing as an intelligent control system. At this stage, following our prior work (Voss et al., 2014), we seek to determine how the commander communicates to accomplish different tasks with the robot, while we limit the information made available in passing from the robot's sensors and camera to the commander by way of the stand-in. In future phases, we will progressively automate away this actor's role, replacing the audio that the stand-in hears with what is "understood" by automatic natural language semantic interpretation within a dialog manager, and replacing the joystick that it uses to navigate as the robot

Proceedings of the 25th International Conference on Computational Linguistics, pages 9–16,
Dublin, Ireland, August 23-29 2014.

with "actions" as automatically generated from micro-controller commands produced by transformation of semantic commands.

In this paper, we report *work-in-progress* that maintains face validity of selected configurations of resources and people, as would be available in emergency circumstances. From an off-site post, we ask human commanders (C) to perform an exploratory task in collaboration with a remotely located human robot-navigator (Rn) who actually controls the navigation of, but cannot see, the physical robot (R). We restrict the information Rn receives from R by imposing network bandwidth restrictions comparable to real circumstances which limit what Rn is able to communicate to C. We then examine the commander/robot dialogs and task performance under these varied conditions.

To better understand the capabilities and language required in such configurations, we constructed multi-modal corpora of time-synced dialog, video, and LIDAR files recorded during task sessions. We can now examine commander/robot dialogs while replaying what C and Rn saw, to identify the impact of varying the shared visual information on discourse, and to assess task performance under these varied conditions. We hypothesized that more explicit, mututally available information (visual or verbal) between participants would yield better understanding with more common ground, leading to more task success. We also hypothesized that exploration in a more complex physical environment would lead both to more dialog, as needed in resolving references to more locations, and also then on occasion, to less overall task success. We have found in preliminary analyses that, with more explicit *visual* information, some Cs reduce their level of communication, with fewer requests for images from Rn. In one such case, this led to the Rn getting lost. We also noticed that some Cs increased their level of *verbal* communication, requesting far more still images from the robot when Rn could not itself see the robot's images (as opposed to when Rn had access to sent images). Taken together, these observations suggest—contrary to our hypothesis that more information is better, especially in a complex environment—that there may be a "teeter totter" effect in the communication between C and Rn as visual information varies. When Rn has access to more of the robot's visual information, C communicates less with Rn, possibly assuming more shared information than is correct. Whereas when Rn is able to see less, C communicates more with Rn, possibly compensating for the lack of certainty Rn expresses.

2 Related Work

For human-robot communication in joint exploration tasks, we wish to understand two issues. The first is "scene to text": when exploring new locations, how do people talk about what they see, and how does that inform how they want robot team members to communicate about what they "see" while exploring? The second is "text to scene": given natural language instructions, how do people move about in new locations, and how does that impact their expectations of robot navigation? These issues span both generation and understanding of spatial language. There exists a large literature on spatial language, starting several decades ago (Talmy, 1983; Anderson et al., 1991; Gurney et al., 1996; Bloom et al., 1996; Olivier and Gapp, 1998) *inter alia*. This work yielded linguistic insights into the underlying structure of spatial expressions, that has led more recently to annotation efforts like SpaceML (Morarescu, 2006) and spatial role labeling (Kordjamshidi et al., 2010). These results, theoretical and computational, have been incorporated into NLP research, such as spoken dialog systems (Meena et al., 2014).

For "scene to text" processing, starting from a robot's perception of the scene or environment, exploiting even known dependencies among objects (spatial relations, relative motion, etc.) is a central problem in computer vision research. In the current state of robotics, the perceived world (a.k.a. semantic perception) derived from data collected by the robot is limited by what is available within its immediate sensor and video reach (Hebert et al., 2012). Within computational linguistic research, (Feng and Lapata, 2013) have tackled going from news images to text, leveraging the news story content as contextual knowledge, and automatically generating captions describing the image content as relevant for the story. For "text to scene" processing, a robot "understanding" a commander's language entails going beyond linguistic semantic interpretation down to the the robot controller level, as in, for example, Kress-Gazit et al. (2008). Within computational linguistics, Srihari and Burhans (1994) tackled going from text to images, exploiting the conventions and spatial language in news caption to identify people by their relative positions in accompanying images. More recently Coyne et al. (2011) presented work for text-to-graphics generation, grounding conceptual knowledge in relational semantic encoding of lexical meanings from FrameNet. These one-way, directional approaches provide strong evidence that text and image modalities can each inform the processing of the other, and that, with concurrent audio and video streaming data, the alignment of time-stamped files across the two data modalities should also yield additional benefits in shared structural analyses and disambiguating references.[1]

3 Approach

In previous work, we had teams search a series of buildings, where all information from the Rn to C was strictly limited to text (Voss et al., 2014). While verbal descriptions of scenery were successfully elicited during exploratory missions, the communication was painfully slow and this scenario yielded unrealistic results from our stand-in: we would not expect a robot to generate the complex verbal descriptions we collected. Furthermore we also learned that our equipment could be adjusted for transmission of LIDAR map data and video stream from the robot to Rn and then to C. In this second study, we allowed individual map and image updates to be sent to C, but only on request. This work provides more explicitly shared knowledge between C and Rn, with its form and quantity more realistically varied and dynamic.

Equipment: We used an iRobot PackBot equipped with a forward-facing Kinect camera and a Hokuyo LIDAR sensor.[2] We use GPS and inertial sensors for Simultaneous Localization and Mapping (SLAM). Each participant had their own laptop with speakers and separate push-to-talk microphones. For navigating the robot, the Rn pushed a joystick on an X-box controller that was held. Additionally for transmitting visual information available from the robot during the missions, the Rn pushed separate buttons on the same controller to transfer image and map data to C, but only at C's request.

Pre-pilot Design: We conducted training sessions at one location and test sessions at a second location. A top down view of these sites is provided in Figure 1. We asked participants to perform distinct missions (task conditions) in the training and test sessions, with different levels of visual information available to Rn (vision conditions). Due to wireless networking timeouts and hardware integration difficulties, a number of sessions ended prematurely. Descriptive statistics for the sessions are in Table 1.

	Vision Condition		
Task Condition - quality of dataset	LIDAR only	LIDAR + Image last-sent	Video + LIDAR + Image last-sent
Mission 1 - complete	–	–	6 sessions (77 min)
Mission 1 - partial	–	–	1 session (1 min)
Mission 2 - complete	4 sessions (57 min)	2 sessions (28 min)	2 sessions (18 min)
Mission 2 - partial	11 sessions (15 min)	3 sessions (3 min)	–

Table 1: Total #sessions attempted by configuration (different task & vision conditions)

Vision Conditions: The Rn always saw (i) a continuously updated LIDAR map built up progressively from the robot's sensors as the Rn navigated the robot using the joystick on an X-box controller. On the map during training, the Rn could also see (ii) an avatar shape for the robot's location based on GPS and (iii) an arrow for the robot's facing direction generated by its internal components (updated intermittently by GPS). However the GPS signal was also sporadic during these sessions, causing confusion for Rn navigating the robot. As a result, during test sessions, we turned off the GPS to avoid this source of confusion, mirroring what actual operators do in this scenario. During test sessions, the Rn only saw (iii) the arrow, again within (i) the streamed LIDAR map. Beyond these Rn screen specifics, we ran three conditions controlling for the visual information that the C and Rn could see. During mission 1 (training), Rn was given "full" view of the streaming video, any specific images sent to C at C's request, and the map with arrow and avatar. During mission 2 (test) in one "partially blinded" condition, the Rn

[1]We are also eager to learn more from recent research examining streaming multimodal data for how and where the composition of natural language and the composition of visual scenes can inform one another (Barbu et al., 2012) and (Barbu et al., 2013).

[2]iRobot, PackBot, Kinect, and Hokuyo are all trademarks or registered trademarks.

Figure 1: On left side: view of Mission 1 courtyard and building, with doorways marked. On right side: view of Mission 2 courtyards and buildings.

saw no video, but could see the specific images he sent to C as well as the map with arrow, and in the other even “more blinded” condition, Rn saw only the map with arrow. By contrast, the C only ever saw what the Rn sent (by pushing buttons) as snapshots at C’s request. During all conditions — independent of what was presented to Rn (“full’ view in mission 1, partially blinded or more-blinded in mission 2) — C could always request an updated snapshot image from the video feed or an updated snapshot map from the LIDAR feed or both. As a result, Rn’s view was “pushed” and current from the robot’s streaming data, whereas the C’s view had to be “pulled,” requiring C to ask for more snapshots. Note that in Rn’s more-blinded condition, images were passed to C with Rn’s button push, but Rn could not see the images.

Mission 1: Enter courtyard and building via safe doorways. We hypothesized a robot with the ability to carry on limited conversation regarding simple navigation and exploration, but without sufficient vision capabilities to analyze more subtle clues about whether a doorway was safe to enter. We designed the task to simulate a low-bandwidth condition where constant transmission of the map and video information is impossible. The robot was placed in one of two undisclosed positions outside the courtyard surrounding a building. All sessions adopted the L+I+V vision condition. The site for this mission was a

Figure 2: Robot-navigator’s screen during Mission 1: upper left is static Image (clip from video, most recently sent to Commander), upper right is video window, gray-scale background is LIDAR map

single rectangular building enclosed by a single rectangular courtyard. The site for mission 2 was more complex, consisting of 5 buildings in a complex series of interconnected courtyards (see Figure 1). There are five doorways into the courtyard and two doorways into the building. These doorways are marked as safe or unsafe in a way that C can recognize but Rn cannot (C is given a key to the meaning of objects placed just beyond open doorways as symbols). The participants are not informed about doorway location or safety status. Figure 2 shows Rn's screen during a mission 1 session. The grey-scale background is an overhead, 2D view of a 3D map being built on the fly by combining various sensor data, which contains a white robot avatar and blue arrow indicating its current pose. C's view is similar, but without video. Success on this task was gauged by whether the robot stayed safe in gaining entry to the house.

Mission 2: Find and classify all building doorways within a compound.
As noted above and shown in Figure 1, the location in this mission had a more complex layout. The robot's location within the compound was not disclosed to C nor Rn (no clues were provided), so that the C and Rn team would need to work hard to place the robot on the map. The team was tasked with thoroughly exploring the compound to capture images of each building doorway. In the LIDAR-only (L) condition, Rn sees only the grey-scale map, whereas in the LIDAR and image condition (L+I) Rn sees the most recently sent image as well as the grey-scale map (same screen layout as in Figure 2 but without video window in upper right). Success on this mission was gauged both by the number of doors (open or closed) that were identified and photographed and by whether the participants were lost at some stage in the exploration.

4 Observations and Preliminary Results

We recorded rich, multi-modal datasets including: dialogue between C and Rn, video, LIDAR 3D point clouds, scene classification output on video frames, and robot pose. The data is used to build up a 3D model of the scene, and automatically align RGB images to the model by mapping pixels to 3D regions. Examples of scene classification performance can be seen in Figure 3. The data for each run consists of a ROS bag file (Quigley et al., 2009) and two audio files.[3]

Figure 3: left: view from robot camera. right: automated scene classification. Mix of colors indicates probability of belonging to a particular class. Classes found in this scene include sky, foliage, building, grass, concrete, and asphalt. Performance degrades in lighting conditions unattested in training data.

4.1 Results from Session Path Analysis

Figure 4 shows an overhead 2D view of the final 3D map built using the SLAM module. An orange line depicts the robot's path from mission start to finish, with ordinal numbers indicating the robot's high level trajectory (the robot traveled from "start" to "1", then to the location marked by "2", etc., finally ending on the location marked by "15"). Doorways that were successfully captured in images sent to C are highlighted with a green solid-lined circle, whereas doorways that were passed by are indicated with

[3]A bag file stores nano-second accuracy timestamped, discrete data *messages*, such as an individual video frame, the fact that a joystick button was pressed, or the robot's current velocity.

Mission 1 Sessions (duration)	Vision Condition	Total # Images sent	# Images sent with (any) door	# Images sent with safe door	Task Success: Stayed **S**afe? Gained **E**ntry?
1 (21 min.)	L + I + V	0	0	0	S, E
2 (5 min.)	L + I + V	0	0	0	N, E
3 (17 min.)	L + I + V	3	3	2	S, E
4 (15 min.)	L + I + V	8	7	2	S, E
5 (13 min.)	L + I + V	12	7	4	S, E

Table 2: Mission 1 sessions: These training sessions provided the robot-navigators (Rn) with "full" real-time vision, i.e., their screens displayed all sensed data, as collected by the physical robot (R)

Mission 2 Sessions (duration)	Vision Conditions (**L**IDAR) (**I**mage)	Total #Images (sent w/o map)	Total #Maps (sent w/o img)	Total # Im & Map (sent one, then other)	# deictic refs by C, Rn	# refs to past by C, Rn	Task Success: # **D**oors id? Got **L**ost? **R**ecovered?
A (21 min.)	L map	27	7	5	13, 2	6, 3	9, n/a , n/a
B (20 min.)	L map + I	7	9	7	7, 2	7, 2	7, L, R

Table 3: Mission 2 per-session events: request and reference types, task success.

a dotted line. There is a point in the run depicted where Rn states that he is "lost", which is marked in the figure by a green dot at step 10.

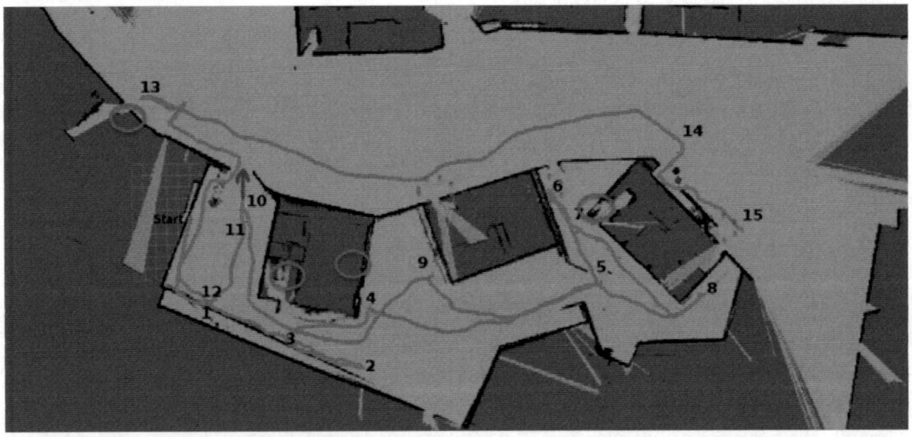

Figure 4: Robot path during Mission 2 session, doorways marked

4.2 Language Phenomena in Dialogs

Referring Expressions: There were few named environment features, necessitating the use of referring expressions. Participants often used pronouns ('behind it'), deictic expressions ('that wall'), and both definite and indefinite noun phrase descriptors ('a wall directly in front of you'). The frequency of referring expressions other than proper names highlights the need for a dialog manager to robustly handle human-robot dialog in our setting. In six mission 2 dialogs consisting of 6,593 words total, we annotated 1,593 referring expressions - 1,213 definite and 380 indefinite. The most common were first and second person singular pronouns (287 and 245), definite expressions of the form *the x* (265) and indefinite expressions of the form *a(n) x* (256). Most references are to things, either in the physical ('face the doorway') or software ('update your map') environment, though there are references to events as well ('do that again').

Lexical Ambiguity: The same objects were sometimes referred to as 'doors' or 'doorways,' although by a dictionary definition, those refer to somewhat different things. Based on context, the robot would need to be able to understand which sense was intended.

Spatial Relations: Since these were navigation and observation tasks, much of the discussion involved spatial language pertaining to object configurations and robot paths. There were references to distances and angles, both specific ('turn 15 degrees to your right') and vague ('turn around.') The robot was asked to 'follow the wall', 'go north', and to travel 'around,' 'behind,' and 'near' various objects.
Clarifications and Suggestions in Dialogs: When uncertain about the meaning of commands, Rn sometimes asked for clarification. At other times, Rn reminded C of its capabilities when appropriate: 'Would you like me to send you an updated map?'

4.3 The Role of Shared Visual Information

Participants were generally able to use both image and map data in conjunction with dialog to gain enough common ground to communicate about the environment and accomplish the tasks at hand. For example, after discussing environment features against the backdrop of an updated 2D map, we were often surprised at the extent to which C apparently kept track of R's location using dialog alone without further map updates, as evidenced by C's ability to correctly use Rn's egocentric frame of reference in verbal descriptions (recall that the robot avatar remained static on C's map between updates). In such cases C and R took advantage of mutually accessible visual information - their 2D maps were identical during discussion. The role of mutually accessible information for achieving common ground is further supported by the fact that C requested significantly more images in the LIDAR-only condition, when Rn could not see those sent images (see Table 3). Although shared visual knowledge proved useful for resolving referring expressions, C and Rn rarely mentioned the media explicitly ('the building' vs 'the building in the image you sent me'). In this way, the transfer of visual information served to introduce entities into their discourse, but was taken for granted and not called out per se.

5 Ongoing Work

We have found in preliminary analyses that, with more explicit *visual* information, some Cs reduce their level of communication, with fewer requests for images from Rn. In one such case, this led to the Rn getting lost. We also noticed that some Cs increased their level of *verbal* communication, requesting far more still images from the robot when Rn could not itself see the robot's images (as opposed to when Rn had access to sent images). Taken together, these observations suggest—contrary to our hypotheses that more information is better, especially in a complex environment—that there may be a "teeter totter" effect in the communication between C and Rn as visual information varies. When Rn "sees as the robot" with access to more transmitted visual information, C communicates less with Rn, possibly assuming more shared information than is correct. Whereas when Rn "sees" less, C communicates more with Rn, possibly compensating for the lack of certainty Rn expresses. We plan to extend our analysis of how C and Rn communicate uncertainty, and look at how this topic is addressed in first aid and military manuals (US Dept. of the Army, 1993).

We are currently developing a framework to automate many of the tasks currently performed by Rn. Our studies and data collections so far are best understood in the context of the capabilities and limitations of the overall system we are in the process of building. A crucial gap to address is associating referring expressions with corresponding concrete spatial structures in the 3D map. Consider one sentence spoken by the commander in one of the dialogues: "When you get to the wall, turn left and drive along the wall until you reach either a corner or what you believe to be a door." To interpret this correctly, the robot must understand an entire set of points as a single object or part of an object, so it can recognize doors, walls, and corners in the combined vision and point-cloud. Moreover, it needs to plan a path that obeys the constraint "along the wall" and stops at some point which may be a door or a corner, that has not yet been observed. Thus, objects need to be represented independent of the observed world map.[4] At present, scene parsing techniques can analyze images and assign each pixel a probability of belonging to a particular object class (wall, stucco, road, etc.) allowing us to propagate these labels to corresponding points in the 3D model of the scene. In the future, we will use the 3D model to resolve visual ambiguities and attach labels to particular objects that persist from one video frame to the next.

[4]Resolving references to unvisited locations is a largely unexplored problem (Williams et al., 2013; Duvallet et al., 2013).

Acknowledgements

We thank members of the Asset Control and Behavior Branch at ARL for participation in our study and for continuing to provide the technical support that makes our work possible. The work of Taylor Cassidy was funded by IBM under the International Technology Alliance in Network & Information Sciences.

References

A. Anderson, M. Bader, E. Bard, E. Boyd, G.M. Doherty, S. Garrod, S. Isard, J. Kowtko, J. McAllister, C. Sotillo, H.S. Thompson, and R. Weinert. 1991. The HCRC Map Task Corpus. *Language and Speech*, 34:351–366.

A. Barbu, A. Bridge, D. Coroian, S. J. Dickinson, S. Mussman, S. Narayanaswamy, D.l Salvi, L. Schmidt, J. Shangguan, J. M. Siskind, J. W. Waggoner, S. Wang, J. Wei, Y. Yin, and Z. Zhang. 2012. Large-scale automatic labeling of video events with verbs based on event-participant interaction. *CoRR*, abs/1204.3616.

A. Barbu, S. Narayanaswamy, and J. Siskind. 2013. Saying what you're looking for: Linguistics meets video search. *CoRR*, abs/1309.5174.

P. Bloom, M. Peterson, L. Madel, and M. F. Garrett, editors. 1996. *Language and Space*. The MIT Press.

B. Coyne, D. Bauer, and O. Rambow. 2011. Vignet: Grounding language in graphics using frame semantics. In *ACL Workshop on Relational Models of Semantics (RELMS 2011)*.

F. Duvallet, T. Kollar, and A. Stentz. 2013. Imitation learning for natural language direction following through unknown environments. In *IEEE Intl. Conference on Robotics and Automation (ICRA)*, pages 1047–1053.

Y. Feng and M. Lapata. 2013. Automatic caption generation for news images. *IEEE Transactions on Pattern Analysis and Machine Intelligence*, 35:4:797–812.

J. Gurney, E. Klipple, and C. Voss. 1996. Talking about what we think we see: natural language processing for a real-time virtual environment. *IEEE International Joint Symposia on Intelligence and Systems*.

M. Hebert, J. A. Bagnell, M. Bajracharya, K. Daniilidis, L. H. Matthies, L. Mianzo, L. Navarro-Serment, J. Shi, and M. Wellfare. 2012. Semantic perception for ground robotics. In R. E. Karlsen; D. W. Gage; C. M. Shoemaker; G. R. Gerhart, editor, *SPIE Proceedings Vol. 8387: Unmanned Systems Technology XIV*.

P. Kordjamshidi, M. Van Otterlo, and Marie-Francine Moens. 2010. Spatial Role Labeling: Task Definition and Annotation Scheme. In *Proceedings of Language Resources and Evaluation Conference*.

H. Kress-Gazit, G. E. Fainekos, and G. J. Pappas. 2008. Translating Structured English to Robot Controllers. *Advanced Robotics Special Issue on Selected Papers from IROS*, Vol. 22, No. 12:1343–1359.

R. Meena, J. Boye, G. Skantze, and J. Gustafson. 2014. Crowdsourcing street-level geographic information using a spoken dialogue system. In *Proceedings of SIGDIAL*. Association for Computational Linguistics.

P. C. Morarescu. 2006. Principles for annotating and reasoning with spatial information. In *LREC*.

P. Olivier and K-P. Gapp, editors. 1998. *Representation and Processing of Spatial Expressions*. Lawrence Erlbaum Associates, Hillsdale, NJ, USA.

M. Quigley, K. Conley, B. Gerkey, J. Faust, T. B. Foote, J. Leibs, R. Wheeler, and A. Y. Ng. 2009. ROS: an open-source robot operating system. In *ICRA Workshop on Open Source Software*.

R. K. Srihari and D. T. Burhans. 1994. Visual semantics: Extracting visual information from text accompanying pictures. In *Proc. Of Twelfth National Conference on Artificial Intelligence (AAAI-94)*, pages 793–798.

L. Talmy. 1983. How Language Structures Space. In Jr. H. L. Pick and L. P. Acredolo, editors, *Spatial Orientation: Theory, Research, and Application*, pages 225–282. Plenum Press, London.

US Dept. of the Army. 1993. *Physical fitness training: Field manual 3-25.26*. Washington, D.C.

C.R. Voss, T. Cassidy, and D. Summers-Stay. 2014. Collaborative Exploration in Human-Robot Teams: What's in Their Corpora of Dialog, Video, & LIDAR Messages? In *Proceedings of EACL Dialog in Motion Workshop*.

T. E. Williams, R. Cantrell, G. Briggs, P. W. Schermerhorn, and M. Scheutz. 2013. Grounding natural language references to unvisited and hypothetical locations. In *AAAI*.

TUHOI: Trento Universal Human Object Interaction Dataset

Dieu-Thu Le
DISI, University of Trento
Povo, 38123, Italy
dle@disi.unitn.it

Jasper Uijlings
University of Trento, Italy
University of Edinburgh, Scotland
jrr.uijlings@ed.ac.uk

Raffaella Bernardi
DISI, University of Trento
Povo, 38123, Italy
bernardi@disi.unitn.it

Abstract

This paper describes the Trento Universal Human Object Interaction dataset, TUHOI, which is dedicated to human object interactions in images.[1] Recognizing human actions is an important yet challenging task. Most available datasets in this field are limited in numbers of actions and objects. A large dataset with various actions and human object interactions is needed for training and evaluating complicated and robust human action recognition systems, especially systems that combine knowledge learned from language and vision. We introduce an image collection with more than two thousand actions which have been annotated through crowdsourcing. We review publicly available datasets, describe the annotation process of our image collection and some statistics of this dataset. Finally, experimental results on the dataset including human action recognition based on objects and an analysis of the relation between human-object positions in images and prepositions in language are presented.

1 Introduction

Visual action recognition is generally studied on datasets with a limited number of predefined actions represented in many training images or videos (Ikizler et al., 2008; Delaitre et al., 2011; Yao and Li, 2010; Yao et al., 2011). Common methods using holistic image or video representation such as Bag-of-Words have achieved successful results in retrieval settings (Ayache and Quenot, 2008). Though these predefined lists of actions are good for many computer vision problems, this cannot work when one wants to recognize *all* possible actions. Firstly, the same action can be phrased in several ways. Secondly, the number of actions that such systems would have to recognize in real life data is huge: the number of possible interactions with all possible objects is bounded by the cartesian product of numbers of verbs and objects. Therefore, the task of collecting images or videos of each individual action becomes infeasible with this growing number. By necessity this means that for some actions only few examples will be available. In this paper we want to enable studies in the direction of recognizing all possible actions, for which we provide a new, suitable human-object interaction dataset.

A human action can be defined as a human, object, and the relation between them. Therefore, an action is naturally recognized through its individual components. Recent advances in computer vision have led to reasonable accuracy for object and human recognition, which makes recognizing the components feasible. Additionally, language can help determining how components are combined. Furthermore, the relative position between human and object can be used to disambiguate different human actions. Perhaps prepositions in natural language can be linked to this relative position between the object and human (e.g., step *out of* a car). To transfer this knowledge from language to vision, it is important that the distribution of the visual actions are sampled similarly as the language data. This requirement is fulfilled when the action frequencies in the dataset mirror the frequencies in which they occur in real life.

To sum up, we aim at building an image dataset which can (1) capture the distribution of human interactions with objects in reality (if an action is more common that the other actions, that action is also observed more frequently in the dataset than the others), (2) provide different ways of describing

[1] Our dataset is available to download at http://disi.unitn.it/ dle/dataset/TUHOI.html

Proceedings of the 25th International Conference on Computational Linguistics, pages 17–24,
Dublin, Ireland, August 23-29 2014.

an action for each image (there are many actions that can be phrased in several ways, for example: fix a bike or repair a bike), (3) help with identifying different verb meanings (for example, the word 'riding' has different implications for 'riding a horse', 'riding a car', and 'riding a skateboard').

2 Available image datasets for human action recognition

A common approach to human action recognition is to exploit visual features using bag-of-features or part-based representation and treat action recognition as a general classification problem (Delaitre et al., 2010; Yao and Li, 2010; Wang et al., ; Laptev, 2005). For common actions, it has been shown that learning the joint appearance of the human-object interaction can be beneficial (Sadeghi and Farhadi, 2011). Other studies recognize actions by their components such as objects, human poses, scenes (Gupta et al., 2009; Yao et al., 2011): (Yao et al., 2011) jointly models attributes and parts, where attributes are verbs and parts are objects and local body parts. These studies rely on suitable training data for a set of predefined actions: (Gupta et al., 2009) tests on a 6 sport action dataset, (Yao and Li, 2010) attempts to distinguish images where a human plays a musical instrument from images where he/she does not, (Delaitre et al., 2010) classifies images to one of the seven every day actions, and (Yao et al., 2011) introduces a dataset containing 40 human actions. Most of these datasets were obtained using web search results such as Google, Bing, Flickr, etc. The number of images varies from 300 to more than 9K images. A comparison of the publicly available datasets with respect to the number of actions and their related objects is given in Table 1.

Dataset	#images	#objects	#actions	Examples of actions
Ikirler (Ikizler et al., 2008)	467	0	6	running, walking, throwing, crouching and kicking
Willow (Delaitre et al., 2011)	968	5	7	interaction with computer, photographing, riding bike
Sport dataset (Gupta et al., 2009)	300	4	6	tennis-forehand, tennis-serve, cricket bowling
Stanford 40 (Yao et al., 2011)	9532	31	40	ride horse, row boat, ride bike, cut vegetables
PPMI (Yao and Li, 2010)	4800	7	7	play violin, play guitar, play flute, play french horn
PASCAL (Everingham et al., 2012)	1221	6	10	jumping, playing instrument, riding horse
89 action dataset (Le et al., 2013)	2038	19	89	drive bus, sail boat, ride bike, fix bike, watch TV
TUHOI dataset	10805	189	2974	sit on chair, use computer, ride horse, play with dog

Table 1: A comparison of available human action datasets in terms of number of objects and actions

As can be seen in Table 1, the Stanford 40 action dataset contains quite a big number of images with 40 different actions. This dataset is good for visually training action recognizers since there are enough images collected for each actions divided into training and test sets. There are some dataset in which human action does not involved any object, these actions are for instance running, walking, or actions where objects are not specified such as catching, throwing. These types of actions are not the target domain of our dataset. We aim at recognizing the human object interactions based on objects. With the same object, some actions are also more common than other actions: for example, sitting on a chair is more commonly observed than standing on a chair. We want to capture such information in our dataset which can reflect the human action distributions on common objects, aiming to sample human actions related to objects in the visual world. Furthermore, how actions can be phrased in different ways, or how verbs can have different meanings when interacting with different objects should also be considered. Some actions can only be performed on some particular objects and are not applicable to some other objects: a person can ride a horse, ride a bike, can feed a horse, but cannot feed a bike. This problem of ambiguity and different word uses have been widely studied in computational linguistics, but have received little attention from the computer vision community.

With the aim of creating a dataset that covers these requirements, we collect our dataset starting from images where humans and objects co-occur together and define the actions we observe in each image instead of collecting images for some predefined human actions. This way of annotating actions in images is more natural and helps creating a more realistic dataset with various human actions that can occur in images generally.

Recently, some good works attempted to generate descriptive sentences from images (Farhadi et al., 2010; Kulkarni et al., 2011). In our dataset we focus on human actions, which, if present, are often the main topic of interest within an image. As such, our dataset can be used as an important stepping stone for generating full image descriptions as it allows for more rigorous evaluation than free-form text.

3 TUHOI, the new human action dataset

ImageNet is a hierarchical image database built upon the WordNet structure. The DET dataset in the ImageNet large scale object recognition challenge 2013[2] contains 200 objects for training and evaluation. With the idea of starting from images with humans and common objects, we chose to use this DET dataset as a starting point to build our human action data.

3.1 The DET dataset: Object categories and labels

The 200 objects in the DET dataset are general, basic-level categories (e.g., monitor, waffle iron, sofa, spatula, starfish). Each object corresponds to a synset (set of synonymous nouns) in WordNet. The DET training set consists of single topic images where only the target object is annotated. As such, most images only contain primarily the object of interest and few actions. It is good for learning object classifiers but is not suitable for learning action recognition. In contrast, the validation dataset contains various images where all object instances are annotated with a bounding box. Many of these images contain actions. Therefore we start the annotation from the validation set.

Dataset	#images	#images having "person"	#object instances	#instances/object (min-max-median)	#"person" instances
Training	395,909	9,877	345,854	438 - 73,799 - 660	18,258
Validation	20,121	5,791	55,502	31 - 12,823 - 111	12,823

Table 2: The statistics of the DET dataset

As can be seen in Table 2, there are 15,668 images having human and 31,081 human instances in these images. We select only images having human since we want to annotate this dataset with human object interactions. Objects related to clothes such as bathing cap, miniskirt, tie, etc. are not interesting for human actions (most of the time, the action associated with these objects is "to wear"). Therefore, we excluded all these objects from the list of 200 objects above, which are: bathing cap, bow tie, bow, brassiere, hat with a wide brim, helmet, maillot, miniskirt, neck brace, sunglasses, tie.

3.2 Human action annotation

Goal Our goal is to annotate these selected images containing humans and objects with their interactions. Each human action is required to be associated with at least one of the given 200 object categories. We used the Crowdflower, a crowdsourcing service for annotating these images. The Crowdflower annotators are required to be English native speakers and they can use any vocabulary to describe the actions as they wish. Every action is composed of a verb and an object (possibly with a preposition).

Annotation guideline For each image, given all object instances appearing in that image (together with their bounding boxes), the annotator has been be asked to assign all human actions associated to each of the object instance in the image (where "no action" is also possible). Every human actions need to have as object one of the object instances given in that image. For example, if the image has a bike and a dog, the annotator will assign every human actions associated to "bike" and "dog". Every image has been annotated by at least 3 annotators, so that each action in the image can be described differently by different people. Some examples of annotated images in our dataset are given in Figure 1.

3.3 Results of the annotation and some statistics

In total, there are 10,805 images, which have been annotated with 58,808 actions, of which 6,826 times it has been annotated with "no action" (11.6%). On average, there are 4.8 actions annotated for each image (excluding "no action"), of which there are 1.97 unique action/image. Some other statistics of the dataset are given in Table 3: The number of unique verbs per object ranges from 1 (starfish, otter) to 158 (dog). As dogs occur very often in this image dataset (4,671 times), the number of actions associated to it is also larger than other objects.

[2] http://www.image-net.org/challenges/LSVRC/2013/

Figure 1: Examples of annotated images: **Left:** (1) play ping-pong, hold racket; (2) use laptop, hold computer mouse; (3) use microphone, play accordion, play guitar, play violin; (4) talk on microphone, sit on sofa, pour pitcher; (5) play trombone; (6) eat/suck popsicle; (7) listen/use/hear stethoscope; (8) ride bicycle, wear backpack; (9) swing/hold racket, hit tennis ball; **Right:** (1) sit on chair, play violin; (2) wear diaper, sit on chair, squeeze/apply cream; (3) sit on chair, play cello; (4) hold/shake maraca; (5) ride watercraft, wear swimming trunks; (6) cook/use stove, stir mushroom, hold spatula; (7) drive/row watercraft; (8) sit on chair, pet dog, lay on sofa; (9) click/type on computer keyboard

Number of unique actions (verb + object): 2,974 actions Number of unique verbs: 860 verbs
Verbs that are used most frequently (verb (#occurrences)): play (13043), hold (7731), ride (4765), sit (3535), sit on (1501) drive (1491), wear (1441), eat (1175), hit (1168), pet (970), use (897), walk (787), stand (756) touch (509), carry (507), blow (384), sail (323), kick (297), lead (290), throw (246), strum (239) stand on (223), run (223)
Verbs that are used least frequently (occur only once): dirty, swing over, twist, beats, walks, ay, curl face, shit, sail in, n‘, see by, forge, draw, tag10, sling, rides, walk across, no image available, waving drag, award, preform, strumb, died, land, unload, tricks, cooked, time, fasten, fall over, holed, leap over, pull up
Objects go with the largest number of verbs (object (#unique verbs)): dog (158), car (80), table (79), watercraft (68) horizontal bar (56), chair (54), cart (52), whale (50), bicycle (48), cattle (42), soccer ball (41), balance beam (38) band aid (38), motorcycle (37), flower pot (35), ladle (35), guitar (35), horse (35), ski (34), bus (34)
Objects that go with the least number of verbs (object (#unique verbs)): milk can (5), pitcher (5), scorpion (4), bear (4), pretzel (4), sheep (4), frog (4), mushroom (4), printer (4), pineapple (4), ruler (3), guacamole (3), isopod (3), chime (3), plate (rack (3), strawberry (3), porcupine (3), ant (3), toaster (3), bagel (3), jellyfish (3), dragonfly (2), lion (2), zebra (2), goldfish (2), hamster (2), fig (2), squirrel (2), bee (2), centipede (2), koala (bear (2), snail (2), pomegranate (2), armadillo (2), otter (1), starfish (1)

Table 3: Some statistics of the human action dataset

For some images, the annotators find many different ways to describe the action in the image. In our data, a set of images was selected to be annotated by more than three people in order to facilitate sanity checks. An example of such image which has been annotated by many people is given in Figure 2. The annotators have found many verbs to describe the action: feeding, leading, running with, touching, giving a treat to, etc.

Splitting training and test set For each object in our human action dataset, we split half of the images for training and the other half is used for testing. The splitting process is done such that actions that occur in test set also occur in training set to guarantee that the training set contains at least one image for each action occurring in the test set.

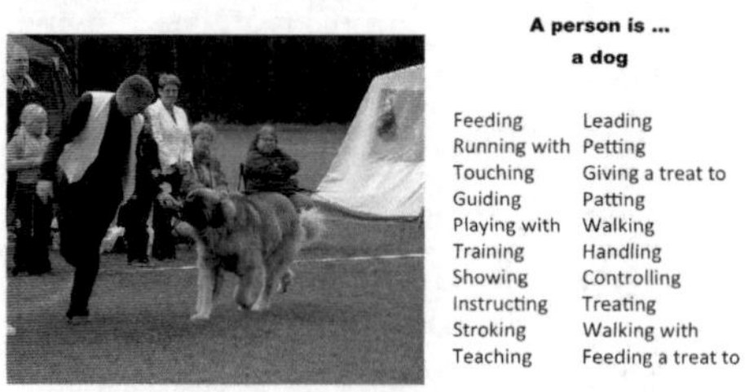

Figure 2: Many different ways to describe an action in an image

Evaluating human action classification in our dataset To evaluate the performance of the human action classification on this dataset, we use two different measurements: the accuracy and the traditional precision, recall and F1 score. The accuracy reflects the percentage of predictions that are correct. We calculate within how many images, the classifier assigns the correct actions for a given object i:

$$Accuracy_i = \frac{\text{number of images that the classifier predicts correctly}}{\text{total number of images}} \quad (1)$$

If the output of the classifier is one of the three annotated actions by human, then the action predicted is considered to be correct. The accuracy of the whole system is the average accuracy over all objects, with n is the total number of objects.

$$Accuracy = \frac{\sum_{i=1}^{n} Accuracy_i}{n} \quad (2)$$

This metric gives us the general performance of the system and easy to interpret. However, it gives higher weights to actions that occur more often in the dataset. For example, if there are many actions "ride bike" occurring in the dataset, the accuracy of the whole system depends mostly on the performance of the class "ride bike". For actions that occur more rarely such as "fix bike", then the accuracy of the class "fix bike" will have little effect to the accuracy of the whole system.

To better analyze the results of the system and evaluate each action individually, we use the precision, recall and F1 score for each class in the classifier. More specifically, as this classifier is the multi-class classifier, these metrics are computed using a confusion matrix:

$$Precision_i = \frac{M_{ii}}{\sum_j M_{ji}}; Recall_i = \frac{M_{ii}}{\sum_j M_{ij}} \quad (3)$$

where M_{ij} is the value of the row i, column j in the confusion matrix. The confusion matrix is oriented such that a given row of the matrix corresponds to the value of the "truth", i.e., correct actions assigned by human, and a given column corresponds to the value of action assigned by the classifier. Finally, the precision, recall and F1 score of the whole system are calculated as the average score over all actions.

4 Experiments

In this part, we use our newly collected dataset for building a general human action classifier based on objects. We analyze the relative positions between humans and objects in each image and use this information to help classifying human actions. Finally, we discuss the relations between human-object positions with prepositions that are used in language for describing human actions.

4.1 Classifying human actions based on human-object positions

In this experiment, we used Forest Random classification method to classify an image to an action given an object. The features used for this classifier are positions of the object and the person appearing in that image. We compare this classifier when using position with a classifier using no position information to see whether position information helps in classifying human actions and in which cases.

Extracting features To extract the features of objects and persons' positions in the images, we take the bounding box of the first object instance annotated in that image. There are images with more than one object instance (for example, there are several 'bike' in an image, so we do not know what 'bike' we are talking about). We use the four coordinates of the bounding boxes of the object and person in the image as features for the classifier.

Results of the classifier To compare whether position information can help in recognizing actions or not, we design a naive classifier which learns from the probability of a verb given an object to assign an action for each image from the training image dataset.

	Accuracy	Precision	Recall	F1
Without position	74.2%	0.40	0.26	0.29
With position	72.1%	0.65	0.29	0.36

Table 4: Results of the classifier with and without position information

Object	Without position	With position	Object	Without position	With position
baseball	0.36	0.52	bus	0.57	0.73
face powder	0.33	1	hair spray	0.73	0.74
harmonica	0.07	0.97	horizontal bar	0.42	0.45
hotdog	0.29	0.57	motorcycle	0.80	0.82
turtle	0.43	0.71	water bottle	0.56	0.65

Table 5: Objects with higher accuracy when using position information

The results of the systems with and without position are report in Table 4. It shows that the accuracy of the classifier without position is higher than when including the position (74.2% in compared to 72.1%). However the precision, recall and F1 of the classifier using position are all higher than without position. It's due to the fact that the classifier without position blindly assigns each image to the most probable action (i.e., actions that occurs most often with a given object learned from the training set), so it obtains better overall accuracy when testing on all images. However, for other possible actions, this classifier is unable to disambiguate actions and the performance of this classifier on less frequent actions is worst than when including position information into the classifier. Generally, when taking into account all possible actions, the position-based classifier has better average precision, recall and F1 score (28.6% without position in compared with 35.8% using position).

To further analyze which objects and actions, the position information helps better, we compare the accuracy of each individual objects. Table 5 reports main objects that have higher accuracy when using position. We want to be able to predict which kind of actions that positions will help in recognizing them through the knowledge we learn from language. This prediction will help us to learn how to include the position information inside our human action recognizer since not all actions can be disambiguated by positions. We divide the actions into two groups: one group for which we found position information increase the classification results. Another group for which we found position information to decrease the classification results.

4.2 From prepositions in language to relative positions between human and object in images

In this section, we want to learn how prepositions in language can be used to determine which positions are useful in action classification, i.e., if they belong to the first group or the second group in the previous experiment.

The relative positions between human and object in images are useful in analyzing their interactions. For example, when a person is riding a horse, the person is usually on the top of the horse, and when a person is feeding a horse, then the person is usually standing next to the horse. In spoken English, sometimes prepositions can be used as an indicator to the relations between human and object positions.

We want to exploit the connection between human-object positions in images and prepositions that link human, verb and object in language. Intuitively, if an action implies a strong positional relation between the human and the object, we expect to find specific, distinguishing prepositions in language. For example, in language you usually say "sit *on* chair", where the preposition *on* suggests a specific spatial relation between the human and the chair. When an action does not imply a strong positional relation, such as "play", we expect no specific prepositions.

***Links* in language models** To test this hypothesis, we use TypeDM (Baroni and Lenci, 2010), a distributional memory that has been built from large scale text corpora. This model contains weighted <word-link-word> tuples extracted from a dependency parse of corpora. The relations between words are characterized by their "link". Some of these links are prepositions that connect verbs and objects together. Examples of some tuples with word-link-word and their weights are provided in Figure 3.

Number of links and link entropy We want to determine whether there is any correlation between human-object relative positions in images and the associated prepositions from language models. To do this, we record two metrics: the number of links, where we count how many different links that connect verbs and objects in the language model; and the entropy of each action A^i verb-object pair (where the human is implicit) is $H(A^i)$ defined by: $H(A^i) = -\sum_{l_j \in L^i} p(l_j) \times \log p(l_j)$

where L^i is the set of all links that occur between verb and object of action i; $p(l_j)$ is the probability of the link l_j of the action A^i:

bicycle-n	by	ride-v	11.2994
bicycle-n	in	ride-v	6.7795
bicycle-n	of	ride-v	2.4167
bicycle-n	on	ride-v	278.4273
drum-n	against	play-v	3.5056
drum-n	behind	play-v	4.7656
drum-n	by	play-v	2.4393
drum-n	in	play-v	8.9440
drum-n	of	play-v	2.9940
drum-n	on	play-v	185.8888
drum-n	over	play-v	2.8841
accordion-n	on	play-v	174.7606
ant-n	over	hold-v	3.3807
apple-n	in	hold-v	0.3519
apple-n	on	hold-v	1.1309

Figure 3: Examples of word-link-word and their weights in the distributional memory

$$p(l_j) = \frac{weight(l_j)}{\sum_{l_k \in L_i} weight(l_k)} \tag{4}$$

where $weight(l_j)$ is the weight given by the TypeDM of link j in action i.

Generally, the entropy for each action allows seeing whether a link is predictable for a given pair of verb-object or not: when a link is predictable, the entropy is expected to be low (contain little information), which might correspond to the case that the position information will be useful in predicting actions and the other way around.

	Number of links	Entropy
Group 1 (position helps)	8	1.05
Group 2 (position doesn't help)	15.3	1.36

Table 6: Actions that can be disambiguated by positions (Group 1) vs. actions that cannot be disambiguated by positions (Group 2) and their links in the language model

Results The result shown in Table 6: for the first group (with position is better), the average number of links per relation (verb - object) is 8 and the average entropy is 1.05; the average number of links per relation for the second group is almost twice more, 15.3, and their average entropy is also higher, 1.36. It shows that verbs which have many different ways of linking to an object might not have a *representative* relative position between the person and object, hence more difficult to be classified based on their positions. Verbs that have less links to an object tend to have more *fixed* relative positions between persons and objects, hence it might be helpful to use position information in classification.

A qualitative analysis We further examine actions where this statement does not apply, i.e., actions with high number of links and high entropy but belong to group 1 (position information helps) and actions with low number of links and entropy belonging to group 2. For the first case, typical actions which have high number of links/entropy are: ride car, ride bus, ride train, pull cart, light lamp. The large number of links of these actions seem to come from relations which do not describe the human/object interaction itself. For example, the links associated with 'ride bus' do not all actually refer to 'ride a bus' but to ride another object in a position with respect to the bus: ride after bus, ride behind bus, ride before bus. These cause extra links which are not related to the action itself. Similarly, actions pull of/around/behind/below/on cart, there is another object which is moved to a specific position with regards to the cart.

For the second case, examples of typical actions with low links but for which positions information doesn't help are hold harmonica, wear diaper, hold ladle, spread cream, hold racket, apply lipstick. These actions are related to objects, for which their positions depends a lot on the human pose (e.g., hold something). These actions in the language model do not contain many links as we expected: the most possible link between hold, harmonica is *in*, which probably means hold harmonica *in* your hand.

Instead of looking at actions, we look into typical verbs where position information helps in classifying actions and verbs where position information doesn't help. For the first group, the most frequent verbs are: chop, cut, drink, feed, lean, sit on, sleep, look at, put on, shake, shoot, wash, catch. For the second group, the most frequent verbs are: clean, cook, lift, punch, sing, spray, spread. It can be observed that verbs related to some particular poses or relative positions between human and object are better with the position information (chop, drink, sit on, sleep), and verbs related to more various human poses and unspecific are not helped by the position information (cook, sing, spray, clean).

Generally, there is a relation between prepositions in language and the relative positions between human-object in images. Although this statement does not hold in every cases, for example when the prepositions refer to the positions between another action (e.g., ride) and that object (e.g., after a bike), this can be potentially solved by better NLP parsing and analyses of verb phrases. Furthermore, actions that cannot be disambiguated by positions are usually related to different human poses, while actions that have some particular human poses can be classified using position information.

5 Conclusion

In this paper, we have introduced the Trento Universal Human Object Interaction image dataset, TUHOI. This dataset contains more than two thousand human actions associated with 189 common objects in images. The main characteristics of this dataset are that it follows the actual human action distribution observed in images, it captures different ways of describing an action and it enables the study of how verbs are used differently with different objects in images. Additionally, we performed some preliminary experiments in which we show that action recognition can benefit from using position information. Finally, we showed that this position information is related to prepositions that can be extracted from a general language model.

References

Stephane Ayache and Georges Quenot. 2008. Video Corpus Annotation using Active Learning. In *European Conference on Information Retrieval (ECIR)*, pages 187–198, Glasgow, Scotland, mar.

Marco Baroni and Alessandro Lenci. 2010. Distributional memory: A general framework for corpus-based semantics. *Computational Linguistics*.

Vincent Delaitre, Ivan Laptev, and Josef Sivic. 2010. Recognizing human actions in still images: a study of bag-of-features and part-based representations. In *BMVC*. BMVA Press.

Vincent Delaitre, Josef Sivic, and Ivan Laptev. 2011. Learning person-object interactions for action recognition in still images. In *NIPS*.

M. Everingham, L. Van Gool, C. K. I. Williams, J. Winn, and A. Zisserman. 2012. The PASCAL Visual Object Classes Challenge 2012 (VOC2012) Results.

Ali Farhadi, Mohsen Hejrati, Amin Sadeghi, Peter Young, Cyrus Rashtchian, Julia Hockenmaier, and David Forsyth. 2010. Every picture tells a story: Generating sentences for images. In *ECCV*.

Abhinav Gupta, Aniruddha Kembhavi, and Larry S. Davis. 2009. Observing human-object interactions: Using spatial and functional compatibility for recognition. *IEEE Trans. Pattern Anal. Mach. Intell.*, 31(10), October.

Nazli Ikizler, Ramazan Gokberk Cinbis, Selen Pehlivan, and Pinar Duygulu. 2008. Recognizing actions from still images. In *ICPR*, pages 1–4. IEEE.

Girish Kulkarni, Visruth Premraj, Sagnik Dhar, Siming Li, Yejin Choi, Alexander Berg, and Tamara Berg. 2011. Babytalk: Understanding and generating simple image descriptions. In *CVPR*.

Ivan Laptev. 2005. On space-time interest points. *Int. J. Comput. Vision*, 64(2-3):107–123, September.

Dieu Thu Le, Raffaella Bernardi, and Jasper Uijlings. 2013. Exploiting language models to recognize unseen actions. In *ICMR*.

Amin Sadeghi and Ali Farhadi. 2011. Recognition using visual phrases. In *CVPR*.

Heng Wang, Alexander Kläser, Cordelia Schmid, and Cheng-Lin Liu. Dense trajectories and motion boundary descriptors for action recognition.

Bangpeng Yao and Fei-Fei Li. 2010. Grouplet: A structured image representation for recognizing human and object interactions. In *CVPR*, pages 9–16.

Bangpeng Yao, Xiaoye Jiang, Aditya Khosla, Andy Lai Lin, Leonidas J. Guibas, and Li Fei-Fei. 2011. Action recognition by learning bases of action attributes and parts. In *ICCV*.

Concept-oriented labelling of patent images based on Random Forests and proximity-driven generation of synthetic data

Dimitris Liparas
Information Technologies Institute
Centre for Research and Technology Hellas
Thermi-Thessaloniki, Greece
dliparas@iti.gr

Anastasia Moumtzidou
Information Technologies Institute
Centre for Research and Technology Hellas
Thermi-Thessaloniki, Greece
moumtzid@iti.gr

Stefanos Vrochidis
Information Technologies Institute
Centre for Research and Technology Hellas
Thermi-Thessaloniki, Greece
stefanos@iti.gr

Ioannis Kompatsiaris
Information Technologies Institute
Centre for Research and Technology Hellas
Thermi-Thessaloniki, Greece
ikom@iti.gr

Abstract

Patent images are very important for patent examiners to understand the contents of an invention. Therefore there is a need for automatic labelling of patent images in order to support patent search tasks. Towards this goal, recent research works propose classification-based approaches for patent image annotation. However, one of the main drawbacks of these methods is that they rely upon large annotated patent image datasets, which require substantial manual effort to be obtained. In this context, the proposed work performs extraction of concepts from patent images building upon a supervised machine learning framework, which is trained with limited annotated data and automatically generated synthetic data. The classification is realised with Random Forests (RF) and a combination of visual and textual features. First, we make use of RF's implicit ability to detect outliers to rid our data of unnecessary noise. Then, we generate new synthetic data cases by means of Synthetic Minority Over-sampling Technique (SMOTE). We evaluate the different retrieval parts of the framework by using a dataset from the footwear domain. The results of the experiments indicate the benefits of using the proposed methodology.

1 Introduction

The vast number of patent documents submitted to patent offices worldwide calls for the need of advanced patent search technologies, which could deal effectively with the complexity and the unique characteristics of patents. The majority of existing patent retrieval techniques and search engines rely upon text, given the fact that the ideas and the innovations to be patented are described in text format in the claims and the disclosure parts of the patent. However, we should not overlook the fact that most of the patents include a drawings section, which contains figures, drawings and diagrams as a means to further describe and understand the patented inventions.

In the recent years, the Intellectual Property and Information Retrieval communities, motivated by the interest in patent image search, have directed their efforts towards the development of systems that have the ability to search in patents by considering both textual and visual information. Following the latest trends and challenges in image retrieval, the most recent studies in patent image search deal with concept extraction and classification using visual features (e.g. Csurka et al., 2011; Vrochidis et al., 2012). The concept extraction techniques involve the identification of images with common characteristics that fall into a specific semantic category or depict a specific concept. The motivation behind the interest in patent concept-based search is revealed by the following scenario presented in (De Marco, 2010): a patent searcher searches for a dancing shoe that incorporates a rotating heel with ball bearings; at first, the patent searcher recognises the main concepts of the invention (e.g. dancing shoe) and based on them keywords and relevant classification areas are defined. In many cases the important information is described with figures. Therefore, it would be important if the patent searcher could directly retrieve patents, which include figures depicting these concepts. The main obstacle of this ap-

Proceedings of the 25th International Conference on Computational Linguistics, pages 25–32,
Dublin, Ireland, August 23-29 2014.

proach is the need for a significant number of annotated images required during the training phase for developing models for each concept/category, something that is arduous and time-consuming (due to the specific nature of these images, it is not easy to retrieve training instances from the web).

To deal with the aforementioned restriction, we present an approach for concept extraction from patent images with the ability to supplement a small manually annotated dataset by means of automatic synthetic data cases generation. The proposed methodology is based on a supervised machine learning framework using Random Forests (RF) trained with textual and visual features. RF's advantage of handling multiclass classification tasks directly eliminates the need to develop a classification model for each concept separately. Moreover, its outlier detection technique carries out a suitable pre-processing of the data. The main contribution and the research objective of this paper is the examination of concept extraction based on multimodal classification, coupled with RF construction driven by synthetic data and outlier elimination. While the research works up to date apply Synthetic Minority Over-sampling Technique (SMOTE) for the purpose of overcoming imbalanced-related problems, the proposed approach extends the application of SMOTE to the generation of synthetic cases in an already balanced dataset. To the best of our knowledge, there isn't any relevant literature concerning the application of SMOTE to multiclass datasets that are balanced but contain a relatively small amount of training instances per class (which is the case in this study).

The rest of the paper is organised as follows: In Section 2 we provide the theoretical background of our study. In Section 3, the related work is presented. The feature extraction process and the architecture of the proposed framework are analysed in Sections 4 and 5, respectively. Section 6 describes the conducted experiments, as well as the results. Finally, concluding remarks are provided in Section 7.

2 Theoretical background

Random Forests (RF) is an ensemble learning method for classification and regression (Breiman, 2001). Its inherent ability to learn multiclass classification problems (without the need to convert the multiclass problem into a set of binary classification problems) makes it one of the most attractive machine learning algorithms. The fundamental idea of the methodology is the construction of a multitude of decision trees. RF operates on two sources of randomness. Firstly, each decision tree is grown on a different bootstrap sample drawn randomly from the training data. Secondly, at each node split during the construction of a decision tree, a random subset of p variables is selected from the original variable set and the best split based on these p variables is used. For predicting an unknown case, the predictions of the trees constituting the RF are aggregated (majority voting for classification / averaging for regression). For a RF consisting of N trees, the equation for predicting the class label l of a case y through majority voting is the following:

$$l(y) = argmax_c(\sum_{n=1}^{N} I_{h_n(y)=c}) \tag{1}$$

where I the indicator function and h_n the nth tree of the RF.

Among other things, RF can provide an internal estimate of its generalisation error. This is achieved by the out-of-bag (OOB) error estimate. For each tree that is constructed, only 2/3 of the original data cases are used in that particular bootstrap sample. The rest 1/3 of the instances (OOB data) are classified by the constructed tree and therefore, used for testing its performance. The OOB error estimate is the averaged prediction error for each training case y, using only the trees that do not include y in their bootstrap sample. Moreover, RF has a built-in mechanism for detecting outliers. Within the RF context, cases whose proximities to all other cases in the data are generally small can be considered outliers (Breiman, 2001). When a RF is constructed, all the training cases are put down each tree and their proximity matrix is computed, based on whether pairs of cases end up in the same terminal node of a tree. From this proximity matrix, an outlier measure for each case is derived. Cases whose outlier measure values exceed a specified threshold are detected as outliers. For a more thorough analysis of the core concepts of RF, see (Breiman, 2001).

Synthetic Minority Over-sampling Technique (SMOTE) is an approach for constructing efficient classifiers from imbalanced datasets (Chawla et al., 2002). A dataset can be defined as imbalanced if its classes are not evenly represented. The basic notion of the technique is the synthetic generation of new minority class examples, based on the nearest neighbours of these cases, coupled with the under-sampling of the majority class cases (Chawla et al., 2002).

3 Related work

Since our proposed framework deals with patent image classification, we report previous work related to patent image concept extraction and to the classification methodologies involved in this study.

3.1 Patent image search and classification

The first attempts in patent image search were based on the extraction of visual low level features with a view of retrieving visually similar images based on the query by visual example paradigm. Within this context, several systems have been developed, including PATSEEK (Tiwari and Bansal, 2004) and PatMedia image search engine (Vrochidis et al., 2010).

More recently, research in patent image search moved towards concept extraction and classification. The two main approaches followed for concept generation in multimedia content are: "content-based" and "text-based". The content-based analysis uses visual low-level features to represent the multimedia content. In such a work (Csurka et al., 2011) the authors extract SIFT-like local orientation histograms and they build visual vocabularies specific to patent images using Gaussian mixture model (GMM). Then the images are represented by Fisher features and linear classifiers are employed for the categorisation. On the other hand, text-based representation uses the indexing of media according to text that can be associated to it, such as titles or descriptions in associated metadata files. Although text-based representation can be considered as reliable, it depends on the existence and the quality of the annotations. Finally, other recent works consider both visual and textual information. For example, in (Vrochidis et al., 2012) the authors propose a supervised machine learning framework to extract semantic concepts from patent images by combining visual and textual information. Although the aforementioned studies deal with patent image concept extraction and classification, none of them considers the use of synthetically generated data to leverage the classification performance.

3.2 Random Forests/SMOTE

Over the years, RF has been successfully applied to a wide range of disciplines. More specifically, several studies dealing with image classification can be found in the relevant literature (see for example (Bosch et al., 2007)). In this domain, a number of modifications of the RF algorithm have been proposed (Moosmann et al., 2008; Xu et al., 2012). In addition, there has been some research addressing the outlier detection mechanism provided by RF (Zhang and Zulkernine, 2006).

Regarding SMOTE, many studies dealing with class imbalance problems have used this method to overcome such issues. Among others, (Wang, 2008; Gao et al., 2011) can be listed. Moreover, several improvements of the original algorithm have been introduced (Chawla et al., 2003; Wang et al., 2006).

In general, RF, as many other popular machine learning methods, needs a large amount of training data, in order to achieve good performance and be able to generalise to new, unknown instances. For any given classification problem, obtaining large datasets that contain existing training examples is not always feasible, therefore a need to create new synthetic data arises. Although existing applications of SMOTE are dealing with balancing imbalanced data (Wang, 2008; Gao et al., 2011), in this work we use SMOTE with the sole purpose of generating synthetic cases, in order to enrich and improve the training procedure of RF in a patent image classification framework.

4 Feature extraction from patent images

In this Section we briefly describe the extraction of visual and textual features from the patent images.

4.1 Visual features

The extraction of global concepts requires the employment of global visual features, which can capture the special characteristics of patent images (i.e. they are mostly black and white and depict technical drawings). Given the fact that general case image representation features consider colour and texture, which are absent in most of patent images, it is evident that we need to apply an algorithm that takes into account the geometry and the pixel distribution of these images. To this end, we employ the

Adaptive Hierarchical Density Histograms (AHDH) as visual feature vectors, due to the fact that they have shown discriminative power between binary complex drawings (Sidiropoulos et al., 2011).

The AHDH feature vector is generated based on the following steps. First, the algorithm involves a pre-processing phase for noise reduction, coordinate calculation and normalisation. Then, the first geometric centroid of the image plane is calculated and the image area is split into four regions based on the position of this centroid. In the following, the feature vector is initialised by estimating the distribution of the black points in each region. This procedure is repeated in a recursive way for a manually specified number of iterations (e.g. Fig. 1), and after each iteration, the feature vector is updated. This non-segmentation point-density orientated technique combines high accuracy at low computational cost as it represents the image with a low dimension feature vector (i.e. around 100 features).

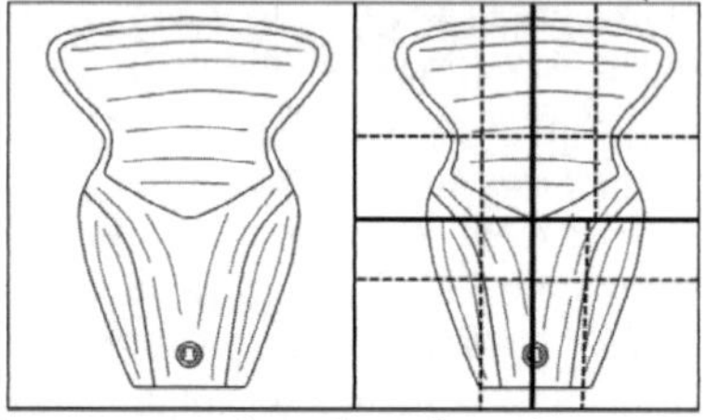

Fig. 1. The image is iteratively split to new regions based on the geometric centroids.

4.2 Textual features

Each figure of the patent document is linked to a description and caption found within the text. In order to exploit these textual descriptions, we apply a bag of words approach to model each figure with a vector. The bag of words model is a simplifying assumption used in natural language processing and information retrieval. In this model, a text (such as a sentence or a document) is represented as an unordered collection of words, disregarding grammar and even word order.

To generate such a vector we define a lexicon, which includes the most frequent words of this dataset. Then for each figure and based on the associated description we calculate a weight for each word included in the lexicon. The textual annotations are stemmed using the Porter stemming algorithm and the frequent stop words (e.g. and, so, etc.) are removed. The weight of each term is calculated with the well-established metric tf-idf (term frequency multiplied with the inverse document frequency).

5 Proposed methodology framework

The flowchart of the proposed concept extraction and classification framework (training phase) is depicted in Fig. 2. Next, the different steps and components of the framework are described in detail.

First, the **patent images and the captions associated to them are extracted** from the patent and in the following step the **visual and textual features are generated**, according to the procedures described in Section 4. In this approach we treat each modality's features independently. Thus, two different feature vectors (one for each modality) are formulated.

In the training phase, the feature vectors from each modality serve as input for the **construction of a RF** (section 2), from which we proceed to the **detection of possible outliers**. The latter is achieved in the following way: for each RF, the corresponding dataset's training cases are put down each tree. If a pair of cases end up in the same terminal node of a tree, their proximity is increased by 1. This is repeated for every pair of cases and all trees in the RF. In order to obtain the final proximity values we normalise them (divide them by the number of trees). Thus, if a dataset consists of N cases, a $N \times N$ proximity matrix is derived. From this proximity matrix a measure that indicates the outlierness of each case is computed. In general, since the RF algorithm is based on randomisation and in order to obtain robust and reliable estimations about potential outliers, we suggest that the RF construction for the outlier detection and elimination step is repeated several times for each modality and the resulting outlier measure values from the constructed RFs are averaged. In this way, the randomisation factor is minimised and the outliers can be detected with more confidence. We note that we opted to follow this approach. The cases that are identified as outliers are eliminated from further processing.

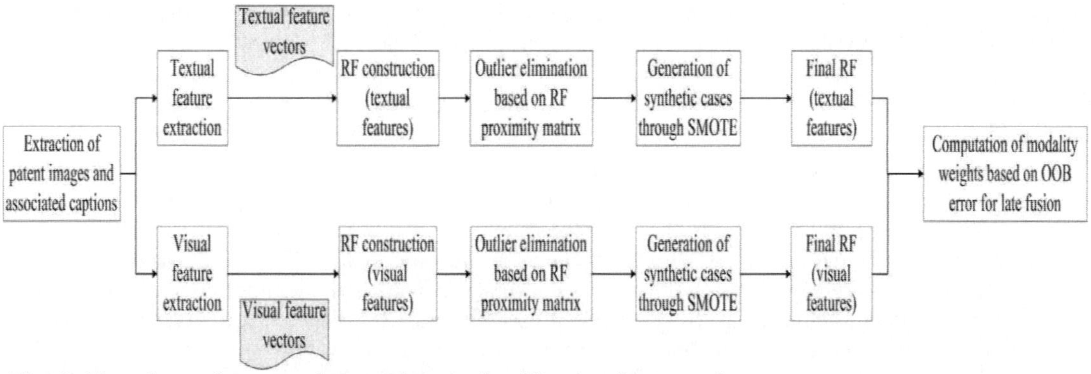

Fig. 2. Flowchart of proposed patent image classification framework

Next, the over-sampling procedure of SMOTE is employed, in order to **artificially generate new cases** and supplement the existing ones. The resulting larger datasets can lead to a better and more efficient RF training. It is important to note that the classes of the dataset used in this study are balanced in the first place. Therefore, we apply SMOTE not for balancing the classes of the training data, which was its main application to date (Section 2), but for introducing new training cases. According to (Chawla et al., 2002), SMOTE over-samples each case by introducing synthetic examples along the line segments joining a number (the number depends on the amount of over-sampling required) of that case's nearest neighbours. The over-sampling procedure is applied to each modality's dataset and to each concept separately. In this way the final datasets are created and correspondingly, the **final RFs for the textual and visual features are constructed**.

Finally, for the **formulation of the final RF predictions, a late fusion strategy is applied** as follows: from the OOB error estimate (for the entire data set) of each modality's RF, the corresponding OOB accuracy values are computed. These values are normalised (by dividing them by their sum) and serve as weights for the two modalities. During the testing phase, when the RF predicts a case, it outputs probability estimates per class for that case. The probability outputs P_t and P_v from the textual and visual RFs respectively are multiplied by their corresponding modality weights W_t and W_v and summed, in order to produce the final RF predictions as in the following equation:

$$P_{fused} = W_t P_t + W_v P_v \tag{2}$$

6 Experimental design - Results

6.1 Dataset description – Experimental setup

The dataset[1] was manually extracted from around 300 patents. It contains around 1000 patent images depicting parts of footwear. The feature vectors that were generated (Section 4) for this dataset consist of 100 visual and 250 textual features. With the help of professional patent searchers we selected the following 8 concepts for this domain: cleat, ski boot, high heel, lacing closure, heel with spring, tongue, toe caps and roller skates (Vrochidis et al., 2012). The procedure of associating the patent images with the figure text descriptions was carried out manually. This was done in order to acquire quality data and consequently, draw safer conclusions on the concept extraction method. The images were manually annotated with the support and advice of professional patent searchers.

For our experiments, the dataset was randomly split into training and test sets. We kept 2/3 of the images for training purposes, whereas the rest (1/3) were used as test set, in order to estimate the classification scheme's performance. We note here that because of the fact that RF provides an internal estimate of its performance on cases that do not participate in its training procedure (the OOB error estimate), no cross-validation was required. Moreover, since SMOTE is applied during the training phase, it is important to mention that the test set contains only real (not synthetic) data.

[1] Available for download at http://mklab.iti.gr/files/concepts-patent_images.rar

Regarding the parameters of the methods involved in the experiments, we selected and applied the following setting: The number of trees used for the construction of each RF was set based on the OOB error estimate. After conducting several experiments and gradually increasing the number of trees, we noticed that the OOB error estimate was stabilised after using 1000 trees and no longer improved. Hence, the number of trees was set to 1000. Moreover, for each node split during the growing of each tree, the number of the subset of variables used to determine the best split was set to $\sqrt{k}$, where k is the total number of features of the dataset (according to (Breiman, 2001)). Concerning the RF outlier detection and elimination procedure, (Breiman, 2003) states that a case can be considered an outlier if its outlier measure value is higher than 10. We note that after choosing this configuration, approximately 2% of the textual modality's cases were detected as outliers and discarded, keeping the rest of the cases for further processing, while for the visual modality no outliers were detected. Finally, the SMOTE oversampling rate for each concept in both modalities datasets was set to 500%, i.e. for each case 5 new synthetic cases were generated, based on this case's nearest neighbours.

6.2 Results

In order to evaluate the performance of the proposed methodology, we computed the precision, recall and F-score measures for each concept, along with their corresponding macro-averaged values. Table 1 summarises the test set results from the application of RF to the initial dataset, without any outlier deletion and without the use of SMOTE. The results refer to each modality separately, as well as to their fused (according to the OOB error estimates) output scores (Visual + Textual). Since the F-score takes into account precision and recall simultaneously, we consider it the most important metric for the evaluation of the results. Moreover, since we are handling this classification problem in a multiclass manner, we are more interested in the macro-average value of F-score. The results verify the notion mentioned in Section 1 that textual data is a very reliable source of information for the patent retrieval, since the textual modality achieves a macro-averaged F-score value of 73.7%, compared to 67.4% for the visual modality. However, the late fusion of the outputs of each modality's RF provides us with improved results compared to the ones provided by each single modality, as evident from the corresponding macro-averaged F-score value (81.8%). This suggests that the visual and textual modalities can complement each other in the patent image classification task. If we observe the results for each concept independently, we notice that the textual features do not outperform the visual ones only for the "Ski boot", "High heel" and "Lacing" concepts. On the other hand, the fused results are better than the corresponding visual and textual results for every concept, with only the exception of "Tongue", where the textual features achieve the same performance (89.9% for the F-score).

Concepts	**Visual**			**Textual**			**Visual + Textual**		
	Prec.	Rec.	F-score	Prec.	Rec.	F-score	Prec.	Rec.	F-score
Cleat	73.3%	55.9%	63.4%	70.1%	67.8%	68.9%	82.4%	79.6%	80.9%
Ski boot	94.4%	69.4%	80%	74.1%	81.6%	77.6%	76.2%	91.8%	83.2%
High heel	63.6%	83%	71.9%	51.7%	76.2%	61.5%	76.4%	93.2%	83.9%
Lacing	51.5%	71.7%	59.9%	62.8%	47.8%	54.2%	76.3%	63%	69%
Spring	70.5%	73.8%	72.1%	89.6%	61.9%	73.2%	90.6%	69%	78.3%
Tongue	76.6%	46.9%	58.1%	88.2%	91.8%	89.9%	88.2%	91.8%	89.9%
Toe caps	70.6%	55.8%	62.2%	83.8%	72.1%	77.5%	82.9%	79.1%	80.9%
Roller	64.3%	80.6%	71.5%	89.1%	85.1%	87%	90.6%	86.5%	88.5%
Macro-average	**70.6%**	**67.1%**	**67.4%**	**76.2%**	**73%**	**73.7%**	**82.9%**	**81.7%**	**81.8%**

Table 1. Precision, recall and F-score test set results (without outlier deletion and without SMOTE)

In Table 2 we report the test set results from the RF application to the dataset after the deletion of the detected outliers and the use of SMOTE. While a minor degradation for the F-scores of some of the concepts for both modalities (compared to the RF application to the original dataset) is obvious, it seems that in average RF has benefited from the outlier elimination procedure and the generation of new cases through SMOTE, as the macro-averaged F-scores have been improved (69.5% for the visual and 75.7% for the textual features). In this case, the visual-based classification performs better than the textual-based one only for the "High heel" and "Lacing" concepts. The fusion of the modalities outperforms each one of them (84.2%) and moreover, there is a 2.4% improvement compared to the fused results for the initial dataset. Finally, in Figs. 3 and 4 the first 6 results for the "Ski boot" and "Tongue" concepts (respectively), using the final dataset, are presented. The precision achieved for this set of results is 83.3% (5/6) for the "Ski boot" and 100% (6/6) for the "Tongue" concept.

Concepts	Visual			Textual			Visual + Textual		
	Prec.	Rec.	F-score	Prec.	Rec.	F-score	Prec.	Rec.	F-score
Cleat	66.1%	66.1%	66.1%	79.2%	71.2%	75%	89.1%	83.1%	85.9%
Ski boot	85.7%	73.5%	79.1%	77.7%	85.7%	81.5%	80.4%	83.7%	81.9%
High heel	68.6%	81.4%	74.4%	76.9%	67.8%	72%	80.6%	84.7%	82.6%
Lacing	50%	76.1%	60.3%	42.4%	60.9%	50%	67.3%	76.1%	71.4%
Spring	68.1%	71.4%	69.7%	73.9%	81%	77.3%	90.2%	88.1%	89.1%
Tongue	78.3%	59.2%	67.4%	86.3%	89.8%	88%	88.2%	91.8%	89.9%
Toe caps	72.2%	60.5%	65.8%	90.6%	67.4%	77.2%	89.7%	81.4%	85.3%
Roller	74.2%	73.1%	73.6%	90%	80.6%	85%	90.5%	85.1%	87.7%
Macro-average	**70.4%**	**70.1%**	**69.5%**	**77.1%**	**75.5%**	**75.7%**	**84.5%**	**84.2%**	**84.2%**

Table 2. Precision, recall and F-score test set results (with outlier deletion and SMOTE)

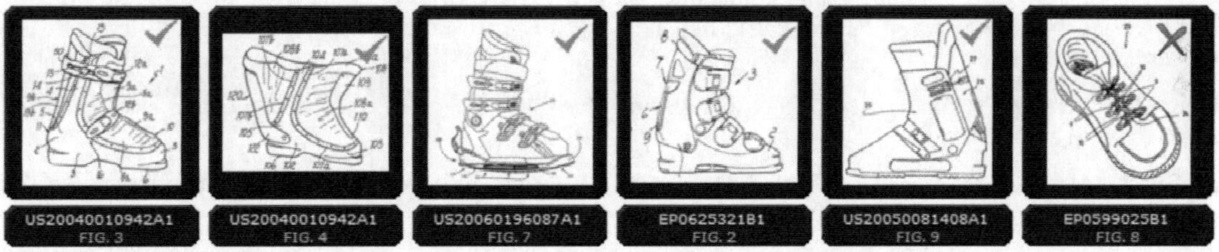

Fig. 3. Results for the "Ski boot" concept. The green tics indicate the correct results.

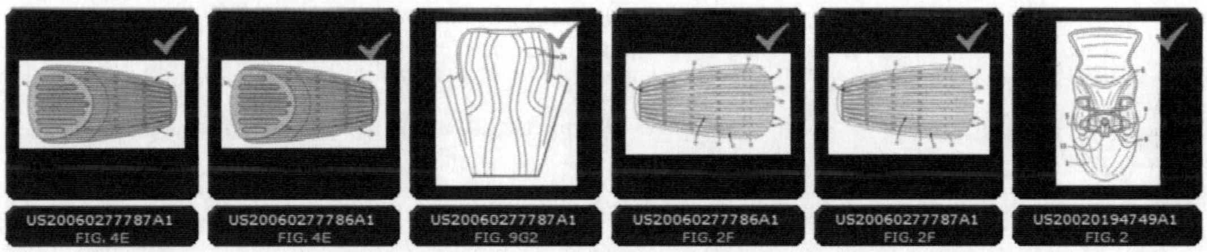

Fig. 4. Results for the "Tongue" concept. The green tics indicate the correct results.

7 Conclusions

In this study a concept extraction and multimodal classification framework for patent images trained with synthetic data, is introduced. The implicit ability of RF to deal effectively with multiclass classification problems and to perform a suitable filtering of the data, according to how well the dataset's instances fit in its construction procedure, coupled with the benefits of using an over-sampling technique such as SMOTE, provide a final result that leads to enhanced classification performance.

The application of this framework could augment existing (mainly text-based) patent search systems. Although the framework has been tested with a limited set of concepts, the methodology based on RF is scalable and the application of SMOTE minimises the need for training data. In addition the application of the concept extraction methodology to patents that belong to the same IPC (International Patent Classification) class and/or groups will allow for targeting only a specific set of concepts (relevant to the corresponding IPC class). The concept-based retrieval functionality will enable patent examiners to search in patent figures based on their visual content and therefore speed up and improve the performance of patent search tasks for patent invalidation and competitive intelligence research.

Our recommendations for future work include the testing of different parameter settings than the one used in this study and the evaluation of their performance, the expansion of the experiments with a very large set of concepts and finally, the investigation of alternative multimodal fusion approaches, such as the one presented in (Roller and Schulte im Walde, 2013).

Acknowledgment: This work was supported by MULTISENSOR project (FP7-610411).

Reference

Anna Bosch, Andrew Zisserman, and Xavier Munoz. 2007. *Image classification using random forests and ferns*. In ICCV, 1-8.

Leo Breiman. 2001. *Random Forests*. In Machine Learning, 45(1): 5-32.

Leo Breiman. 2003. *Manual – Setting up, using and understanding random forests v4.0*. http://oz.berkeley.edu/users/breiman/ Using_random_forests_v4.0.pdf.

Nitesh V. Chawla, Kevin W. Bowyer, Lawrence O. Hall, and W. Philip Kegelmeyer. 2002. *SMOTE: Synthetic Minority Over-Sampling Technique*. Journal of Artificial Intelligence Research, 16: 321-357.

Nitesh V. Chawla, Aleksandar Lazarevic, Lawrence O. Hall, and Kevin W. Bowyer. 2003. *SMOTEBoost: Improving prediction of the minority class in boosting*. In 7th European Conference on Principles and Practice of Knowledge Discovery in Databases, 107–119.

Gabriela Csurka, Jean-Michel Renders, and Guillaume Jacquet. 2011. G. *XRCE's Participation at Patent Image Classification and Image-based Patent Retrieval Tasks of the Clef-IP 2011*. In: Proceedings of CLEF 2011, Amsterdam

Dominic De Marco. 2010. *Mechanical Patent Searching: A Moving Target*. Patent Information Users Group (PIUG), Baltimore, USA

Ming Gao, Xia Hong, Sheng Chen, and Chris J. Harris. 2011. *A combined SMOTE and PSO based RBF classifier for two-class imbalanced problems*. Neurocomputing, 74:3456–3466.

Frank Moosmann, Eric Nowak, and Frederic Jurie. 2008. *Randomized clustering forests for image classification*. IEEE Transactions on PAMI, 30(9): 1632-1646.

Stephen Roller and Stephen Schulte im Walde. 2013. *A multimodal LDA model integrating textual, cognitive and visual modalities*. In Proceedings of the 2013 Joint Conference on Empirical Methods in Natural Language Processing and Computational Natural Language Learning, 1146–1157, Seattle, Washington, USA

Panagiotis Sidiropoulos, Stefanos Vrochidis, and Ioannis Kompatsiaris. 2011. *Content-based binary image retrieval using the adaptive hierarchical density histogram. Pattern Recognition Journal*, 44(4):739–750.

Avinash Tiwari and Veena Bansal. 2004. PATSEEK: *Content Based Image Retrieval System for Patent Database*. In: Proceedings International Conference on Electronic Business, Beijing, China

Stefanos Vrochidis, Symeon Papadopoulos, Anastasia Moumtzidou, Panagiotis Sidiropoulos, Emanuele Pianta, and Ioannis Kompatsiaris. 2010. *Towards Content-based Patent Image Retrieval; A Framework Perspective. World Patent Information Journal*, 32(2):94-106.

Stefanos Vrochidis, Anastasia Moumtzidou, and Ioannis Kompatsiaris. 2012. *Concept-based Patent Image Retrieval. World Patent Information Journal*, 34(4):292-303.

Juanjuan Wang, Mantao Xu, Hui Wang, and Jiwu Zhang. 2006. *Classification of imbalanced data by using the SMOTE algorithm and locally linear embedding*. In 8th International Conference on Signal Processing, 3:16–20.

He-Yong Wang. 2008. *Combination approach of SMOTE and biased-SVM for imbalanced datasets*, Proc. of the IEEE Int. Joint Conf. on Neural Networks, IJCNN 2008, Hong Kong (PRC), 22-31.

Baoxun Xu, Yunming Ye, and Lei Nie. 2012. *An improved random forest classifier for image classification*. In Information and Automation (ICIA), 2012 International Conference on IEEE, 795-800.

Jiong Zhang and Mohammad Zulkernine. 2006. *A Hybrid Network Intrusion Detection Technique Using Random Forests*. In Proceedings of IEEE First International Conference on Availability, Reliability and Security (ARES'06).

Exploration of functional semantics of prepositions from corpora of descriptions of visual scenes

Simon Dobnik[1] and **John D. Kelleher**[2*]
[1]University of Gothenburg, Centre for Language Technology,
Dept. of Philosophy, Linguistics & Theory of Science, Gothenburg, Sweden
[2]Dublin Institute of Technology, Applied Intelligence Research Centre,
School of Computing, Dublin, Ireland
simon.dobnik@gu.se, john.d.kelleher@dit.ie

Abstract

We present a method of extracting functional semantic knowledge from corpora of descriptions of visual scenes. Such knowledge is required for interpretation and generation of spatial descriptions in tasks such as visual search. We identify semantic classes of target and landmark objects related by each preposition by abstracting over WordNet taxonomy. The inclusion of such knowledge in visual search should equip robots with a better, more human-like spatial cognition.

1 Introduction

Visual search is an area of growing research importance in mobile robotics; see (Sjöö, 2011; Kunze et al., 2014) among others. Visual search involves directing the visual sensors of a robot with the goal of locating a specific object. Several recent approaches have integrated non-visual (often linguistically motivated information) into the visual search process. The intuition behind this is that if the robot knows that object X is often located *near/on/...* object Y then in situations where Y is visually salient it may be easier for the system to search by first locating Y and then use relational information to direct the search for X. A key component of these approaches to visual search is the definition of spatial semantics of the relational information. Appropriately modelling these semantics is crucial because fundamentally it is these models that define the scope of the visual search in relation to Y.

In language spatial relations between objects are often expressed using *locative expressions* such as "the apple above a bowl", "the computer is on the shelf" and "the plane is over the house". In these expressions a *target* object is located relative to a *landmark* object using a *preposition* to describe the spatial relation. Crucially, there are differences between prepositions with respect to how their spatial relations are defined. The semantics of some prepositions can be modelled in terms of geometric primitives whereas the semantics of other prepositions are sensitive to the functional relations between the target and the landmark (Coventry and Garrod, 2004). Consider the example "Alex is at her desk". This description refers to a situation where Alex is not only geometrically proximate to her desk but also where she is sitting down and working. The extra constraints are coming from the functional relations that normally exist between an individual and a desk.

Returning to visual search, being able to identify whether a given preposition is primarily geometric of functional is important because this classification informs the design of the spatial semantics for the preposition and hence the appropriate definition of the search relative to the landmark object. In this paper we present some ongoing experiments which attempt to develop techniques that can classify prepositions as geometric or functional.

2 Spatial descriptions

(Coventry and Garrod, 2004) show in the experiments with human observers of images of a man in the rain holding an umbrella where the umbrella is providing a varying degree of protection from the rain that "above" is more sensitive to the geometrical component than "over" and that "over" is more

[*] Both authors are equal contributors.

Proceedings of the 25th International Conference on Computational Linguistics, pages 33–37,
Dublin, Ireland, August 23-29 2014.

sensitive to the object function component than "above". Descriptions of "the umbrella is over a man" were considered acceptable even in cases where the umbrella was held horizontally but was providing protection from the rain.

Modelling of functional knowledge in the computational models of meaning of spatial prepositions is not straightforward. Humans (and even expert linguists) do not seem to have clear intuitions what the functional component of each preposition sense may be and hence they must be confirmed experimentally (Garrod et al., 1999). This may take significant time for various combinations of prepositions and target and landmark objects. One needs to develop a complex ontology of object properties and then associate spatial prepositions with rules that pick out certain properties of objects for a particular preposition sense (for examples of such rules see (Garrod et al., 1999, p.170)).

In this paper we describe a method of extraction of these meaning components from a corpus of descriptions of visual scenes automatically. Unlike in the psycho-linguistic experiments described above we examine general corpora that obtain a wide and unrestricted set of images that humans described freely. The purpose of the experiment is to investigate whether functional knowledge can be extracted from contextual language use. For example, can we make generalisations about the semantics of the arguments that a particular prepositional sense takes automatically. Furthermore, we are also interested if the distinctions between geometric and functional sensitivity of prepositions reported experimentally could be determined this way. This information would allow us to weight the contributions of the geometric and functional knowledge when generating and interpreting spatial descriptions of scenes. We hypothesise, that if a preposition is sensitive to functional meaning then there will be functional relations between target and landmark objects that it is used with and consequently the preposition will will be much more restrictive or specific in the semantic type of targets and landmarks that it requires. Other prepositions may be more sensitive to the satisfaction of the geometric constraint and hence we expect that they will co-occur with objects of more general semantic types.

3 Datasets and extraction of spatial descriptions

The goal of this work is to analyse the semantics of linguistic expressions that are used to describe the relative location of objects in visual contexts. We base our analysis on two corpora of image descriptions: specifically, the IAPR TC-12 Benchmark corpus (Grubinger et al., 2006)[1] which contains 20,000 images and multi-sentence descriptions and the 8K ImageFlickr dataset (Rashtchian et al., 2010)[2] which contains 8108 images. In both corpora the situations and events represented by images are described by several sentences which contain spatial descriptions with prepositions: in the first case all sentences are by a single annotator and in the second case each sentence is by a different annotator. The descriptions are geometrically constrained by the visual context. On the other hand, the describers' choice of the target and the landmarks objects and the preposition in these descriptions will tell us about their functional semantics. The main pre-processing step was to extract parts of spatial expressions used in the image descriptions. Once extracted each spatial expression was stored in a type with the following structure: ⟨preposition, target, landmark⟩. To do this extraction we first parsed both corpora of linguistic descriptions for dependencies (Marneffe et al., 2006) using Stanford CoreNLP tools[3]. Then we wrote several extraction rules that matched dependency parses and extracted all three parts of spatial expressions that we are looking for. All words were lemmatized and converted to lower case, compound prepositions such as "on the left side of" were rewritten as single words and names, etc. were converted to their named entity categories such as "person". The extracted patterns from both corpora were combined into a single dataset from which we can determine their frequency counts.

4 Determining conceptual categories of objects

The intuition behind our experiment is that functionally defined prepositions can be distinguished from geometrically defined prepositions by virtue of the fact that the functional relations between the target

[1]http://imageclef.org/photodata

[2]http://nlp.cs.illinois.edu/HockenmaierGroup/8k-pictures.html

[3]http://nlp.stanford.edu/software/corenlp.shtml

and landmark objects that are encoded in the semantics of functional prepositions result in less variance across the object types that occur with geometric prepositions. In other words, the target objects that occur with a functional preposition will be more semantically similar to each other than the target objects that occur with a geometric preposition. Likewise the landmark objects that occur with a functional preposition will be more semantically similar than the landmark objects that occur with a geometric preposition. In order to test this intuition we need to be able to cluster the target and landmark objects that occur with a given preposition into conceptual categories. We can then define patterns that describe the pairs of conceptual categories that a preposition occurs with. Based on the intuition that functional prepositions occur with more specific object classes we would expect that functional prepositions generate more patterns of use and that the patterns include more specific classes of objects.

To determine conceptual categories that objects of prepositions belong to, WordNet (Fellbaum, 1998) appears to be an ideal tool. It contains taxonomies of words that were constructed by humans using their intuitions. While certain classification of words in the ontology are not entirely unproblematic it is nonetheless considered a gold-standard resource for lexical semantics. In particular, we are interested in finding out given a certain preposition what are the possible semantic classes of its target and landmark objects. To determine the class synset (a sense in WordNet terminology) that covers a bag of words best we use the *class-labelling algorithm* of Widdows (2003). Given a list of words, this algorithm finds hypernyms which subsume as many as possible words in the list, as closely as possible. The algorithm works by first defining the set of all possible hypernyms for the words in the list. In then computes a score for each of the hypernyms: a hypernym score is incremented by a small positive value for each word it subsumes (this positive value is defined as 1 divided by the square of the vertical distance in the hierarchy between the hypernym and the word) and decremented by a small negative value g for each word it does not subsume. The algorithm returns the hypernym with the highest score. Widdows (2003) sets g to 0.25 for lists that contain 5 words on average. The lists in our experiments are much longer so we scale g to the length of the list input: $g = 0.25 \times \frac{5}{list\ length}$. Given a bag of nouns we use the class-labelling algorithm to determine the bets matching hypernym. Words that are subsumed by this hypernym are labelled as belonging to this class and are removed from the bag of words. The algorithm is repeated on the remaining words recursively until all words from the bag of words are exhausted. The procedure allows us to greedily create classes of words that are most general categories representing these words, the level of generality can be tweaked by the parameter g. The bag of words is allowed to contain duplicates as these are indicators of coherent classes. Duplicate words are all covered by a common hypernym and hence this hypernym will be given more weight in the overall scoring. The hypernyms introduced by infrequent and non-similar words are given less weight. This filters words that may be included due to an error.

5 Patterns of prepositional use

The algorithm for class-labelling of words backed by the WordNet ontology allows us to predict the typical classes or semantic types of the landmark and the target objects related by a preposition. From these several patterns can be generated. Such patterns can be used both in the interpretation of visual scenes (visual search) or generation of spatial referring expressions that optimally constrain the set of intended objects. We create the patterns by collecting all targets and all landmarks that occur with a particular preposition. We apply the class labelling on the bags of words representing the targets and the landmarks to obtain a set of classes representing targets and landmarks. Finally, for every tuple ⟨target, preposition, landmark⟩ we replace target and landmark with target class and landmark class and collect a set of ⟨target class, preposition, landmark class⟩ patterns. This method assumes that targets and landmarks are semantically independent of each other. Below are some examples of patterns that our algorithm has found (the notation for the names of the objects corresponds to the names of synsets in the WordNet taxonomy, the numbers in brackets indicate the number of examples out of total examples covered by this pattern): (i) travel.v.01 over object.n.01 (9/713), sunlight.n.01 over object.n.01 (13/713), bridge.n.01 over object.n.01 (23/713), bridge.n.01 over body_of_water.n.01 (42/713), air.v.03 over object.n.01 (36/713), artifact.n.01 over body_of_water.n.01 (42/713), artifact.n.01 over object.n.01

(175/713),...(ii) breeze.n.01 above body_of_water.n.01 (8/183), person.n.01 above artifact.n.01 (9/183), artifact.n.01 above steer.v.01 (14/183), artifact.n.01 above entrance.n.01 (16/183) artifact.n.01 above artifact.n.01 (27/183),...(iii) person.n.01 under tree.n.01 (7/213), shirt.n.01 under sweater.n.01 (8/213), person.n.01 under body_of_water.n.01 (11/213), person.n.01 under artifact.n.01 (13/213) artifact.n.01 under artifact.n.01 (16/213), person.n.01 under structure.n.01 (17/213), artifact.n.01 under structure.n.01 (21/213),...(iv) box.n.05 below window.n.08 (1/14), crown.n.04 below script.n.01 (2/14),...[4] The patterns show that different prepositions which are seemingly synonyms when considering geometry ("over"/"above" and "below"/"under") do relate different types of objects and from the labels of the semantic classes we may speculate what kind of semantic knowledge the relations are sensitive to. Importantly, the labels of the classes and different patterns extracted show that there may be several distinct and even unrelated situations that a preposition is referring to. Consider for example, person.n.01 under tree.n.01, shirt.n.01 under sweater.n.01 (8/213), person.n.01 under body of water.n.01 are denoting three different kinds of situations which require distinct and unrelated geometric arrangements. Overall, the results indicate that the method is able to extract functional knowledge which is a reflection of the way humans conceptualise objects and relations between them and which may be useful for improving visual processing of scenes.

Another question we set off to answer is whether from the patterns one can determine the functional and geometric bias of a preposition. As noted previously, our application of the class labelling algorithm is greedy and attempts to cover a large number of words. The more words are generalised over the more generic classes are created. To counter this confounding factor we down-sampled the dataset by creating, for the results we report here, 50 samples of 20 randomly chosen words. The same procedure for creating patterns of prepositional use was applied as before. On each sampling iteration we estimate for each preposition **(i) the average depth of the target and landmark hypernyms** in the WordNet taxonomy, **(ii) the number of patterns created**, and **(iii) the entropy of the patterns** over the examples in the dataset. Finally, we average all values obtained from iterations and we rank the prepositions by the ascending values of the these measures as shown below:

(i) on (3.17), near (3.55), with (3.66), next to (3.83), of (3.95), between (4.17), in front of (4.26), above (4.27), over (4.48), around (4.52), behind (4.65), from (4.74), at (4.89), under (4.93), for (4.97), through (5.27), in (5.45)

(ii) on (10.5), with (11.5), near (12), next to (12.1), between (12.6), of (12.6), above (12.7), around (13), in front of (13.1), over (13.7), from (13.8), behind (13.9), for (14.2), under (14.3), in (14.5), through (15.1), at (15.2)

(iii) on (2.74), next to (3.05), with (3.07), near (3.1), between (3.2), of (3.29), above (3.33), around (3.36), in front of (3.39), over (3.48), from (3.5), behind (3.51), for (3.59), under (3.62), in (3.62), through (3.75), at (3.76)

With small variations all measures (i), (ii) and (iii) rank the prepositions very similarly. Items at the beginning of the list are used with target and landmark objects that belong to more general classes (i), they are covered by a lower number of preposition patterns (ii), and the entropy of these patterns is low (iii)[5]. Hence, we expect that items at the top of the lists are less affected by the type of the target and landmark objects than items at the bottom of the lists. They are the prepositions where the geometric component is stronger to determine the spatial relation. On the other hand, prepositions at the bottom of the list rely more on the functional component of meaning. The results predict the observations from the literature. Although, being sometimes quite close "above" precedes "over" in respect to to all three measures. "Below" was not processed in this study as there were too few examples but "under" is found at the tail of the list. The ranking of other prepositions also aligns with our intuitions. For example, "on", appearing as the head of the list, requires a contact between objects (a geometric notion), whereas "in", appearing in the tail of the list requires that the target is constrained by the landmark (a functional notion).

[4]There are only 14 examples of "below" in the dataset for which nearly always unique patterns were created.

[5]Entropy balances between the number of classes and the frequency of items in them. Low entropy indicates that there is a tendency of items clustering in small number of specific classes rather rather than being equally dispersed over classes.

6 Conclusions and further work

In the preceding discussion we have demonstrated a method of extracting (i) functional semantic knowledge – required for the generation and interpretation of spatial descriptions – from the corpora of descriptions referring to visual scenes and (ii) made predictions about the bias of spatial descriptions to functional knowledge. We hope that this information can facilitate visual search as it further restricts the set of possible situations and objects involved. We have constructed several patterns of preposition use and have shown that a preposition such as "under" may refer to several distinct situations constrained by the knowledge of object function and that these situations would require geometric representations that are likely to be quite different. This knowledge should allow us to create different routines for visual search that could be applied over a wide set of domains and would better approximate the way humans perceive and reason about space. The applicability of this information for visual search must be properly evaluated in a visual application. Estimating the functional or geometric bias of prepositions informs us for their modelling but more importantly confirms that the patterns extracted here follow the experimental observations reported in the literature.

In the procedure we have made several design choices: the choice of the corpora and the way the corpora is processed and information extracted, the algorithm with which words are labelled for semantic classes and finally the method with which patterns are created. For example, before class labelling we could use an algorithm that clusters words of similar hypernym depth into discrete classes over which hypernyms are generalised. This would allow us to distinguish better between different situations that a preposition is referring to. When creating patterns we assume that target and landmark objects are independent of each other. However, this may not necessarily be the case. For example, the category of the target object may constrain the category of the landmark which means that the latter category should only be generalised over landmark words that occur with some target category.

References

Kenny R Coventry and Simon C Garrod. 2004. *Saying, seeing, and acting: the psychological semantics of spatial prepositions*. Psychology Press, Hove, East Sussex.

Christiane Fellbaum. 1998. *WordNet: an electronic lexical database*. MIT Press, Cambridge, Mass.

Simon Garrod, Gillian Ferrier, and Siobhan Campbell. 1999. In and on: investigating the functional geometry of spatial prepositions. *Cognition*, 72(2):167–189.

Michael Grubinger, Paul D. Clough, Henning Müller, and Thomas Deselaers. 2006. The IAPR benchmark: A new evaluation resource for visual information systems. In *Proceedings of OntoImage 2006: Workshop on language resources for content-based mage retrieval during LREC 2006*, Genoa, Italy, 22 May. European Language Resources Association.

Lars Kunze, Chris Burbridge, and Nick Hawes. 2014. Bootstrapping probabilistic models of qualitative spatial relations for active visual object search. In *AAAI Spring Symposium 2014 on Qualitative Representations for Robots*, Stanford University in Palo Alto, California, US, March, 24–26.

Marie-Catherine De Marneffe, Bill MacCartney, and Christopher D. Manning. 2006. Generating typed dependency parses from phrase structure parses. In *Proceedings of Int'l Conf. on Language Resources and Evaluation (LREC)*, pages 449–454, Genoa, Italy. European Language Resources Association.

Cyrus Rashtchian, Peter Young, Micah Hodosh, and Julia Hockenmaier. 2010. Collecting image annotations using Amazon's Mechanical Turk. In *Proceedings of the NAACL HLT 2010 Workshop on creating speech and language data with Amazon's Mechanical Turk*, Los Angeles, CA, 6 June. North American Chapter of the Association for Computational Linguistics (NAACL).

Kristoffer Sjöö. 2011. *Functional understanding of space: Representing spatial knowledge using concepts grounded in an agent's purpose*. Ph.D. thesis, KTH, Computer Vision and Active Perception (CVAP), Centre for Autonomous Systems (CAS), Stockholm, Sweden.

Dominic Widdows. 2003. Unsupervised methods for developing taxonomies by combining syntactic and statistical information. In *Proceedings of the 2003 Conference of the North American Chapter of the Association for Computational Linguistics on Human Language Technology*, volume 1, pages 197–204. Association for Computational Linguistics.

A Poodle or a Dog? Evaluating Automatic Image Annotation Using Human Descriptions at Different Levels of Granularity

Josiah K. Wang[1] **Fei Yan**[2] **Ahmet Aker**[1] **Robert Gaizauskas**[1]

[1] Department of Computer Science, University of Sheffield, UK
[2] Centre for Vision, Speech and Signal Processing, University of Surrey, UK

{j.k.wang, ahmet.aker, r.gaizauskas}@sheffield.ac.uk f.yan@surrey.ac.uk

Abstract

Different people may describe the same object in different ways, and at varied levels of granularity ("poodle", "dog", "pet" or "animal"?) In this paper, we propose the idea of 'granularity-aware' groupings where semantically related concepts are grouped *across* different levels of granularity to capture the variation in how different people describe the same image content. The idea is demonstrated in the task of automatic image annotation, where these semantic groupings are used to alter the results of image annotation in a manner that affords different insights from its initial, category-independent rankings. The semantic groupings are also incorporated during evaluation against image descriptions written by humans. Our experiments show that semantic groupings result in image annotations that are more informative and flexible than without groupings, although being too flexible may result in image annotations that are less informative.

1 Introduction

Describing the content of an image is essential for various tasks such as image indexing and retrieval, and the organization and browsing of large image collections. Recent years have seen substantial progress in the field of visual object recognition, allowing systems to automatically annotate an image with a list of terms representing concepts depicted in the image. Fueled by advances in recognition algorithms and the availability of large scale datasets such as ImageNet (Deng et al., 2009), current systems are able to recognize thousands of object categories with reasonable accuracy, for example achieving an error rate of 0.11 in classifying $1,000$ categories in the ImageNet Large Scale Visual Recognition Challenge 2013 (ILSVRC13) (Russakovsky et al., 2013).

However, the ILSVRC13 classification challenge assumes each image is annotated with only *one* correct label, although systems are allowed up to five guesses per image to make the correct prediction (or rather, to match the ground truth label). The problem with this is that it becomes difficult to guess what the 'correct' label is, especially when many other categories can equally be considered correct. For instance, should a system label an image containing an instance of a dog (and possibly some other objects like a ball and a couch) as "dog", "poodle", "puppy", "pet", "domestic dog", "canine" or even "animal" (in addition to "ball", "tennis ball", "toy", "couch", "sofa", *etc.*)? The problem becomes even harder when the number of possible ways to refer to the same object instance increases, but the number of prediction slots to fill remains limited. With so many options from which to choose, how do we know what the 'correct' annotation is supposed to be?

In this paper, we take a *human-centric* view of the problem, motivated by the observation that humans are likely to be the end-users or consumers of such linguistic image annotations. In particular, we investigate the effects of grouping semantically related concepts that may refer to the same object instance in an image. Our work is related to the idea of *basic-level* categories (Biederman, 1995) in Linguistics, where most people have a natural preference to classify certain object categories at a particular level of granularity, *e.g.* "bird" instead of "sparrow" or "animal". However, we argue that what one person considers

Proceedings of the 25th International Conference on Computational Linguistics, pages 38–45, Dublin, Ireland, August 23-29 2014.

'basic-level' may not necessarily be 'basic-level' to another, depending on the person's knowledge, expertise, interest, or the context of the task at hand. For example, Rorissa (2008) shows that users label groups of images and describe individual images differently with regards to the level of abstraction. The key idea behind our proposed '*granularity-aware*' approach is to group semantically related categories *across* different levels of granularity to account for how different people would describe content in an image differently.

We demonstrate the benefits of the 'granularity-aware' approach by producing a re-ranking of visual classifier outputs for groups of concept nodes, *e.g.* WordNet synsets. The concept nodes are grouped across different levels of specificity within a semantic hierarchy (Section 3.1). This models better the richness of the vocabulary and lexical semantic relations in natural language. In this sense these groupings are used to alter the results of image annotation in a manner that affords different insights from its initial, category-independent rankings. For example, if the annotation mentions only "dog" but not "poodle", a system ranking "poodle" at 1 and "dog" at 20 will have a lower overall score than a system ranking "dog" at 1, although both are equally correct. Grouping ("poodle" or "dog") however will allow a fairer evaluation and comparison where both systems are now considered equally good. The 'granularity-aware' groupings will also be used in evaluating these re-rankings using textual descriptions written by humans, rather than a keyword-based gold-standard annotation. The hypothesis is that by modeling the variation in granularity levels for different concepts, we can gain a more informative insight as to how the output of image annotation systems can relate to how a person describes what he or she perceives in an image, and consequently produce image annotation systems that are more human-centric.

Overview. The remainder of the paper is organized as follows: Section 2 discusses related work. Section 3 describes our proposed 'granularity-aware' approach to group related concepts across different levels of granularity. It also discusses how to apply the idea both in automatic image annotation, by re-ranking noisy visual classifier outputs in a 'granularity-aware' manner, and in evaluation of classifier outputs against human descriptions of images. The results of the proposed method are reported in Section 4. Finally, Section 5 offers conclusions and proposes possible future work.

2 Related work

Work on automatic image annotation traditionally relies heavily on image datasets annotated with a fixed set of labels as training data. For example, Duygulu et al. (2002) investigated learning from images annotated with a set of keywords, posing the problem as a machine translation task between image regions and textual labels. Gupta and Davis (2008) includes some semantic information by incorporating prepositions and comparative adjectives, which also requires manual annotation as no such data is readily available. Recent work has moved beyond learning image annotation from constrained text labels to learning from real world texts, for example from news captions (Feng and Lapata, 2008) and sports articles (Socher and Fei-Fei, 2010).

There is also recent interest in treating texts as richer sources of information than just simple bags of keywords, for example with the use of semantic hierarchies for object recognition (Marszałek and Schmid, 2008; Deng et al., 2012b) and the inclusion of attributes for a richer representation (Lampert et al., 2009; Farhadi et al., 2009). Another line of recent work uses textual descriptions of images for various vision tasks, for example for recognizing butterfly species from butterfly descriptions (Wang et al., 2009) and discovering attributes from item descriptions on fashion shopping websites (Berg et al., 2010). There has also been interest in recent years in producing systems that annotate images with full sentences rather than just a list of terms (Kulkarni et al., 2011; Yang et al., 2011). We consider our work to complement the work of generating full sentences, as it is important to filter and select the most suitable object instances from noisy visual output. The shift from treating texts as mere labels to utilizing them as human-centric, richer forms of annotations is important to gain a better understanding of the processes underlying image and text understanding or interpretation.

Deng et al. (2012b) address the issue of granularity in a large number of object categories by allowing classifiers to output decisions at the optimum level in terms of being accurate and being informative, for example outputting "mammal" rather than "animal" while still being correct. Their work differs from ours in that the semantic hierarchy is used from *within* the visual classifier to make a decision about its output, rather than for evaluating existing outputs. More directly related to our work is recent work by Ordonez et al. (2013), which incorporates the notion of basic-level categories by modeling word 'naturalness' from text corpora on the web. While their focus is on obtaining the most 'natural' basic-level categories for different encyclopedic concepts as well as for image annotation, our emphasis is on accommodating different levels of naturalness, not just a single basic level. We adapt their model directly to our work, details of which will be discussed in Section 3.1.

3 Granularity-aware approach to image annotation

The proposed 'granularity-aware' approach to image annotation consists of several components. We first define semantic groupings of concepts by considering hypernym/hyponym relations in WordNet (Fellbaum, 1998) and also how people describe image content (Section 3.1). The groupings are then used to re-rank the output of a set of category-specific visual classifiers (Section 3.2), and also used to produce a grouped 'gold standard' from image captions (Section 3.3). The re-ranked output is then evaluated against the 'gold standard', and the initial rankings and 'granularity-aware' re-rankings are compared to gain a different insight into the visual classifiers' performance as human-centric image annotation systems.

3.1 Semantic grouping across different granularity levels

The goal of semantic grouping is to aggregate related concepts such that all members of the group refer to the same instance of an object, even across different specificity levels. In particular, we exploit the hypernym/hyponym hierarchy of WordNet (Fellbaum, 1998) for this task. WordNet is also the natural choice as it pairs well with our visual classifiers which are trained on ImageNet (Deng et al., 2009) categories, or *synsets*.

The WordNet hypernym hierarchy alone is insufficient for semantic grouping as we still need a way to determine what constitutes a reasonable group, *e.g.* putting all categories into a single "entity" group is technically correct but uninformative. For this, we draw inspiration from previous work by Ordonez et al. (2013), where a 'word naturalness' measure is proposed to reflect how people typically describe image content. More specifically, we adapt for our purposes their proposed approach of mapping encyclopedic concepts to basic-level concepts (mapping "*Grampus griseus*" to the more 'natural' "dolphin"). In this approach, the task is defined as learning a translation function $\tau(v, \lambda) : V \mapsto W$ that best maps a node v to a hypernym node w which optimizes a trade-off between the 'naturalness' of w (how likely a person is to use w to describe something) and the distance between v and w (to constrain the translation from being too general, *e.g.* "entity"), with the parameter λ controlling this trade-off between naturalness and specificity. Formally, $\tau(v, \lambda)$ is defined as:

$$\tau(v, \lambda) = \underset{w \in \Pi(v)}{\arg\max} \, [\, \lambda \, \phi(w) - (1 - \lambda) \, \psi(w, v) \,] \quad (1)$$

where $\Pi(v)$ is the set of hypernyms for v (including v), $\phi(w)$ is naturalness measure for node w, and $\psi(w, v)$ is the number of edges separating nodes w and v in the hypernym structure of WordNet.

For our work, all synsets that map to a common hypernym w are clustered as a single semantic group G_w^λ:

$$G_w^\lambda = \{v : \forall_v \, \tau(v, \lambda) = w\} \quad (2)$$

In this sense, the parameter $\lambda \in [0, 1]$ essentially also controls the average size of the groups: $\lambda = 0$ results in no groupings, while $\lambda = 1$ results in synsets being grouped with their most 'natural' hypernym, giving the largest possible difference in the levels of granularity within each group.

Estimating the naturalness function using Flickr. Ordonez et al. (2013) use n-gram counts of the Google IT corpus (Brants and Franz, 2006) as an estimate for term naturalness $\phi(w)$. Although large, the corpus might not be optimal as it is a general corpus and may not necessarily mirror how people describe image content. Thus, we explore a different corpus that (i) better reflects how humans describe image content; (ii) is sufficiently large for a reasonable estimate of $\phi(w)$. The Yahoo! Webscope Yahoo Flickr Creative Commons 100M (YFCC-100M) dataset (Yahoo! Webscope, 2014) fits these criteria with 100 million images containing image captions written by users. Hence, we compute term occurrence statistics from the title, description, and user tags of images from this dataset. Following Ordonez et al., we measure $\phi(w)$ as the maximum log count of term occurrences for all terms appearing in synset w.

Internal nodes. Unlike Ordonez et al. (2013), we do not constrain v to be a leaf node, but instead also allow for internal nodes to be translated to one of their hypernyms. We could choose to limit visual recognition to leaf nodes and estimate the visual content of internal nodes by aggregating the outputs from all its leaf nodes, as done by Ordonez et al. (2013). However, since the example images in ImageNet are obtained for internal nodes pretty much in the same way as leaf nodes (by querying "dog" rather than by combining images from "poodle", "terrier" and "border collie") (Deng et al., 2009), the visual models learnt from images at internal nodes may capture different kinds of patterns than from their hyponyms. For example, a model trained with ImageNet examples of "dog" might capture some higher-level information that may otherwise not be captured by merely accumulating the outputs of the leaf nodes under it, and *vice versa*.

3.2 Re-ranking of visual classifier output

The visual classifier used in our experiments (Section 4.2) outputs a Platt-scaled (Platt, 2000) confidence value for each synset estimating the probability of the synset being depicted in a given image. The classifier outputs are then ranked in descending order of these probability values, and are treated as image annotation labels.

As mentioned, these rankings do not take into consideration that some of these synsets are semantically related. Thus, we aggregate classifier outputs within our semantic groupings (Section 3.1), and then re-rank the scores of each *grouped* classifier. Formally, the new score of a classifier c, $\rho_c(G_w^\lambda)$, for a semantic group G_w^λ is defined as:

$$\rho_c(G_w^\lambda) = \max_{v \in G_w^\lambda} p_c(v) \tag{3}$$

where v is a synset from the semantic group G_w^λ, and $p_c(v)$ is the original probability estimate of classifier c for synset v. I.e., the probability of the most probable synset in the group is taken as the probability of the group.

To enable comparison of the rankings against a gold standard keyword annotation, a word label is also generated for each semantic group. We assign as the semantic group's label $\ell(G_w^\lambda)$ the first term of synset w, the common hypernym node to which members of the group best translates. Note that the term merely acts a label for evaluation purposes and should not be treated as a word in a traditional sense. We also merge semantic groups with the same label to account for polysemes/homonyms, again taking the maximum of ρ_c among the semantic groups as the new score.

The semantic grouping of synsets is performed independently of visual classifier output. As such, we only need to train each visual classifier *once* for each synset, without requiring re-training for different groupings since we only aggregate the *output* of the visual classifiers. This allows for more flexibility since the output for each semantic group is only aggregated at *evaluation time*.

3.3 Evaluation using human descriptions

The image dataset used in our experiments (Section 4.1) is annotated with five full-sentence captions per image but *not* keyword labels. Although an option would be to obtain keyword annotations via crowdsourcing, it is time consuming and expensive and also requires validating the annotation quality. Instead, we exploit the existing full-sentence captions from the dataset to automatically generate a gold standard keyword annotation for evaluating our ranked classifier outputs. The use of such captions is also in line with our goal of making the evaluation of image annotation systems more human-centric. For each caption, we extract nouns using the open source tool FreeLing (Padrö and Stanilovsky, 2012).

	λ										
	0.0	0.1	0.2	0.3	0.4	0.5	0.6	0.7	0.8	0.9	1.0
Semantic Grouping	0.3450	0.3450	0.3548	0.3735	0.4025	0.4417	0.4562	0.4702	0.4834	0.5059	0.5395
Random Grouping	0.3450	0.3450	0.3493	0.3529	0.3585	0.3689	0.3823	0.4067	0.4241	0.4359	0.4467
Number of groups	1294	1294	1237	1105	949	817	693	570	474	419	368

Table 1: Results of re-ranking with semantic groupings. The first two rows show the average NDCG scores for the proposed groupings and the random baseline groupings, for different groupings formed by varying λ. The bottom row shows the number of semantic groups formed for different values of λ.

For each image, each noun is assigned an individual relevance score, which is the number of captions that mentions the noun. This upweights important objects while downweighting less important objects (or errors from the annotator or the parser). The result is a list of nouns that humans use to describe objects present in the image, each weighted by its relevance score. We assume nouns that appear in the same WordNet synset ("bicycle" and "bike") are synonyms and that they refer to the same object instance in the image. Hence, we group them as a single label-group, with the relevance score taken to be the maximum relevance score among the nouns in the group.

Since there are only five captions per image, the proposed approach will result in a *sparse* set of keywords. This mirrors the problem described in Section 1 where systems have to 'guess' the so-called 'correct' labels, thus allowing us to demonstrate the effectiveness of our 'granularity-aware' re-rankings.

In order to compare the annotations against the re-rankings, we will need to map the keywords to the semantic groupings. This is done by matching the nouns to any of the terms in a semantic group, with a corresponding label $\ell(G_w^\lambda)$ for each group (Section 3.2). Nouns assigned the same label are merged, with the new relevance score being the maximum relevance score among the nouns. If a noun matches more than one semantic group (polyseme/homonym), we treat all groups as relevant and divide the relevance score uniformly among the groups. Evaluation is then performed by matching the semantic group labels against the image annotation output.

4 Experimental evaluation

Our proposed method is evaluated on the dataset and categories as will be described in Section 4.1, by re-ranking the output of the visual classifiers in Section 4.2. The effects of semantic groupings are explored using different settings of λ (see Section 3.1).

Baseline. To ensure any improvements in scores are not purely as a result of having a shorter list of concepts to rank, we compare the results to a set of baseline groupings where synsets are grouped in a random manner. For a fair comparison the baselines contain the same number of groups and cluster size distributions as our semantic groupings.

4.1 Dataset and Object Categories

The Flickr8k dataset (Hodosh et al., 2013) is used in our image annotation experiments. The dataset contains 8,091 images, each annotated with five textual descriptions. To demonstrate the notion of granularity in large-scale object hierarchies, we use as object categories synset nodes from WordNet (Fellbaum, 1998). Ideally, we would like to be able to train visual classifiers for all synset categories in ImageNet (Deng et al., 2009). However, we limit the categories to only synsets with terms occurring in the textual descriptions of the Flickr8k dataset to reduce computational complexity, and regard the use of more categories as future work. This results in a total of 1,372 synsets to be used in our experiments. The synsets include both *leaf nodes* as well as *internal nodes* in the WordNet hierarchy.

4.2 Visual classifier

Deep learning (LeCun et al., 1989; Hinton and Salakhutdinov, 2006) based approaches have become popular in visual recognition following the success of deep convolutional neural networks

(CNN) (Krizhevsky et al., 2012) in the ImageNet Large Scale Visual Recognition Challenge 2012 (ILSVRC12) (Deng et al., 2012a). Donahue et al. (2013) report that features extracted from the activation of a deep CNN trained in a fully supervised fashion can also be re-purposed to novel generic tasks that differ significantly from the original task. Inspired by Donahue et al. (2013), we extract such activation as feature for ImageNet images that correspond to the 1,372 synsets, and train binary classifiers to detect the presence of the synsets in the images of Flickr8k. More specifically, we use as our training set the 1,571,576 ImageNet images in the 1,372 synsets, where a random sample of 5,000 images serves as negative examples, and as our test set the 8,091 images in Flickr8k. For each image in both sets, we extracted activation of a pre-trained CNN model as its feature. The model is a reference implementation of the structure proposed in Krizhevsky et al. (2012) with minor modifications, and is made publicly available through the Caffe project (Jia, 2013). It is shown in Donahue et al. (2013) that the activation of layer 6 of the CNN performs the best for novel tasks. Our study on a toy example with 10 ImageNet synsets however suggests that the activation of layer 7 has a small edge. Once the 4,096 dimensional activation of layer 7 is extracted for both training and test sets, 1,372 binary classifiers are trained and applied using LIBSVM (Chang and Lin, 2011), which give probability estimates for the test images. For each image, the 1,372 classifiers are then ranked in order of their probability estimates.

4.3 Evaluation measure

The systems are evaluated using the Normalized Discounted Cumulative Gain (NDCG) (Wang et al., 2013) measure. This measure is commonly used in Information Retrieval (IR) to evaluate ranked retrieval results where each document is assigned a relevance score. This measure favours rankings where the most relevant items are ranked ahead of less relevant items, and does not penalize irrelevant items.

The NDCG at position k, $NDCG_k$, for a set of test images $\mathcal{I}$ is defined as:

$$NDCG_k(\mathcal{I}) = \frac{1}{|\mathcal{I}|} \sum_{i=1}^{|\mathcal{I}|} \frac{1}{IDCG_k(i)} \sum_{p=1}^{k} \frac{2^{R_p} - 1}{\log_2(1+p)} \tag{4}$$

where R_p is the relevance score of the concept at position p, and $IDCG_k(i)$ is the ideal discounted cumulative gain for a perfect ranking algorithm at position k, which normalizes the overall measure to be between 0.0 to 1.0. This makes the scores comparable across rankings regardless of the number of synset groups involved. For each grouping, we report the results of $NDCG_k$ for the largest possible k (*i.e.* the number of synset groups), which gives the overall performance of the rankings.

4.4 Results

Table 1 shows the results of re-ranking the output of the visual classifiers (Section 4.2), with different semantic groupings formed by varying λ. The effects of the proposed groupings is apparent when compared to the random baseline groupings. As we increase the value of λ (allowing groups to have a larger range of granularity), the NDCG scores also consistently increase. However, higher NDCG scores do not necessarily equate to better groupings, as semantic groups with too much flexibility in granularity levels may end up being less informative, for example by annotating a "being" in an image. The informativeness of the groupings is a subjective issue depending on the context, and makes an interesting open question. To provide insight into the effects of our groupings, Figure 1 shows an example where at low levels of λ (rigid flexibility), the various dog species are highly ranked but none of them is considered relevant by the evaluation system. However, at $\lambda = 0.5$ most dog species are grouped as a "dog" semantic group resulting in a highly relevant prediction, while at the same time allowing the "sidewalk" group to rise higher in the rankings. At higher levels of λ, however, the semantic groupings become less informative when superordinate groups like "being", "artifact" and "equipment" are formed, suggesting that higher flexibility with granularity levels may not always be more informative.

5 Conclusions and future work

We presented a 'granularity-aware' approach to grouping semantically related concepts across different levels of granularity, taking into consideration that different people describe the same thing in different

dog (5)
road (2)
pavement (1)
street (1)

$\lambda = 0.0$ score: 0.241	$\lambda = 0.3$ score: 0.480	$\lambda = 0.5$ score: 0.941	$\lambda = 0.8$ score: 0.943	$\lambda = 1.0$ score: 0.944
beagle	beagle	***dog***	***dog***	***dog***
boston_terrier	boston_terrier	animal	animal	animal
corgi	***dog***	leash	leash	leash
basset	basset	kitten	being	being
hound	hound	pet	bird	bird
spaniel	spaniel	penguin	***sidewalk***	***sidewalk***
border_collie	border_collie	***sidewalk***	cat	cat
terrier	terrier	cat	artifact	artifact
dachshund	dachshund	artifact	student	sport
pup	pup	person	baseball	chair
st_bernard	bulldog	student	chair	child
bulldog	springer_spaniel	goat	child	device
springer_spaniel	leash	livestock	frisbee	ball
leash	kitten	rabbit	ball	slope
kitten	pet	duck	slope	equipment
pet	penguin	baseball	equipment	fabric
dog	***sidewalk***	chair	fabric	rug
sheepdog	doberman	child	rug	seat
penguin	collie	frisbee	seat	support
sidewalk	cat	spectator	support	stick

Figure 1: Example re-ranking of our visual classifier by semantic groupings, for selected values of λ. Words directly below the image indicate the 'gold standard' nouns extracted automatically from its corresponding five captions. The number next to each noun indicate its relevance score. For each re-ranking, we show the labels representing the semantic groupings. ***Italicized labels*** indicate a match with the (grouped) 'gold standard' nouns (see Section 3.3).

ways, and at varied levels of specificity. To gain insight into the effects of our semantic groupings on human-centric applications, the proposed idea was investigated in the context of re-ranking the output of visual classifiers, and was also incorporated during evaluation against human descriptions. We found that although the groupings help provide a more human-centric and flexible image annotation system, too much flexibility may result in an uninformative image annotation system. Future work could include (i) exploring different ways of grouping concepts; (ii) incorporating the output of visual classifiers to improve both groupings and rankings; (iii) using information from more textual sources to improve image annotation; (iv) taking the approach further to generate full sentence annotations. We believe that these steps are important to bridge the semantic gap between computer vision and natural language.

Acknowledgements

The authors would like to acknowledge funding from the EU CHIST-ERA D2K programme, EPSRC grant reference: EP/K01904X/1.

References

Tamara L. Berg, Alexander C. Berg, and Jonathan Shih. 2010. Automatic attribute discovery and characterization from noisy web data. In *Proceedings of ECCV*, volume 1, pages 663–676.

Irving Biederman. 1995. Visual object recognition. In S. F. Kosslyn and D. N. Osherson, editors, *An Invitation to Cognitive Science, 2nd edition, Volume 2, Visual Cognition*, pages 121–165. MIT Press.

Thorsten Brants and Alex Franz. 2006. Web 1T 5-gram Version 1. In *Linguistic Data Consortium*.

Chih-Chung Chang and Chih-Jen Lin. 2011. LIBSVM: A library for support vector machines. *ACM Transactions on Intelligent Systems and Technology*, 2(3):1–27. `http://www.csie.ntu.edu.tw/~cjlin/libsvm`.

Jia Deng, Wei Dong, Richard Socher, Li-Jia Li, Kai Li, and Li Fei-Fei. 2009. ImageNet: A large-scale hierarchical image database. In *Proceedings of CVPR*.

Jia Deng, Alexander C. Berg, Sanjeev Satheesh, Hao Su, Aditya Khosla, and Li Fei-Fei. 2012a. ImageNet large scale visual recognition challenge (ILSVRC) 2012. `http://image-net.org/challenges/LSVRC/2012/`.

Jia Deng, Jonathan Krause, Alexander C. Berg, and Li Fei-Fei. 2012b. Hedging your bets: Optimizing accuracy-specificity trade-offs in large scale visual recognition. In *Proceedings of CVPR*.

Jeff Donahue, Yangqing Jia, Oriol Vinyals, Judy Hoffman, Ning Zhang, Eric Tzeng, and Trevor Darrell. 2013. DeCAF: A deep convolutional activation feature for generic visual recognition. arXiv:1310.1531 [cs.CV].

Pinar Duygulu, Kobus Barnard, Nando de Freitas, and David A. Forsyth. 2002. Object recognition as machine translation: Learning a lexicon for a fixed image vocabulary. In *Proceedings of ECCV*, pages 97–112.

Ali Farhadi, Ian Endres, Derek Hoiem, and David A. Forsyth. 2009. Describing objects by their attributes. In *Proceedings of CVPR*.

Christiane Fellbaum, editor. 1998. *WordNet: An Electronic Lexical Database*. MIT Press, Cambridge, MA.

Yansong Feng and Mirella Lapata. 2008. Automatic image annotation using auxiliary text information. In *Proceedings of the 46th Annual Meeting of the Association for Computational Linguistics: Human Language Technologies*, pages 272–280. Association for Computational Linguistics.

Abhinav Gupta and Larry S. Davis. 2008. Beyond nouns: Exploiting prepositions and comparative adjectives for learning visual classifiers. In *Proceedings of ECCV*, pages 16–29.

Geoffrey E. Hinton and Ruslan R. Salakhutdinov. 2006. Reducing the dimensionality of data with neural networks. *Science*, 313:504–507.

Micah Hodosh, Peter Young, and Julia Hockenmaier. 2013. Framing image description as a ranking task: Data, models and evaluation metrics. *Journal of Artificial Intelligence Research*, 47:853–899.

Yangqing Jia. 2013. Caffe: An open source convolutional architecture for fast feature embedding. `http://caffe.berkeleyvision.org`.

Alex Krizhevsky, Ilya Sutskever, and Geoffrey Hinton. 2012. ImageNet classification with deep convolutional neural networks. In *Advances in Neural Information Processing Systems*.

Girish Kulkarni, Visruth Premraj, Sagnik Dhar, Siming Li, Yejin Choi, Alexander C. Berg, and Tamara L. Berg. 2011. Baby talk: Understanding and generating simple image descriptions. In *Proceedings of CVPR*.

Chris H. Lampert, Hannes Nickisch, and Stefan Harmeling. 2009. Learning to detect unseen object classes by between-class attribute transfer. In *Proceedings of CVPR*.

Y. LeCun, B. Boser, J. Denker, D. Henerson, R. Howard, W. Hubbard, and L. Jackel. 1989. Backpropagation applied to handwritten zip code recognition. *Neural Computation*, 1(4):541–551.

Marcin Marszałek and Cordelia Schmid. 2008. Constructing category hierarchies for visual recognition. In David Forsyth, Philip Torr, and Andrew Zisserman, editors, *Proceedings of ECCV*, volume 5305 of *Lecture Notes in Computer Science*, pages 479–491. Springer Berlin Heidelberg.

Vicente Ordonez, Jia Deng, Yejin Choi, Alexander C. Berg, and Tamara L. Berg. 2013. From large scale image categorization to entry-level categories. In *Proceedings of ICCV*.

Lluís Padró and Evgeny Stanilovsky. 2012. Freeling 3.0: Towards wider multilinguality. In *Proceedings of the Language Resources and Evaluation Conference*, LREC '12, Istanbul, Turkey, May. ELRA.

John C. Platt. 2000. Probabilities for SV machines. *Advances in Large-Margin Classifiers*, pages 61–74.

Abebe Rorissa. 2008. User-generated descriptions of individual images versus labels of groups of images: A comparison using basic level theory. *Information Processing and Management*, 44(5):1741–1753.

Olga Russakovsky, Jia Deng, Jonathan Krause, Alexander C. Berg, and Li Fei-Fei. 2013. ImageNet large scale visual recognition challenge (ILSVRC) 2013. `http://image-net.org/challenges/LSVRC/2013/results.php`.

Richard Socher and Li Fei-Fei. 2010. Connecting modalities: Semi-supervised segmentation and annotation of images using unaligned text corpora. In *Proceedings of CVPR*, pages 966–973.

Josiah Wang, Katja Markert, and Mark Everingham. 2009. Learning models for object recognition from natural language descriptions. In *Proceedings of BMVC*.

Yining Wang, Liwei Wang, Yuanzhi Li, Di He, Wei Chen, and Tie-Yan Liu. 2013. A theoretical analysis of NDCG ranking measures. In *Proceedings of the 26th Annual Conference on Learning Theory (COLT 2013)*.

Yahoo! Webscope. 2014. Yahoo! Webscope dataset YFCC-100M. `http://labs.yahoo.com/Academic_Relations`.

Yezhou Yang, Ching Lik Teo, Hal Daumé, III, and Yiannis Aloimonos. 2011. Corpus-guided sentence generation of natural images. In *Proceedings of EMNLP*, pages 444–454.

Key Event Detection in Video using ASR and Visual Data

Niraj Shrestha **Aparna N. Venkitasubramanian** **Marie-Francine Moens**
KU Leuven, Belgium
{niraj.shrestha, Aparna.NuraniVenkitasubramanian,
Marie-Francine.Moens}@cs.kuleuven.be

Abstract

Multimedia data grow day by day which makes it necessary to index them automatically and efficiently for fast retrieval, and more precisely to automatically index them with key events. In this paper, we present preliminary work on key event detection in British royal wedding videos using automatic speech recognition (ASR) and visual data. The system first automatically acquires key events of royal weddings from an external corpus such as Wikipedia, and then identifies those events in the ASR data. The system also models name and face alignment to identify the persons involved in the wedding events. We compare the results obtained with the ASR output with results obtained with subtitles. The error is only slightly higher when using ASR output in the detection of key events and their participants in the wedding videos compared to the results obtained with subtitles.

1 Introduction

With the increase of multimedia data widely available on the Web and in social media, it becomes necessary to automatically index the multimedia resources with key events for information search and mining. For instance, it is not possible to manually index all the frames of a video. Automatically indexing multimedia data with key events makes the retrieval and mining effective and efficient.

Event detection is an important and current research problem in the field of multimedia information retrieval. Most of the event detection in video is done by analyzing the visual features using manually transcribed data. In this paper, we propose key event detection in British royal wedding videos using automatic speech recognition (ASR) data and where possible also to recognize the actors involved in the recognized events using visual and textual data. An event is something that happens at a certain moment in time and at a certain location possibly involving different actors. Events can be quite specific as in this case the key events are the typical events that make up a royal wedding scenario. For example, events like 'design of cake/dress/bouquet', 'couple heading to Buckingham palace', 'appearing on balcony' etc. are key events in British royal wedding video. Figure 1 shows an example of a frame containing an event with its actors, together with the associated subtitle and ASR output. While most works in this domain have focussed on clean textual content such as manual transcripts or subtitles, which are difficult to acquire, we use the output of an ASR system. While the event detection and name-face alignment problem by itself is already quite difficult, the nature of the ASR text adds an additional complexity. ASR data is noisy and inaccurate, it does not contain some parts of the actual spoken text, and does not contain sentence boundaries. Figure 2 illustrates this problem. For the key events, the system first acquires the necessary knowledge from external corpora - in our case Wikipedia articles associated with royal weddings. Then the system identifies the key events in the ASR data. The system also models name and face alignment to identify the persons involved in the wedding events. We perform named entity recognition in the text associated with a window of frames to first generate a noisy label for the faces occurring in the frames and this rough alignment is refined using an Expectation-Maximization (EM) algorithm. We compare the results obtained with the ASR output with results obtained with subtitles. The error is only slightly

Proceedings of the 25th International Conference on Computational Linguistics, pages 46–53,
Dublin, Ireland, August 23-29 2014.

Sub-title: "Outside, fully 150,000 people with unbounded enthusiasm acclaimed Princess Margaret and her husband when they appeared on the balcony.... "
ASR: "outside only a hundred and 50 people on TV and using it as a ... "

Figure 1: An example of a frame containing an event with associated subtitle and ASR output

higher when using ASR output in the detection of key events and their participants in the wedding videos compared to the results obtained with subtitles. The methodology that we propose can be applied for the detection of many different types of video events.

2 Related work

Event detection has some relationship with Topic Detection and Tracking (TDT) and with concept detection. TDT regards the detection and tracking over time of the main event of a news story and is a challenging problem in the field of text and visual analysis. Although widely studied in text (Allan, 2002), (Allan et al., 2005), (Mei and Zhai, 2005), (Wang et al., 2007), (Zhao et al., 2007), topic detection in video is still not well studied. An event in this context is usually broader in scope than the events we want to recognize in wedding videos in this paper. In the multimedia research community, most of the works focus on concept detection like in (Liu et al., 2008), (Yang et al., 2007), (Snoek et al., 2006) rather than event detection. A concept detection task is different from event detection as a concept can be defined as any object or specific configuration of objects. Any frame then can be labelled with some concept descriptor (e.g., church, cake, etc.). While in an event, there is a start and end time in between which something happens, and in video, an event is represented by a sequence of frames.

Event detection is a challenging problem which is not well studied. Only few event detection systems that process video exist. They recognize events such as goal, run, tackle in a soccer game, or recognize specific actions in news video (e.g., meeting of two well-known people) or in a surveillance video (e.g., unusual event). Event detection in video is often related to sports like basketball (Saur et al., 1997), soccer (Yow et al., 1995) and baseball (Kawashima et al., 1998) (Rui et al., 2000). (Wang et al., 2008) developed a model based on a multi-resolution, multi-source and multi-modal bootstrapping framework that exploits knowledge of sub-domains for concept detection in news video. (Adam et al., 2008) developed an algorithm based on multiple local monitors which collect low-level statistics to detect certain types of unusual events in surveillance video.

Most of these works rely only on visual analysis (e.g., detection of certain motion patterns) to identify events in video and the event detection is performed with a supervised learning method, where a model is trained on manually annotated examples of known events. In this paper, we propose a novel idea in which the system learns events from an external corpus like Wikipedia and identifies those events in the ASR or subtitle data of the video. In addition, we identify the persons involved in an event based on the analysis of visual and textual data.

Sub-title

In May 1973, it was announced that Princess Anne was to marry a young lieutenant from the Queen's Dragoon Guards, Mark Phillips. Anne , the Queen 's only daughter , was the first of her four children to marry . Princess Anne , of course , is very much her own person and had always declared that she would marry for love and so she married a fellow equestrian . He joined the regiment that I was in . And Mark was a popular figure because he was good-looking , he was a great sportsman , and we quite like sportsmen , and , of course , he was marrying a princess . And so this brought a spark of light to people 's lives , and he was bound to be popular . And a man in uniform with tight trousers always looks great .....

ASR Transcription

in May 19 73 it was announced that Princess Diana was to marry the young left hander from the Queen's Dragoon Guards officers found the Queen's and indeed also was the first of four children to marry Kansas and of course it is very much a person has always declared she would marry for love and stationary defender Christian he joined the return to London smokers to quit for good because he's good looking he was grateful when we quite liked sports and of course American church service brought a spark of life because life nun who founded the popular and a man in uniform were tight trousers or disgraced ......

Figure 2: An example showing sub-title vs. ASR data

3 Methodology

The main objective of this work is to identify and index key events in videos using ASR data along with key actors involved in the event. We start by identifying key events related to a certain domain, using external corpora. In addition, the proposed method involves pre-processing of the textual and visual data.

At 11.30, Elizabeth entered the abbey on her father's arm, but they did not head straight down the aisle as expected.

Figure 3: Sequence of frames showing the anchor talking about an event of the wedding, but there is no visual appearance of the event.

3.1 Acquiring background knowledge

Our approach for identifying key events in weddings exploits external text corpora. We use two corpora:

1. A genre-specific corpus: a set of pages specific to the topic, for example, from Wikipedia - to identify events associated with the topic.

2. A generic corpus, used to weigh the events identified in the genre-specific corpus.

The process is as follows. We first collect content from Wikipedia articles relevant for Britain's royal weddings[1] in the form of nine documents. These articles include both pages related to weddings, such as these of Diana and Charles, that were mentioned in our test videos as well as pages about other British royal weddings not shown in the videos, such as the wedding of Kate and William. This set of articles formed our wedding corpus for learning typical wedding events. The generic corpus is formed by all English Wikipedia articles.

From each document of this corpus we extract events together with their arguments (subject and object arguments) using a state-of-the-art event annotator[2]. This tool uses linguistic features such as the results of a dependency parse of a sentence, to detect the events and their arguments in a text. Next, we use a data mining technique to find frequent word patterns that signal the event and its arguments in the wedding articles, we keep each event that has sufficient support in the wedding articles and weigh it by a factor that is inversely proportional to the frequency of this event in the more general corpus. We keep the N highest weighted events from the obtained ranked list, where N is determined by whether we want to keep the most common wedding events or include also more rare events. The list obtained has items such as 'to announce engagement', 'to make dress', 'to make cake' etc, which are typical for weddings. We report here on preliminary work and acknowledge that the methodology can be largely refined.

3.2 Detecting person names

In royal wedding videos, there are many persons who appear in the video like anchor, interviewee, the persons married or to be married, the dress designer, the bouquet designer, the cake maker, the friends etc. As in this preliminary work we are only interested in the brides and bridegrooms (which are also the most important persons when indexing the video) we use a gazetteer with their names for recognizing the names in the texts.

3.3 Detecting the faces of persons

In the video key frames are extracted at the rate of 1 frame per second using (ffmpeg, 2012), which ensures that no faces appearing in the video are omitted. To detect the faces in the video, a face detector tool from (Bradski, 2000) is used. Next, we extract the features from the faces detected in the video. Although there are several dedicated facial feature extraction methods such as (Finkel et al., 2005),(Strehl and Ghosh, 2003), in this implementation, we use a simple bag-of-visual-words model (Csurka et al., 2004).

Once feature vectors are built, clustering of the bounding boxes of the detected faces is performed. Each object is, then, compared to the cluster centers obtained and is replaced with the closest center. The clustering is done using Elkan's k-means algorithm (Jain and Obermayer, 2010) which produces the same results as the regular k-means algorithm, but is computationally more efficient. This accelerated algorithm eliminates some distance calculations by applying the triangle inequality and by keeping track of lower and upper bounds for distances between points and centers. This algorithm, however, needs the number k of clusters present in the data. Since we are primarily interested in the brides and bridegrooms and since there are seven weddings shown in the video, we experiment with values of k equal to 7*2 = 14. Although this approach very likely introduces errors in the clustering as we do not know beforehand how many persons apart from the couple appear in the chosen key frames, it showed to be a better strategy than trying to align all persons mentioned in the texts. The clustering is performed using an Euclidean distance metric.

3.4 Name and face alignment

If a key frame contains a face, then we identify the corresponding ASR or subtitle data that co-occur in a fixed time window with this frame. Further, the names occurring in the textual data are listed as possible names for the frame. As a result, it is possible that an entity mentioned in the text is suggested for several

[1]http://en.wikipedia.org/wiki/Category:British_royal_weddings

[2]http://ariadne.cs.kuleuven.be/TERENCEStoryService/

Table 1: Names and faces alignment results on subtitle vs. ASR data on events

	Subtitle			ASR		
	P	R	F_1	P	R	F_1
Textual	38.095	21.622	27.586	36.585	17.857	24
EM	41.304	25.676	31.667	40.426	22.619	29.008

Table 2: WinDiff score on event identification on subtitle vs. ASR data on the union setting

Subtitle	ASR
11.06	13.80

key frames. However, when there is no corresponding text, or when the text does not contain person entities, no name is suggested for the key frame.

Name and face alignment in royal wedding video is difficult and complicated since the video contains many other faces of persons mentioned above. Sometimes the anchor or designer talks about the couple involved in the wedding, but there is no appearance of this couple in the corresponding video key frame as shown in figure 3.

We minimize this problem of name and face alignment by using the EM algorithm cited in (Pham et al., 2010). Alignment is the process of mapping the faces in the video to the names mentioned in the textual data. For each frame, the most probable alignment scheme has to be chosen from all possible schemes. The EM algorithm has an initialization step followed by the iterative E- and M-steps. The E-step estimates the likelihood of each alignment scheme for a frame, while the M-step updates the probability distribution based on the estimated alignments over all key frames of the video.

3.5 Event identification in subtitle and ASR data with person involvement (if any)

Once the system has learned the events from the Wikipedia data, it identifies the events from the subtitles. The process is as follow: the system scans each subtitle for the key words from the event list. If the key word appears in the subtitle data, then it is treated as the occurrence of the event and stores the set of frames that co-occur with that subtitle. The name and face alignment module already might have yielded a list of names present in this subtitle if there is any person involved. If that is the case, then the names are assigned to the events identified.

The same process is repeated using ASR data.

4 Experimental setup

In this section, we describe the dataset, experimental setup and the metrics used for evaluation.

4.1 Datasets and ground truth annotations

The data used in our experiments is the DVD on Britain's Royal Weddings published by the BBC. The duration of this video is 116 minutes at a frame rate of 25 frames per second, and the frame resolution is 720x576 pixels. Frames are extracted at the rate of one frame per second using the ffmpeg tool (ffmpeg, 2012). Faces in the frames are annotated manually using the Picasa tool for building the ground truth for evaluation. This tool is very handy and user-friendly to tag the faces. We have found that there are 69 persons including British wedding couples in the video. The subtitles came along with the DVD which are already split into segments of around 3 seconds. We use the (FBK, 2013) system to obtain the ASR data of the videos. Since the (FBK, 2013) system takes only sound (.mp3 file) as input, we have converted the video into a mp3 file using (ffmpeg, 2012). The obtained ASR data is then in XML format without any sentence boundaries so we have converted the ASR data into segments in the range of three seconds, which is standard when presenting subtitles in video. It is clear that the ASR transcription contains many words that are incorrectly transcribed. It is also visible that the ASR system does not recognize or misspells many words from the actual speech. As mentioned above, we have built a gazetteer of the couples' names. A set of events are recognized by our system as being important in the context of weddings. To evaluate the quality of these events, the events in the video were annotated by two annotators independently. This annotation includes the actual event, and the start and end times of the event. These two sets with annotations form the groundtruth. To be able to compare the system generated events with the ground truth events, we adopt a two-step approach. First, we combine the corresponding ground truth entries from different annotators into one sequence of frames. Suppose one entry in a ground truth file ($GT(a)$) by one annotator contains the following start (x_a) and end (y_a) time range: $GT(a) : [x_a, y_a]$, and the corresponding entry in the other ground truth file ($GT(b)$) (by the second annotator) contains the following start (x_b) and end (y_b) time range: $GT(b) : [x_b, y_b]$. Merging of the ground truth event ranges can be done in different ways, but we report here on the union of the two ranges.

$$GT(a) \cup GT(b) = [min(x_a, x_b), max(y_a, y_b)] \tag{1}$$

4.2 Evaluation Metrics

Let FL be the final list of name and face alignment retrieved by our system for all the faces detected in all frames, and GL the complete ground truth list. To evaluate the name and face alignment task, we use standard precision (P), recall (R) and F_1 scores for evaluation:

$$P = \frac{|FL \cap GL|}{|FL|} \quad R = \frac{|FL \cap GL|}{|GL|} \quad F_1 = 2 \cdot \frac{P \cdot R}{P + R}$$

To evaluate correctness of event segment boundaries, precision and recall are too strict since they penalize boundaries placed very close to the ground truth boundaries. We use the WindowDiff (Pevzner and Hearst, 2002) metric that measures the difference between the ground truth segment GT and the segment SE found by the machine originally designed for text segmentation. For our scenario, this metric is defined as follows:

$$WD(GT, SE) = \frac{1}{M-k} \sum_{i=1}^{M-k} (|b(GT_i, GT_{i+k}) - b(SE_i, SE_{i+k})| > 0) \tag{2}$$

where $M = 7102$, is the number of frames extracted, $k = 1$, is the window size and $b(i, j)$ represents the number of boundaries between frame indices i and j.

5 Results

Events on Wiki (manual)	Events learned by system from wiki	Events identified by system on subtitle	Events identified by system on ASR data
• Meet/ proposed • Engagement announced • Wedding took place/held • Guest arrival • Design/make (wedding) dress • Design/make (wedding) ring • Design/make (wedding) cake • Design/make (wedding) bouquet • Arrived with father • Proceeded/heading/went to Buckingham palace • Appearing on balcony and kissing	• 'place' • 'wear & dress' • 'announce & engagement' • 'make' • 'make & wedding' • 'wedding' • 'watch' • 'marry' • 'ceremony & ceremony' • 'announce' • 'watch & million' • 'royal' • 'create & marriage' • 'make & cake' • 'make & dress' • 'make & ring' • 'wear & full' • 'attend & wedding' • 'create & wedding' • 'receive & wedding' • 'wear & wedding'	• that took place in palaces and castles like Windsor. • To satisfy the public's appetite, a sketch of the dress was released. • And the dress itself, you know, it's so simple, isn't it, for a Royal wedding? • The day after the engagement was announced. • The style of the wedding as well, there was a lot said at the time • the ceremony was to be primarily for family and friends. • when half a million lined the streets, this was a low-key event. • When the cake was put up to finally check	• that took place in palaces and cost loans like the ones that • the dress was released • the announcement of its royal engagement • watch the wedding ceremony before getting d • Princess Margaret s wedding changed everything • the engagement ring maybe a royal family • the Queen Mother s dress which was said to be one of them is the simple • Prince Andrew and Sarah Ferguson s wedding the royal family • was working for Royal cake maker but if you can price

Figure 4: Events learned from the Wikipedia data and their identification in the subtitles and ASR by the system

5.1 Evaluation of the extraction of wedding events from Wikipedia

Figure 4 shows which key events typical for royal weddings the system has learned from Wikipedia data and how it found these events in the subtitles and the ASR data. It is seen from figure 4 that the system could not learn many events that are important to wedding events, but the system recognized the events that it has learned quite accurately in the subtitles and ASR data.

5.2 Evaluation of the event segmentation and recognition

Table 2 shows the results of WinDiff score obtained on subtitles versus ASR data on the union setting discussed in 4.1. Though the error rate is more or less the same, it degrades in ASR data which is obviously due to the different ASR errors. The error rate is increased by 2.74% in ASR data using a window size of 1. Here a window size 1 is equivalent to one second so it corresponds to one frame. In this case the system tries to find the event boundaries in each frame and evaluates these against the ground truth event boundaries.

5.3 Evaluation of the name-face alignments

Table 1 shows the result of the name and face alignment given the detected events. Though the result is not quite satisfactory even after applying the EM algorithm, there are many bottlenecks that need to be tackled. Many parts of the video contain interviews. Interviewees and anchors mostly talk about the couples that are married or are to be married, but the couples are not shown which might cause errors in the name and face alignment.

6 Conclusion and future work

In this paper, we have presented ongoing research on event detection in video using ASR and visual data. To some extent the system is able to learn key events from relevant external corpora. The event identification process is quite satisfactory as the system learns from external corpora. If the system would have learnt the events from external corpora good enough, it might identify events very well from subtitle or ASR data. We are interested in improving the learning process from external corpora in further work. Finding event boundaries in the frame sequence corresponding to a subtitle or ASR data where the event is mentioned is still a challenging problem because an event key word might be identified in a subtitle segment or in a sentence which actually may not correspond to what is shown the aligned frames. We have also tried to implement name and face alignment techniques to identify persons involved in the event. As a further improvement of our system, we need to find how to deal with the many interviews in this type of videos which might improve the alignment of names and faces.

References

A. Adam, E. Rivlin, I. Shimshoni, and D. Reinitz. 2008. Robust real-time unusual event detection using multiple fixed-location monitors. *Pattern Analysis and Machine Intelligence, IEEE Transactions on*, 30(3):555–560, March.

James Allan, Stephen Harding, David Fisher, Alvaro Bolivar, Sergio Guzman-Lara, and Peter Amstutz. 2005. Taking topic detection from evaluation to practice. In *Proceedings of the 38th Annual Hawaii International Conference on System Sciences (HICSS'05) - Track 4 - Volume 04*, HICSS '05, pages 101.1–, Washington, DC, USA. IEEE Computer Society.

James Allan, editor. 2002. *Topic Detection and Tracking: Event-based Information Organization*. Kluwer Academic Publishers, Norwell, MA, USA.

G. Bradski. 2000. Opencv face detector tool. *Dr. Dobb's Journal of Software Tools*. Available at `http://opencv.org/downloads.html`.

Gabriella Csurka, Christopher R. Dance, Lixin Fan, Jutta Willamowski, and Cdric Bray. 2004. Visual categorization with bags of keypoints. In *Workshop on Statistical Learning in Computer Vision, ECCV*, pages 1–22.

FBK. 2013. FBK ASR transcription. Available at `https://hlt-tools.fbk.eu/tosca/publish/ASR/transcribe`.

ffmpeg. 2012. ffmpeg audio/video tool. Available at `http://www.ffmpeg.org`.

Jenny Rose Finkel, Trond Grenager, and Christopher D. Manning. 2005. Incorporating non-local information into information extraction systems by Gibbs sampling. In *Proceedings of ACL*, pages 363–370.

Brijnesh J. Jain and Klaus Obermayer. 2010. Elkan's k-means algorithm for graphs. In *Proceedings of the 9th Mexican International Conference on Artificial Intelligence: Conference on Advances in Soft Computing: Part II*, MICAI'10, pages 22–32, Berlin, Heidelberg. Springer-Verlag.

Toshio Kawashima, Kouichi Tateyama, Toshimasa Iijima, and Yoshinao Aoki. 1998. Indexing of baseball telecast for content-based video retrieval. In *ICIP (1)*, pages 871–874.

Ken-Hao Liu, Ming-Fang Weng, Chi-Yao Tseng, Yung-Yu Chuang, and Ming-Syan Chen. 2008. Association and temporal rule mining for post-filtering of semantic concept detection in video. *Trans. Multi.*, 10(2):240–251, February.

Qiaozhu Mei and ChengXiang Zhai. 2005. Discovering evolutionary theme patterns from text: An exploration of temporal text mining. In *Proceedings of the Eleventh ACM SIGKDD International Conference on Knowledge Discovery in Data Mining*, KDD '05, pages 198–207, New York, NY, USA. ACM.

Lev Pevzner and Marti A. Hearst. 2002. A critique and improvement of an evaluation metric for text segmentation. *Computational Linguistics*, 28(1):19–36.

Phi The Pham, M. F. Moens, and T. Tuytelaars. 2010. Cross-media alignment of names and faces. *IEEE Transactions on Multimedia*, 12(1):13–27, January.

Yong Rui, Anoop Gupta, and Alex Acero. 2000. Automatically extracting highlights for tv baseball programs. In *Proceedings of the Eighth ACM International Conference on Multimedia*, MULTIMEDIA '00, pages 105–115.

Drew D. Saur, Yap-Peng Tan, Sanjeev R. Kulkarni, and Peter J. Ramadge. 1997. Automated analysis and annotation of basketball video. In *Storage and Retrieval for Image and Video Databases (SPIE)*, pages 176–187.

Cees G. M. Snoek, Marcel Worring, Jan C. van Gemert, Jan-Mark Geusebroek, and Arnold W. M. Smeulders. 2006. The challenge problem for automated detection of 101 semantic concepts in multimedia. In *Proceedings of the 14th Annual ACM International Conference on Multimedia*, MULTIMEDIA '06, pages 421–430, New York, NY, USA.

Alexander Strehl and Joydeep Ghosh. 2003. Cluster ensembles — a knowledge reuse framework for combining multiple partitions. *J. Mach. Learn. Res.*, 3:583–617, March.

Xuanhui Wang, ChengXiang Zhai, Xiao Hu, and Richard Sproat. 2007. Mining correlated bursty topic patterns from coordinated text streams. In *Proceedings of the 13th ACM SIGKDD International Conference on Knowledge Discovery and Data Mining*, KDD '07, pages 784–793.

Gang Wang, Tat-Seng Chua, and Ming Zhao. 2008. Exploring knowledge of sub-domain in a multi-resolution bootstrapping framework for concept detection in news video. In *Proceedings of the 16th ACM International Conference on Multimedia*, MM '08, pages 249–258, New York, NY, USA. ACM.

Jun Yang, Rong Yan, and Alexander G. Hauptmann. 2007. Cross-domain video concept detection using adaptive SVMs. In *Proceedings of the 15th International Conference on Multimedia*, MULTIMEDIA '07, pages 188–197, New York, NY, USA. ACM.

Dennis Yow, Boon lock Yeo, Minerva Yeung, and Bede Liu. 1995. Analysis and presentation of soccer highlights from digital video. pages 499–503.

Qiankun Zhao, Prasenjit Mitra, and Bi Chen. 2007. Temporal and information flow based event detection from social text streams. In *Proceedings of the 22nd National Conference on Artificial Intelligence - Volume 2*, AAAI'07, pages 1501–1506.

Twitter User Gender Inference Using Combined Analysis of Text and Image Processing

Shigeyuki Sakaki, Yasuhide Miura, Xiaojun Ma, Keigo Hattori, and Tomoko Ohkuma
Fuji Xerox Co., Ltd. / Japan
6-1, Minatomirai, Nishi-ku, Yokohama-shi, Kanagawa
{sakaki.shigeyuki, yasuhide.miura, xiaojun.ma, keigo.hattori, ohkuma.tomoko}@fujixerox.co.jp

Abstract

Profile inference of SNS users is valuable for marketing, target advertisement, and opinion polls. Several studies examining profile inference have been reported to date. Although information of various types is included in SNS, most such studies only use text information. It is expected that incorporating information of other types into text classifiers can provide more accurate profile inference. As described in this paper, we propose combined method of text processing and image processing to improve gender inference accuracy. By applying the simple formula to combine two results derived from a text processor and an image processor, significantly increased accuracy was confirmed.

1 Introduction

Recently, several researches on profile inference of Social Networking Services (SNS) user conducted by analyzing postings have been reported (Rao and Yarowsky, 2010; Han et al., 2013; Makazhanov et al., 2013). User profile information such as gender, age, residential area, and political preference have attracted attention because they are helpful for marketing, target advertisement, TV viewer rate calculations, and opinion polls. The major approach to this subject is building a machine learning classifier trained by text in postings. However, images posted by a user are rarely used in profile inference. Images in postings also include features of user profiles. For example, if a user posts many dessert images, then the user might be female. Therefore, we assumed that highly accurate profile inference will be available by analyzing image information and text information simultaneously.

As described in this paper, we implement gender inference of Japanese Twitter user using text information and image information. We propose a combined method consisting of text processing and image processing, which accepts tweets as input data and outputs a gender probability score. The combined method comprises of two steps: step 1) two gender probability scores are inferred respectively by a text processor and an image processor; step 2) the combined score is calculated by merging two gender scores with an appropriate ratio. This report is the first describing an attempt to apply the combined method of text processing and image processing to profile inference of an SNS user.

This paper is presented as seven sections: section 2 presents a description of prior work; section 3 presents a description of the annotation data prepared for this study; section 4 introduces the proposed method; section 5 explains preliminary experiments for optimizing the combined method parameter; section 6 presents the experimentally obtained result; section 7 summarizes the paper and discusses future work.

2 Prior Work

Many reports have described studies examining gender inference. The conventional approach to this theme is building a machine learning classifier such as Support Vector Machine (SVM) trained by text features (Burger et al., 2011; Liu et al., 2012). Most of these studies specifically examine improvement of the machine classification methodology rather than expanding features or combining features. Different from these studies, Liu et al. (2013) implemented gender inference with incorporation of a user name into the classifier based on text information. However, the expansion of features

Proceedings of the 25th International Conference on Computational Linguistics, pages 54–61,
Dublin, Ireland, August 23-29 2014.

remains in the text field.

A few reports in the literature describe studies of systems that infer the SNS user gender with information aside from the text. Ikeda et al. (2013) leverages the accuracy of profile inference based on a text feature classifier by combining user cluster information. According to their study, the accuracy of classification that deals only with the user cluster is lower than that of the text classifier. The classifier using both text and cluster information of a user outperforms their text classifier. This research shows that information aside from the text is useful to leverage the performance of profile inference based on text and text information is necessary to achieve high accuracy. However, we introduce image information that is not used by Ikeda et al (2013).

Along with text information and cluster information, images are popular informative elements that are included in SNS postings. An image includes enough information to infer what is printed in itself, and researches to automatically annotate an image with semantic labels are already known (Zhang et al., 2012). Automatic image annotation is a machine learning technique that involves a process by which a computer system automatically assigns semantic labels to a digital image. These studies succeeded in inferences of various objects, such as person, dog, bicycle, chair etc. We supposed that such objects in images posted by a user should be useful clues as to a profile inference of a twitter user. As a matter of fact, gender inference by image information is reported by Ma et al. (2014), which implemented gender inference by processing images in tweets. Their study, which ignored text information, exhibited accuracy of less than 70%. It was much lower than most gender inference work using text feature.

From results of these studies, we concluded that gender inference by text and image information invites further study.

3 Proposed Method

Our proposed method for combining text processing and image processing is presented in Figure 1. First, data of 200 tweets of a user are separated into text data and image data. Each of separated data is analyzed using a dedicated processor, a text processor, and an image processor. Both of the processors

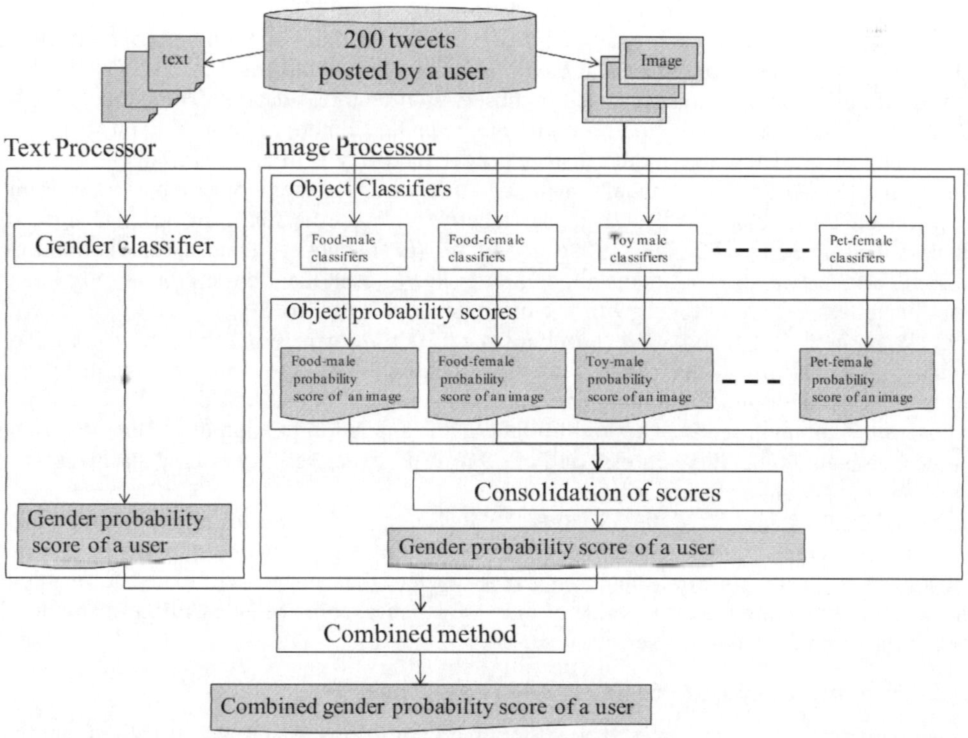

Figure 1. Combined method constitution.

output a user's gender probability score, the upper/lower ends of which respectively correspond to male and female labels. At the end of this process, the combined gender probability score is calculated using two probability scores. In this section, details of the two processors and the method of combining their two results are described.

3.1 Text Processing

The text processor is constructed from a text classifier, which accepts text data in tweets and outputs the gender probability score of a user. We defined the gender classifier in the text processor as an SVM binary classification of a male and female. The SVM classifier is trained based on unigram Bag-of-words with a linear kernel. The cost parameter C is set to 1.0. Then LIBSVM (Chang and Lin, 2001) is used as an implementation of SVM. Because words are not divided by spaces in a Japanese sentence, Kuromoji (Atilika, 2011), a morphological analysis program for Japanese, is used to obtain unigrams.

To combine two results from the text processor and the image processor, it is necessary to calculate each result as a probability value. To retrieve probability scores, we used logistic regression. Logistic function converts a distance from a hyper plane to probability scores of 0.0–1.0. The text classifier is a male and female binary classification. Therefore, the upper and lower ends of the probability score respectively correspond to male and female data. If a score is close to 0.0, then the user has high probability of being male. If it is close to 1.0, then a user is probably female.

3.2 Image Processing

We first tried to infer a Twitter user gender directly by a two-class classifier trained by image feature vector calculated by all images posted by a user. However, with some preliminary experiments, we found that this approach does not work well, since the large variation of objects made the classification difficult with single classifier setting. We, therefore, used the image processing method described by Ma et al. (2014) which uses automatic image annotation classifiers (Zhang et al., 2012) to model human recognition of different gender tendency in images. The method consists of two steps: step 1) annotating images by an image annotation technique at the image level; step 2) consolidating gender scores according to annotation results at the user level.

In the first step, the image labels are defined as the combination of the following two information: the gender tendency in images of a user and the objects that images express. Ma et al. (2014) defined 10 categories of objects in SNS images based on observation on a real dataset. The defined labels are cartoon/illustration, famous person, food, goods, memo/leaflet, outdoor/nature, person, pet, screenshot/capture, and other. They also indicated that gender tendency in images are coherent with user gender, and set three gender labels, male, female, and unknown, for each object label. As a result, 30 labels constructed from object label and gender label (e.g. "male-person") are used in this paper, which is described in section 4.2. Then a bag-of-features (BOF) model (Tsai, 2012; Chatfield et al., 2011) is applied to accomplish the image annotation task. We used local descriptors of SIFT (Lowe, 1999) and image features are encoded with a k-mean generated codebook with size of 2000. We applied LLC (Wang et al, 2010) and SPM (Lazebnik et al, 2006) to generating the final presentation of image features. Then, the 30 SVM classifiers are trained based on the features of training images: each classifier is trained per image label among one-versus-rest strategy. The SVM classifier annotates images of a user by computing scores, and logistic function is applied to the outputs of the image classifiers in order to obtain probability scores. Each of 30 probability scores shows how an image is close to the decision boundary of a particular label.

In the second step, we integrated the 30 scores of labels assigned to images to yield comprehensive scores which imply a user's gender. Two methods are suggested for the second step. One is computing the average of all scores output from each classifier for each of the categories of male and female for a user. The other is computing the mean value of only the highest scores of every image for each of the categories of male and female for a user.

3.3 Combined method of Text Processing and Image Processing

To combine two results derived from text processing and image processing, we used the function below. $Score_{text}$ and $Score_{image}$ respectively represent gender probability scores derived from the text processor and the image processor. In the function, α is set as a ratio of the text score and an image score to combine two scores appropriately. We introduced α as a reliability ratio parameter of the scores by the text processor and the scores by the image processor.

$$Score_{combined} = Score_{text} \times \alpha + Score_{image} \times (1 - \alpha)$$

4 Data

We prepared user annotation data and image annotation data that we used as training data and evaluation data. User annotation data are input data for the text processor, whereas image annotation data are for the image processor. As it is required to prepare a huge number of annotated data as a training corpus, the data is annotated by Yahoo Crowd Sourcing (Yahoo! Japan, 2013). Yahoo Crowd Sourcing is a Japanese crowd sourcing service similar to Amazon Mechanical Turk (Amazon, 2005). Therefore the annotation process aims to obtain annotation based on human recognition rather than to explore truth about users and images of twitter.

4.1 User Annotation Data

We first collected Japanese Twitter users according to their streaming tweets. We ignored heavy users and Twitter bots. A random sampling of tweets revealed that tweets from heavy users include much information that is not useful for profile inference such as short representations of their actions (e.g. "Going to bed now" and "Just waking up"). A Twitter bot is also classed as an uninformative user because it is a program that automatically generates tweets. During data collection, we filtered out those users by setting conditions shown below in Table 1. Finally, we obtained 3976 Twitter users. We gathered tweets on each user up to 200. By executing the processes above, we obtained tweet data of each user corresponding to the user's own 200 tweets.

To obtain gender annotation for this large dataset, we used Yahoo! Crowd Sourcing. As shown in Figure 2(a), we set task for every Twitter user: please infer the gender of the user who posted the tweets in the URL below. In this task, after reading 200 tweets of a user, the gender label of male or female was asked of every Twitter user. To guarantee quality reliability, annotation tasks for one Twitter user were duplicated 10 times by different workers; then a majority vote of 10 annotations was calculated to obtain a gold label.

As a result of the crowd sourcing tasks, 1733 users were reported as male; 2067 users were reported as female. There were 176 users whose votes were split equally between male and female. We re-

Table 1. Filtering conditions used to disqualify heavy users and Twitter bots

User Types	Definition for N	Criteria
Twitter bots	Number of tweets posted from Twitter clients on PC/mobile by a user	N<150
Heavy	Number of Friends or followers of a user	N>200
	Number of Tweets posted in a day by a user	N>10

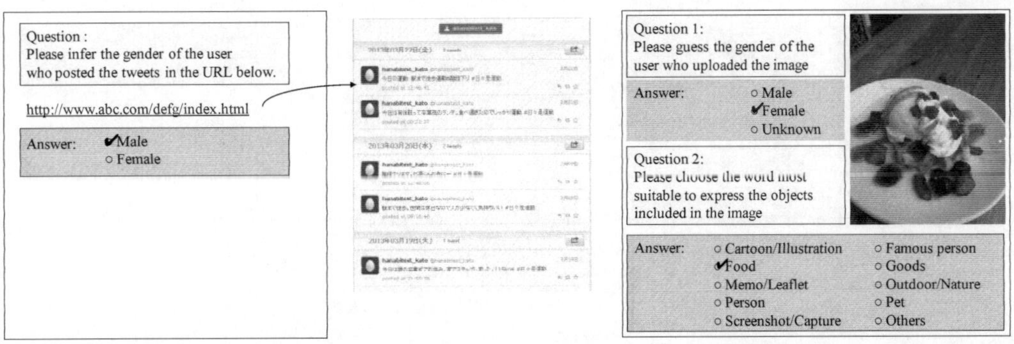

(a) User annotation task (b) Image annotation task

Figure 2. Annotation tasks in crowd sourcing.

moved balanced users from the data. The male and female populations of annotation assumed users are 45.6% and 54.4% respectively. This gender proportion tendency is consistent with those reported from an earlier study showing that Twitter participants are 55% female (Heli and Piskorski, 2009; Burger et al., 2011). Finally, we obtained gender annotation data of 3800 users. We divided these data equally between training data and evaluation data: 1900 users for training data and 1900 users for evaluation data.

4.2 Image Annotation Data

We first made a user list including 1523 users. After checking tweets from these users, we extracted 9996 images. Image annotation processes were also executed by Yahoo Crowd Sourcing.

Our image annotation process refers to rules proposed by Ma et al. (2014). As shown in Figure 2(b), a worker is requested to provide responses of two kinds for every image: Q1. Please guess the gender of the user who uploaded the image; Q2. Please choose the word most suitable to express the objects included in the image. The possible responses for Q1 were male, female, and unknown. Those for Q2 were cartoon/illustration, famous person, food, goods, memo/leaflet, outdoor/nature, person, pet, screenshot/capture, and other. It is sometimes difficult to infer a gender of a user solely based on one image. Therefore, *unknown* is set for Q1. From those responses we obtained multiple labels for every image, such as "male-person". To avoid influence by poor-quality workers, each image was presented to 10 different workers. A summation of 10 annotations was executed to obtain gold label data.

5 Preliminary Experiments

5.1 Image Processing

We compared two consolidation methods, computing the average of all scores and computing the average of the highest scores for 30 object scores. We applied the two method to the training data of the user annotation data, and tested them on the evaluation data. Results show that the accuracy of former method is 60.11. That of the latter is 65.42. The reason the latter method is superior to the former one is probably attributable to noise reduction effects of ignoring low scores.

5.2 Combined method of Text Processing and Image Processing

To estimate the optimal value of α, we conducted a preliminary experiment of the combined method with training data. We first prepared text and image probability scores. The text score is obtained by executing five-fold cross validation of the text processor for training data. We used the probability score derived in section 5.1 as the image score. The accuracies were, respectively, 86.23 and 65.42. Next, the combined formula was applied to these probability scores with moving α from 0 to 1. Figure 3 shows the correlation between accuracy and α. To obtain the α value of the peak, we executed polynomial fitting to a part of the correlation curve where α is 0.1–0.4. By differentiating this function, we calculated the α value of the peak as equal to 0.244 indicated by the arrow in Figure 3. The accuracy reaches 86.73% at the peak, which is 0.50 pt higher than that of the text processor.

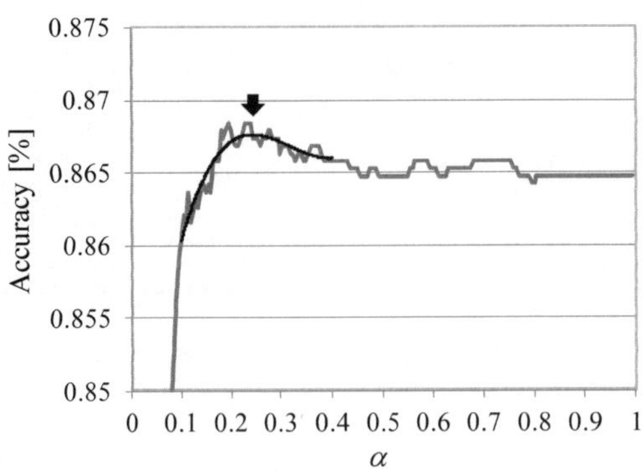

Figure 3. Correlation between accuracy and α in training data.
(Fitting curve function is $0.9519\alpha^3-0.9129\alpha^2+0.2756\alpha+0.8409$)

6 Experimental Results

6.1 Comparing the Accuracies between Three Methods

We executed an evaluation experiment assessing the three methods: text processing, image processing with a selected consolidation method, and the combined method with optimized α (0.235). Each method is applied to evaluation data including 1900 gender-annotated data. Table 2 presents precision, recall, F-measure, and accuracy obtained through the evaluation experiments. The text processing accuracy achieves 84.63%, and image processing accuracy is 64.21%. The combined method achieves 85.11% accuracy, which is 0.48 pt higher than the text processing accuracy.[1] We also confirmed that both the male and female F-measures become higher than text processing. We concluded that significantly increased accuracy obtained using the method combining text processing and image processing.

6.2 Discussion

We expected the optimal value of α to be large, since the accuracy of the text processor is explicitly higher than that of the image processor. However, the actual optimal α resulted to the rather small value, 0.244. This small α is thought to be caused by a characteristic of the image processor's gender scores. Figure 4 (a) and (b) show the distributions of the gender scores derived by the text processor and the image processor. The horizontal axis corresponds to a gender score of a user, ranging from 0, highly probable female, to 1, highly probable male. The two distributions are clearly different from

Table 2. Results obtained using text processing, image processing and combined method. (P, precision; R, recall; F, F-measure; Acc., Accuracy)

	Male			Female			Acc.
	P	R	F	P	R	F	
Text processing	84.65	82.39	83.50	84.62	86.64	83.50	84.63
Image processing	64.68	66.56	65.60	72.10	62.11	66.74	64.21
Combined method (α= 0.244)	84.57	83.72	84.16	85.49	86.34	85.91	85.11

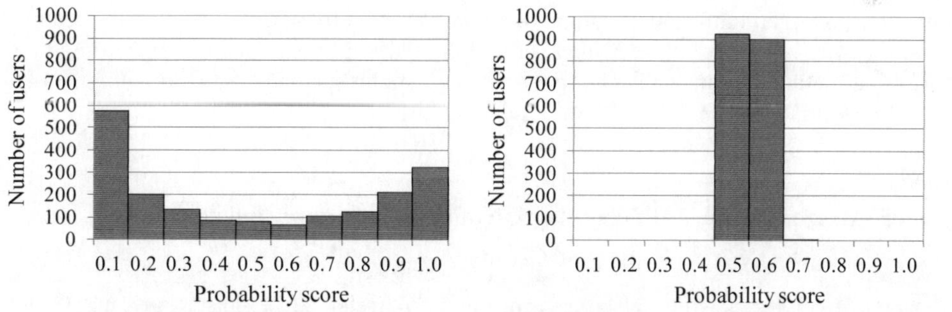

(a) The distribution of the text processing scores (b) The distribution of the image processing scores

Figure 4. The distributions of the probability scores.

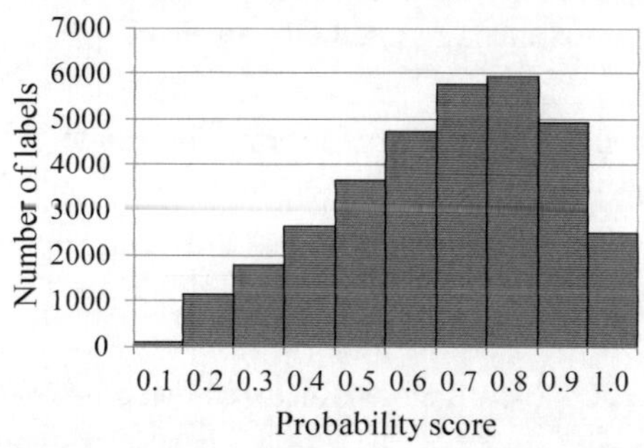

Figure 5. The distribution of the "male-person" score of training data of user annotation data.

[1]Significance improvement with paired t-test (p=0.09<0.1).

each other: the variance of the image scores is much smaller than that of the text. From this characteristic, the image scores were needed to be amplified in order to reflect them in the final result. In terms of α, this amplification corresponds to a small value.

The reason why the variance of the image scores became small is in its calculation process. In the image processor, the gender score of a user is calculated as the mean of the highest object scores extracted from each image. Figure 5 shows a distribution of "male-person" label scores. Though a distribution of each object probability scores centres not at 0.5, highest score selections and the averaging of them leads to a mid-range value, in this case 0.5.

Our intuition behind the introduction of α was to provide a reliability ratio parameter of the text processor and the image processor. But as a matter of fact, this parameter also worked to calibrate the scale difference between the two probability scores. From this observation, a function that includes a reliability parameter and a calibration parameter separately can be considered as an alternative to the proposed function. Using this kind of function will provide further insights about combining a text processing and image processing.

7 Conclusion

As described herein, we assembled two results retrieved by text and image processors respectively to enhance the Twitter user gender inference. Even though the gender inference accuracy already reached 84.63 solely by the text classifier, we succeeded in improving efficiency further by 0.48 pt. Because the image processing in our method is completely independent from the text processing, this combined method is applicable to the other gender prediction methods, just like those of Burger and Liu (Burger, 2011; Liu, 2013). Reported studies about SNS user profile inference targeted basic attributes such as gender, age, career, residential area, etc. More worthwhile attributes for marketing that directly indicate user characteristics are desired to predict, for example, hobbies and lifestyles. Images in tweets are expected to include clues about these profiles aside from gender. As a subject for future work, we will apply our combined method to various profile attributes.

As the combined method in this paper is simple linear consolidation and ignores a capability of analyzing both text and image information at the same time, exploring more suitable combined method is needed. The simplest way to analyze both text and image information simultaneously is early fusion that first creates the large multi-model feature vector constructed by both text and image features and then trains a classifier. Meta classifier which infers final class from the outputs of two modalities is also considerable method for this subject. Applying more sophisticated combined methods is another subject for future work.

References

Amazon. 2005. Amazon Mechanical Turk (2005), Available: http://www.mturk/welcom

Atilika. 2011, Kuromoji. Available: http://www.atilika.org

John D. Burger, John Henderson, Gerorge Kim, Guido Zarrella. 2011. Discriminating Gender on Twitter, In *Proc. of the Conference on Empirical Methods in natural Language Processing*

Ken Chatfield, Victor Lempitsky, Andrea Vedaldi, Andrew Zisserman. 2011. The devil is in the details: an evaluation of recent feature encoding methods, In *Proc. of British Machine Vision Conference 2011*

Chih-Chung Chang, Chih-Jen Lin, 2001. LIBSVM: a Library for Support Vector Machines. Available: http://www.csie.ntu.edu.tw/~cjlin/libsvm

Bo Han, Paul Cook, and Timothy Baldwin. 2013. A Stacking-based Approach to Twitter User Geolocation Prediction, In *Proc. of the 51st Annual meeting of Association for Computational Linguistics*, pages 7-12

Bill Heli, Mikolaj Jan Piskorski. 2009. New Twitter Research: Men Follow Men and Nobody Tweets, *Harvard Business Review*, June 1.

Kazushi Ikeda, Gen Hattori, Chihiro Ono, Hideki Asoh, Teruo Higashino. 2013. Twitter User Profiling Based on Text and Community Mining for Market Analysis, *Knowledge Based Systems 51*, pages 35-47.

Svetlana Lazebnik, Cordelia Schmid, Jean Ponce, 2006. Beyond bags of features: Spatial Pyramid Matching for Recognizing Natural Scene Categories, In *Proc. of Computer Vision and Pattern Recognition 2006,* page 2169-2178

Wendy Liu, Faiyaz Al Zamal, Derek Ruths. 2012. Using Social Media to Infer Gender Composition of Commuter Populations, In *Proc. of the International Association for the Advancement of Artificial Intelligence Conference on Weblogs and Social*

Wendy Liu, Derek Ruths. 2013. What's in a Name? Using First Names as Features for Gender Inference in Twitter, In Symposium on Analyzing Microtext

David G. Lowe. 1999. Object recognition from local scale-invariant features, In *Proc. of the International Conference on Computer Vision*, pages 1150-1157

Matt Lynley. 2012. Statistics That Reveal Instagram's Mind-Blowing Success, Available: http://www.businessinsider.com/statistics-that-reveal-instagrams-mind-blowing-success-2012-4

Xiaojun Ma, Yukihiro Tsuboshita, Noriji Kato. 2014. Gender Estimation for SNS User Profiling Automatic Image Annotation, In *Proc. of the 1st International Workshop on Cross-media Analysis for Social Multimedia*

Aibek Makazhanov, Davood Refiei. 2013. Predicting Political Preference of Twitter Users, In *Proc. of the 2013 IEEE/ACM International Conference on Advances in Social Network and Mining,* pages 298-305

Alan Mislove, Sune Lehmann, Yong-Yeol Ahn, Jukka-Pekka onnela, J. Hiels Rosenquist. 2011. Undersanding the Demographics of Twitter Users, In *Proc. of 5th International AAAI Conference on Weblogs and Social Media*, pages 554-557

Delip Rao and David Yarowsky. 2010. Detecting Latent User Properties in Social Media, In *Proc. of the Neural Information Processing Systems Foundation workshop on Machine Learning for Social Networks*

Chih-Fong Tsai. 2012. Bag-of-Words Representation in Image Annotation: A Review, *International Scholarly Research Notices Artificial Intelligence*, Volume 2012, Article ID 376804, 19 pages

Jinjun Wang, Jinchao Yang, Kai Yu, Fengjun Lv, Thomas Huang, Yihong Gong. 2010. Locality-constrained linear coding for image classification, In *Proc. of Computer Vision and Pattern Recognition 2010,* page 626

Yahoo! Japan. 2013. Yahoo Crowd Sourcing. Available: http://crowdsourcing.yahoo.co.jp/

Dengsheng Zhang, Md Monirul Islam, Guojun Lu. 2012. A review on automatic image annotation, *Pattern Recognition* 45, pages 346-362

Semantic and geometric enrichment of 3D geo-spatial models with captioned photos and labelled illustrations

Christopher B. Jones, Paul L. Rosin and **Jonathan D. Slade**
School of Computer Science & Informatics
Cardiff University
5, The Parade, Cardiff, CF24 3AA
United Kingdom
{JonesCB2, RosinPL, SladeJD}@cardiff.ac.uk

Abstract

There are many 3D digital models of buildings with cultural heritage interest, but most of them lack semantic annotation that could be used to inform users of mobile and desktop applications about their origins and architectural features. We describe methods in an ongoing project for enriching 3D models with generic annotation, derived from examples of images of building components and from labelled plans and diagrams, and with object-specific descriptions obtained from photo captions. This is the first stage of research that aims to annotate 3D models with facts extracted from the text of authoritative architectural guides.

1 Introduction

Geographical data are used in many professional and academic applications in the environmental and social sciences and for personal applications such as navigation and local information search. For many purposes, information referenced to 2D geographical coordinates is quite adequate. There are however a number of applications for which 3D geo-data are either necessary or highly desirable. These include inter-visibility analysis, radio communications, visualization for urban planning, indoor navigation, augmented reality, and mobile and desktop applications that allow the user to be informed about cultural heritage and architectural features of detailed aspects of the built environment. While there are increasing numbers of 3D city models, and individual models of many notable buildings, for some of the 3D geo-data applications the existing models are still inadequate as they usually lack semantic annotation of any sort. There is a requirement therefore to develop effective procedures to annotate 3D building models with descriptive attributes. In a cultural heritage context these could include the materials, origins, people and events associated with them.

In this paper we describe an approach to semantic annotation of 3D building models that forms the basis of a research project that is currently in its early stages. The main premise of the project is that if captioned images and annotated plans and diagrams can be matched, using computer vision methods, to locations on 3D models of buildings, then the textual information content of the captions can be linked to the corresponding parts of the model. The project focuses upon buildings with cultural heritage and builds upon and progresses beyond previous work that has used captioned photos to annotate 3D models, e.g. Simon and Seitz (2008) and Russell et al. (2013). We aim to generate models of buildings that are semantically richer than typical existing models. The approach complements work such as Zhang et al. (2014) in which 3D models were used to enhance and annotate photos.

Social media sites such as Flickr have many freely available photographs of interesting buildings, often accompanied by captions that provide descriptions of an entire building or of parts of a building. While photos on social media are a valuable source of information for well-visited buildings, there are many buildings, particularly less visited ones, that have few or no such photographs with useful captions. There are also however many captioned photos in architectural and cultural heritage guides that describe architectural features and associated historical events with a level of detail and quality of information that is often superior to the content of social media, including that of Wikipedia. Many of these guides

Proceedings of the 25th International Conference on Computational Linguistics, pages 62–67,
Dublin, Ireland, August 23-29 2014.

contain plans and diagrams of the layout of buildings labelled with the names of rooms and associated spaces. The combination of captioned images, annotated plans and diagrams that can be found in social media and in authoritative texts provides a rich source of information that can be used to attach semantic attributes to 3D models of buildings as well as to some 2D cartographic data.

The idea of exploiting captioned photos of buildings to support virtual exploration of buildings was pioneered in the Photo Tourism application of Snavely et al (2008) in which SIFT and related methods of feature matching in computer vision were used to match photos of buildings, compute camera parameters (i.e. pose) and to generate point clouds representing the 3D geometry of buildings (referred to as structure from motion). This enabled applications in which users could view captioned photos of particular parts of a building. It also provided the possibility of matching a new photo to an existing captioned photo and hence automatically tagging the new photo with tags from the already captioned photo or with tags that users manually linked to the 3D geometry. Simon and Seitz (2008) used related methods to annotate 3D point clouds with the captions of the Flickr photos. They presented a segmentation procedure that grouped photos that contain the same 3D points (derived from the SIFT/structure from motion methods) as well as exploiting the fact that 3D points belonging to the same object could be expected to be clustered in space.

Finer granularity annotation of parts of buildings was achieved by Russell et al (2013) who linked items of text in Wikipedia articles about particular buildings to locations in 3D models. The models were created from sets of Flickr images tagged with the respective building name, but annotation of objects within the buildings, such as statues and paintings, was obtained using images found on Google Image search, with search terms obtained from extraction of prepositional and noun phrases in the Wikipedia articles. In Russell et al's application, the 3D building model is essentially a point cloud with no explicit structure, and the users' views of parts of the building consist of the Flickr photos of respective annotated objects.

Our work differs from these approaches in that we employ structured 3D building models, as can be found for example in 3D Warehouse[1]. We exploit the fact that many of these 3D models include texture mapped photos that have been registered to the building geometry. This enables the use of image matching methods to associate captioned photographs with specific parts of the texture mapped images, and hence via the 3D geometry to specific geometric objects on the buildings. The aim is to enrich structured 3D models both semantically and, where necessary, geometrically, using a combination of the texture-mapped imagery, captioned photos, and other annotated resources such as ground plans, that name the rooms or spaces of a building, and diagrams of the elevation (side view) of a building. In the remainder of the paper we provide a summary of the methods. We conclude with a discussion of the future challenges.

2 Methods

2.1 Annotation of 3D models with examples of generic objects

To support the objective of attaching annotation from captions, or other text, to building components such as rooms, doors, windows, arches, clocks etc, it would be useful for their presence to be recorded explicitly in the geometric model, which is not the case for many existing building models. The geometric representation of component objects would serve as a digital record of the building structure and assist applications that guide and inform users of the various aspects of a building. If these objects, such as doors and windows, are generically labelled it will also assist the process of matching caption text to the parts of the building that they describe. Thus while a caption may describe something in the image the question is exactly what part of the 3D model is being described. In some cases the caption will relate to most of the content of the photo image, if for example a particular statue or window has been photographed, but in some cases the described object may occupy just a part of the image. Simon and Seitz (2008) addressed this issue by comparing multiple (hundreds or thousands of) photos with a similar caption and identifying the region that is common to the majority of the photos, but that approach cannot be used when there are very few photos with useful captions. If the 3D model contains generic

[1]https://3dwarehouse.sketchup.com/ also known as Trimble 3D Warehouse and Google 3D Warehouse

annotation then it will be possible in some cases to infer what geometric object the caption is describing, by matching between the generic descriptor in the model and equivalent terms in the caption.

We will therefore develop automated methods to assist in enhancing the geometric detail in order to support semantic annotation. The intention is to use, in the first instance, generic object models to assist in identifying the boundary of prominent building components, such as windows, within the texture mapped imagery or within photos that have been matched to, and hence registered with, the texture maps (see Mayer and Reznik (2006; 2005) for examples of related work in photogrammetry). The vectorised geometric representation of these boundaries will then be added to the building model geometry and labelled with the object category (e.g. "door") of the corresponding object detector.

Previous work on the detection of objects in images of buildings has mostly used template-based methods that require the design of object detectors (e.g. Chen et al (2011)). These methods may not be suitable for application to texture mapped imagery due to the wide range of appearances of objects such as doors and windows as a consequence both of stylistic variation and of variation in the viewpoint, lighting, colour and size. An alternative approach is the bag of visual words BoVW (Sivic and Zisserman, 2003) which involves detecting and describing a set of keypoints (or interest points) in the image. Given a training set of images, vector quantization is applied to cluster the extracted feature vectors to form a dictionary which captures the most frequently occurring patterns (the visual words). An unseen image is represented as a vector of visual word frequencies and image classification is performed by matching the vector to prototypical vectors.

2.2 Exploitation of building plans

As indicated above, annotated plans of buildings, such as may be found in published building guides and in some web documents about specific buildings, provide a potentially useful further source of information about the nature of rooms and spaces in buildings. When 3D building models lack such annotation, as is usually the case, it will be possible to match the plans to the ground projection of the building geometry and hence label the corresponding parts of the building.

In various applications of GIS it is common practice to integrate data from multiple sources in order to generate a representation that retains the best elements of the multiple sources (see Ross et al (2009) for an example that includes 3D data) – in our case we are interested in taking labels of plans in illustrated guides and transferring the labels to the appropriate matching parts of the 3D building. The process requires geometric and semantic matching and is referred to as conflation (Samal et al., 2004), though it is most commonly applied to 2D geographical data. If there is considerable variation in the representation of the same real world objects then it can be helpful to use probabilistic methods such as mutual information (Walter and Fritsch, 1999) and Bayesian learning methods (Jones et al., 1999) that employ multiple sources of evidence for equivalence. Most conflation methods in GIS operate on vector representations. As plans in guides to buildings are typically purely image based, it may be necessary to vectorize them, for which standard GIS methods are again available, prior to application of conflation procedures. An alternative to conventional GIS methods, many of which require some interactive control, has been described in Smart et al (2011), who presented matching methods that entailed rasterizing the projection of poorly structured building geometry prior to raster based matching with a rasterized digital map.

2.3 Feature matching methods and linking captions to models

In computer vision, image feature matching procedures based on SIFT (Scale Invariant Feature Transform) are now widely used (Mikolajczyk and Schmid, 2005). In our project these feature matching methods will support object detection (as explained above) and enable matching of captioned photos to the corresponding objects or regions of a building. The first step is to identify distinctive local regions, or keypoints, of an image, and compute descriptors for each keypoint. Matches between corresponding features in different images are established using measures of similarity between the keypoint descriptors. However, some of these local matches will often be inconsistent at an object (i.e. more global) level. These are eliminated by applying a RANSAC procedure (Fischler and R. Bolles, 1987) to the set of matching keypoints to robustly generate the fundamental matrix representing the perspective transformation between the two images. Those pairs of matching keypoints that are inconsistent with the

Figure 1: Flickr photo and accompanying caption of Big Ben

estimated transformation are identified as outliers, and removed.

Figure 1 illustrates an image and caption from Flickr of Big Ben which is part of the Houses of Parliament in London. It is of interest to match this captioned image to the corresponding part of the 3D model of the building (illustrated in Figure 2b) for purposes of annotation. Applying the SIFT-based matching procedure to compare the Flickr image with the set of texture map images for the 3D model, followed by the RANSAC procedure, results in one of the texture map images containing a strong cluster of matching keypoints for the region around the clock of Big Ben (Figure 2a), i.e. the inlier matched keypoint pairs, represented in the figure with red lines. Other, false matching outlier keypoint pairs are highlighted with dashed cyan lines in Figure 2a. The matched region on the 3D model is highlighted in red in Figure 2b and is based on the convex hull of the matching inlier keypoints. The caption becomes linked in the first instance to this region. In future work we will use other methods to refine this matching region. Initially this could use region growing from the initial set of inlier key points, whereby pixels in the captioned images adjacent to the inlier key points are transformed to the texture map image using the estimated fundamental matrix, and retained if the (dense) SIFT descriptors of the corresponding pixels match. In subsequent work the intention is to match the caption text to the corresponding generically labelled objects on the building model, which in the illustrated example would be the clock and the tower.

2.4 Linking to rich text descriptions

The work described here is a step towards the objective of linking detailed authoritative descriptions of parts of buildings to the corresponding objects in 3D geometric models. Russell et al (2013) have demonstrated such linking between parts of Wikipedia articles to 3D models. It is clear however from their examples that their methods are quite selective and can fail to match interesting descriptions to their respective building components. Their methods depend upon crowdsourcing of suitably captioned photos that match with the authoritative text, which in turn restricts the approach to well-photographed places and objects. While that approach has benefits for popular buildings, the challenge remains to develop more effective methods for detecting references to building components in rich textual descriptions (not just in social media) and to develop methods for linking them to the geometric model that are not entirely dependent upon multiple tagged photographs.

One approach to reducing the dependancy upon captioned photos is to develop effective methods for

(a) (b)

Figure 2: (a) Key point matching between a Flickr image of Big Ben (on the right) and the texture map imagery of a 3D model of the Houses of Parliament that includes Big Ben. Inlier matches are coloured as red lines and outliers as dashed cyan lines. (b) The 3D texture-mapped model of the Houses of Parliament in which the convex hull region of the matching inlier key points is highlighted in red.

understanding localisation expressions that tell the reader where particular objects are to be found. This will involve sophisticated natural language processing to detect and interpret the often vague spatial relations that are employed in descriptions of the locations of environmental objects (Kordjamshidi et al., 2011; Mani et al., 2010). Thus a door may be described as being in the west wall of a church, in which case it may be possible to identify the respective boundary (wall) of the 3D building model and hence the generically labelled geometric object within that wall. Equally, terms such as left and right, and architectural words such as lintel, arch and column, may help to locate a described object without recourse to a captioned photo. When captioned photos are available they may however be exploited to assist in the geometric annotation process. It remains to investigate the refinement and application of these and related methods for the purpose of detailed and authoritative annotation of building models and other 3D representations of the built and the natural world.

3 Concluding Remarks

In this paper we have summarised an approach to semantic and geometric enrichment of 3D building models that exploits a mix of captioned photos from social media with captioned photos and labelled ground plans obtained from illustrated guides. The methods differ from the current state of the art for annotating 3D models in that we employ structured 3D models, rather than 3D point clouds, and we focus on enhancing the geometric representation and generic annotation of objects within these models. Generic annotation, achieved through a combination of computer vision methods and GIS conflation procedures, facilitates the linking of text descriptions of particular types of object to the corresponding components of the 3D model. This will avoid the sometimes prohibitive dependence of existing methods on the presence of multiple captioned photos of all objects of interest. It also paves the way for linking rich textual descriptions in authoritative guides to the corresponding geometric objects.

Acknowledgements

Jonathan Slade is funded by an EPSRC Industrial CASE studentship with Ordnance Survey, GB.

References

Z. Chen, Y. Li, and S. T. Birchfield. 2011. Visual detection of lintel-occluded doors by integrating multiple cues using data-driven MCMC. *Robotics and Autonomous Systems*.

M. Fischler and R. R. Bolles. 1987. Random sample consensus: a paradigm for model fitting with applications to image analysis and automated cartography. In *Readings in computer vision: issues, problems, principles, and paradigms,*.

C.B. Jones, J.M. Ware, and D.R. Miller. 1999. A probabilistic approach to environmental change detection with area-class map data. In *ISD '99 International Workshop on Integrated Spatial Databases, Digital Images and GIS*, volume 1737 of *Lecture Notes in Computer Science*, pages 122–136, Berlin. Springer.

P. Kordjamshidi, M. van Otterlo, and M.F. Moens. 2011. Spatial role labeling: Towards extraction of spatial relations from natural language. *ACM Transactions on Speech and Language Processing*, 8(3).

I. Mani, C. Doran, D. Harris, et al. 2010. SpatialML: annotation scheme, resources, and evaluation. *Language Resources and Evaluation*, 44:263–280.

H. Mayer and S. Reznik. 2005. Building façade interpretation from image sequences. In U Stilla, F Rottensteiner, and S Hinz, editors, *International archives of photogrammetry, remote sensing and spatial information sciences*, volume XXXVI. Joint workshop of ISPRS and DAGM.

H. Mayer and S. Reznik. 2006. MCMC Linked With Implicit Shape Models and Plane Sweeping for 3D Building Facade Interpretation in Image Sequences. In *The International Archives of the Photogrammetry, Remote Sensing and Spatial Information*, volume XXXVI. ISPRS Commission III.

K. Mikolajczyk and C. Schmid. 2005. A performance evaluation of local descriptors. *IEEE Trans. Pattern Anal. Mach. Intell.*, 27(10):1615–1630.

L. Ross, J. Bolling, J. Döllner, and B. Kleinschmit. 2009. Enhancing 3d city models with heterogeneous spatial information: Towards 3d land information systems. In *Lecture Notes in Geoinformation and Cartography*, pages 113–133.

B.C. Russell, R. Martin-Brualla, D.J. Butler, S. M. Seitz, and L. Zettlemoyer. 2013. 3d wikipedia: Using online text to automatically label and navigate reconstructed geometry. *ACM Transactions on Graphics (SIGGRAPH Asia 2013)*, 32(6).

A. Samal, S. Sheth, and K. Cueto. 2004. A feature-based approach to conflation of geospatial sources. *International Journal of Geographical Information Science*, 18(5):459–489.

I. Simon and S.M. Seitz. 2008. Scene segmentation using the wisdom of crowds. In *European Conference on Computer Vision (ECCV)*, pages 541–553.

J. Sivic and A. Zisserman. 2003. Video google: A text retrieval approach to object matching in videos. In *Int. Conf. Computer Vision*, pages 1470–1477.

P.D. Smart, J.A.Quinn, and C.B. Jones. 2011. City model enrichment. *ISPRS Journal of Photogrammetry and Remote Sensing*, 66(2):223–234.

N. Snavely, S.M. Seitz, and R. Szeliski. 2008. Modeling the world from internet photo collections. *Int. J. of Computer Vision*, 80(2):189–210.

V. Walter and D. Fritsch. 1999. Matching spatial data sets: A statistical approach. *International Journal of Geographical Information Science*, 13(5):445–473.

C. Zhang, Gao J., Wang O., Georgel P., Yang R., Davis J., Frahm J.M., and Pollefeys M. 2014. Personal photograph enhancement using internet photo collections. *IEEE Transactions on Vision and Computer Graphics*, 20(2):262–75.

Weakly supervised construction of a repository of iconic images

Lydia Weiland and **Wolfgang Effelsberg** and **Simone Paolo Ponzetto**
University of Mannheim
Mannheim, Germany
{lydia,effelsberg,simone}@informatik.uni-mannheim.de

Abstract

We present a first attempt at semi-automatically harvesting a dataset of iconic images, namely images that depict objects or scenes, which arouse associations to abstract topics. Our method starts with representative topic-evoking images from Wikipedia, which are labeled with relevant concepts and entities found in their associated captions. These are used to query an online image repository (i.e., Flickr), in order to further acquire additional examples of topic-specific iconic relations. To this end, we leverage a combination of visual similarity measures, image clustering and matching algorithms to acquire clusters of iconic images that are topically connected to the original seed images, while also allowing for various degrees of diversity. Our first results are promising in that they indicate the feasibility of the task and that we are able to build a first version of our resource with minimal supervision.

1 Introduction

Figurative language and images are a pervasive phenomenon associated with human communication. For instance, images used in news articles (especially on hot and sensitive topics) often make use of non-literal visual representations like iconic images, which are aimed at capturing the reader's attention. For environmental topics, for instance, a windmill in an untouched and bright landscape surrounded by a clear sky is typically associated by humans with environmental friendliness, and accordingly causes positive emotions. In a similar way, images of a polar bear on a drifting ice floe are typically associated with the topic of global warming (O'Neill and Smith, 2014).

But while icons represent a pervasive device for visual communication, to date, there exists to the best of our knowledge no approach aimed at their computational modeling. In order to enable the overarching goal of producing such kind of models from real-world data, we focus, in this work, on the preliminary task of semi-automatically compiling an electronic database of iconic images. These consist, in our definition, of images produced to create privileged associations between a particular visual representation and a referent. Iconic images are highly recognizable for media users and typically induce negative or positive emotions that have an impact on viewers' attitudes and actions. In order to model them from a computational perspective, we initially formulate iconic image acquisition as a clustering task in which, given a set of initial, manually-selected 'seed' images – e.g., a photo of a polar bear on a drifting ice floe for the topic of global warming, a smokestack for the topic of pollution, etc. – we use their associated textual descriptions in order to collect related images from the Web. We then process these images using state-of-the-art image understanding techniques to produce clusters of semantically similar, yet different images depicting the same topic in an iconic way.

The acquisition of a database of iconic images represents the first step towards a full-fledged model to computationally capture the phenomenon of iconic images in context. Our long-term vision is to cover all three aspects of *content* (what makes an image iconic?), *usage* (in which context are iconic images used?), and *effects* (which negative/positive emotions do iconic images evoke on viewers?) of iconic images. To make this challenging problem feasible, we opt in this preliminary step for an approach that views the task of understanding iconic images as the ability to build a dataset for further research.

Proceedings of the 25th International Conference on Computational Linguistics, pages 68–73,
Dublin, Ireland, August 23-29 2014.

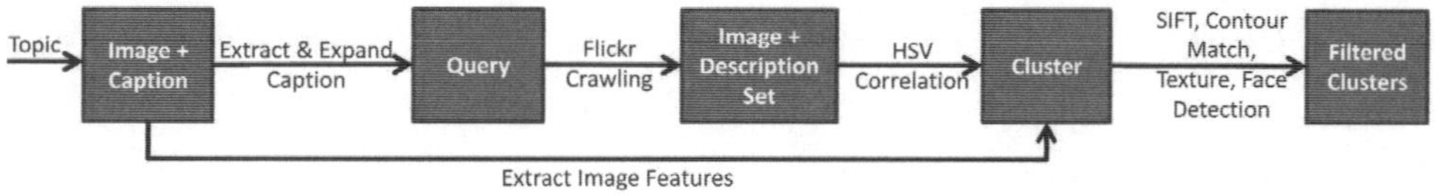

Figure 1: Our framework for the semi-automatic acquisition of iconic images from the Web.

2 Method

Our method for the semi-automatic acquisition of iconic images consists of five phases (Figure 1):

Seed selection. In the first phase of our approach we provide our pipeline with human-selected examples of iconic images that help us bootstrap the image harvesting process. To this end, we initially focus on a wide range of twelve different abstract topics that can be typically represented using iconic images (Table 1). Selecting initial examples describing a visual iconic representation of a topic can be a daunting task, due to their volatile and topic-dependent nature. In this work, we explore the use of Web encyclopedic resources in order to collect our initial examples. We start with the encyclopedic entries from National Geographic Education[1], an on-line resource in which human expert editors make explicit use of prototypical images to visually represent encyclopedic entries like "agriculture", "climate change", etc.. For instance, the encyclopedic entry for "air pollution" contains images of smokestacks, cooling towers release steam, and so on (cf. Table 1). We use these (proprietary) images to provide us with human-validated examples of iconic images, and use these to identify (freely available) similar images within Wikipedia pages based on a Google image search restricted to Wikipedia – e.g., by searching for `smokestack site:wikipedia.org`. We then use Wikipedia to create an initial dataset of iconic visuals associated with the textual descriptions found in their captions.

Text-based image search. In the next step, we make use of a query-by-text approach in order to collect additional data and enlarge our dataset with additional images depicting iconic relations. To this end, we start by collecting the entities annotated within the image captions (e.g., "Cumberland Power Plant at Cumberland City"), and manually determine their relevance to the associated topic (e.g., smokestacks and air pollution). This is because, to build a good query, we need to provide the search systems with a good lexicalization (i.e., keywords) of the underlying information need (i.e., the topic). Consequently, we extract entities from each caption of our initial set of images and use these to query additional data. For each seed, we generate a query by concatenating the entity labels in the captions and send it to Flickr[2]. We then filter the data by retaining only photos with title, description, and tags where both, tags and description (caption and title) contain the query words. This method provides us with around 4000 additional images and text pairs.

Image clustering. Text-based image search results can introduce noise in the dataset, e.g., cases of 'semantic mismatch' where the caption and tags do not appropriately describe the scene found in the image. In this work, we explore the application of image clustering techniques to cope with this issue. For each topic we start with a set of instances made up of the seed images and the crawled one, and group them into clusters based on image similarity measures. Clusters are built by calculating the linear correlation – i.e., which we take as a proxy for a similarity measure – from the HSV-histograms of each image, and applying the K-Means algorithm. Clustering on the basis of HSV-histograms does not take into account the semantic content of images, since images with different meanings can still have the same HSV-histogram. Nevertheless, this approach makes it possible to spot those outliers in the image sets that do not relate well to the other images retrieved with the same query.

Image filtering. The next processing step focuses instead on rule-driven filtering to improve the initial clustering-based filtering. We first apply a face detection and HoG (histogram of gradients) descriptor for

[1]`http://education.nationalgeographic.com`
[2]`http://flickr.com`

Topic	Themes of seed images
Adaption	hummingbird, king snake, koala
Agriculture	cattle, ploughing, rice terraces, tropical fruits
Air	balloon, sky view
Air Pollution	smokestack, Three Mile Island, wildfire
Biodiversity	Amazonas, blue starfish, cornflowers, fungi, Hopetoun Falls
Capital	Capitol Hill, Praça Dos Três, Washington Monument
Climate	Mykonos (mild climate), Sonoran Desert, tea plantation (cool climate)
Climate Change	polar bear, volcano, dry lake
Climate Refugee	climate refugees from Indonesia, Haiti, Pakistan, etc.
Ecosystem	bison, flooded forest, Flynn Reef, harp seal, rainforest, thorn tree
Global Warming	deforestation, flooding, smokestack
Greenhouse Effect	smokestack, steam engine train (smoke emissions)

Table 1: Overview of our covered topics and the themes associated with their seed images.

detecting people (Viola and Jones, 2001; Dalal and Triggs, 2005)[3]. Next, we filter our data as follows. If faces or people are recognized in the picture, and the caption is judged to be related to entities of type person (e.g., farmers iconically depicting the topic of agriculture), the instance is retained in the dataset. On the other hand, if faces and/or people are recognized, but the caption is not related to entities of type person (e.g., a blue linckia, which is a physical object), we filter out the image from the dataset.

Image matching. The filtered clusters we built so far are still problematic in that they do not account for diversity – i.e., we do not want as the outcome of our method to end up with clusters made up only of various pictures of the very same object (e.g., the cooling towers of the Three Mile Island power complex for the topic of air pollution, possibly seen from different perspectives, times of the day, etc.). That is, in our scenario we would like to promote heterogeneous clusters which still retain a high-level semantic match with the initial seeds (e.g., smokestacks or cooling towers belonging to different plants). To this end, we explore in this work an approach that leverages different image matching methods together at the same time to automatically capture these visual semantic matches.

Initially, for each cluster we select the image that minimizes the sum over all squared distances from the other images in the cluster. That is, given a cluster $C = \{c_1 \dots c_n\}$, we collect the image $\hat{c} = \arg\min_{c_i \in C} \sum_{c_j \in C - \{c_i\}} (c_i - c_j)^2$. We call this the *prototype* of the cluster. Several image processing methods are then used to compare the prototype of each cluster with the original seed images, with the aim to detect high-level content similarity (i.e., distinct, yet similar objects such as the smokestacks of different plants, etc.) and account for diversity with respect to our initial seeds. The first method is a template matching approach, based on minimum and maximum values of gray levels, which, together with their location are used to detect similar textures. The matching method is based on a correlation coefficient matching (Brunelli, 2009). In parallel, we explore an alternative approach where images and prototypes are compared using SIFT-based features (Lowe, 2004). Finally, we apply a contour matching method: we use a manually chosen threshold of the largest 10% of contours of an image to reduce the noise from non-characteristic contours like dots, points or other smaller structures. The matching of contours is based on rotation invariant moments (Hu, 1962). When a good match is found, bounding boxes are drawn around the contours.

The three methods provide evidence for potential matches between regions of each input prototype and seed pair. Information from each single method is then combined by intersecting their respective outputs: i) the patch, where the template matching is found is compared against the coordinates where relevant SIFT features are detected (SIFT-Template); ii) the template matching patch is tested for intersection with the bounding boxes of the matched contours (Template-Contour); iii) the bounding boxes of the contours

[3]We focus on face and people detection since these are both well studied areas in computer vision for which a wide range of state-of-the-art methods exist.

Topic	2-matches			all matches		
	P	R	F_1	P	R	F_1
Adaption	100.0	57.2	72.8	66.7	10.9	18.7
Agriculture	50.0	35.4	41.4	0.0	0.0	0.0
Air	84.2	75.6	79.7	66.7	15.8	25.5
Air Pollution	65.9	83.7	73.7	65.1	32.4	43.3
Biodiversity	54.0	40.6	46.3	34.4	8.1	13.1
Capital	61.7	54.6	57.9	50.6	12.6	20.2
Climate	93.7	81.6	87.2	89.1	20.0	32.7
Climate Change	88.5	78.1	83.0	50.0	21.4	30.0
Climate Refugee	40.0	50.0	44.4	0.0	0.0	0.0
Ecosystem	73.7	61.7	67.2	43.3	11.4	18.0
Global Warming	65.9	71.0	68.3	43.0	21.7	28.8
Greenhouse Effect	100.0	81.6	89.9	100.0	34.2	51.0

Table 2: Performance results per topic on iconic image detection (percentages).

are checked for relevant SIFT features (SIFT-Contour). Finally, we group together the prototype with the seed icon of the corresponding topic in case at least two or three of the single matching strategies in i–iii) identify the same regions in the images. This process is repeated until all prototypes have been examined: prototypes for which the no match can be found are filtered out as being not iconic.

3 Evaluation

Dataset statistics. We first provide statistics on the size of the datasets created with our approach. Using HSV correlation we initially generate 1232 clusters with an average size of 27.37 elements per cluster. Additional filtering based on at least two of our image matching methods produces 870 clusters (19.33 elements on average), whereas the more restrictive clustering based on all three methods gives 261 small-sized clusters of only 5.8 instances on average. This is because, naturally, applying matching-based filtering tends to produce a smaller number of clusters with fewer elements.

Gold standard and filtering evaluation. To produce a gold standard for our task, we annotated all of the 4,000 images we retrieved from Flickr. Each image is associated with a keyword query (Section 2): accordingly, we annotated each instance as being iconic or not with respect to the topic expressed by the keywords – e.g., given a picture of Hopetoun Falls, whether it captures the concept of waterfall or not. This is because, in our work, we take keywords as proxies of the underlying topics (e.g., biodiversity is depicted using waterfalls): in this setting, negative instances consist of mismatches between the query text and the picture – e.g., a photography taken near Hopetoun Falls, showing beech trees and thus capturing a query search for "forest" rather than "waterfalls".

We next evaluate our system on the binary classification task of detecting whether an image is iconic or not. In our case, we can quantify performance by taking all images not filtered out in the last step of image matching (and thus deemed as iconic in the final system output), and comparing them against our gold-standard annotations. This way we can compute standard metrics of precision, recall and balanced F-measure. Our results indicate that combining the output of two image matching techniques allows us to reach 59.5% recall and 68.5% precision, whereas requiring all three methods to match reduces precision (46.9%) while drastically decreasing recall (14.3%). The results show that our system is precision-oriented, and that filtering based on the combination of all methods leads to an overall performance degradation. This is because requiring all methods to match gives an over-constrained filtering: our methods, in fact, tend to match all together only with those images which are highly similar to the seeds, thus not being able to produce heterogeneous clusters.

We finally compute performance metrics for each single topic in turn, in order to experimentally investigate the different degrees of performance of our system, and determine whether some topics are more difficult than others (Table 2). Our results indicate that some topics are indeed more difficult than others – e.g., our system exhibits perfect precision on "adaptation" and "greenhouse effect" vs. much poorer one on "biodiversity" or "climate refugee". This is because some topics are bootstrapped from less heterogeneous, and hence 'easier', sets of seed images (e.g., all smokestacks, as in "greenhouse effect", are very similar to each other). In general, this seems to point out that one of the key challenges in our scenario is to produce highly precise clusters, while allowing for image diversity as a trade-off.

Error analysis. We finally looked at the output of our system, in order to better understand its performance, as well as problems and future challenges. Examples of a few sample clusters are shown in Figure 2. These clusters show that, thanks to our method, we are able to collect quite diverse, yet iconic images retaining a topical affinity with the original seeds – e.g., the poster on fighting deforestation or the drawing used to depict air pollution. Due to the noise of our base image processing components, however, we also suffer from wrong matches such as the picture of a mobile phone for the topic of wildfire, where the meaning of a rapidly spreading conflagration is related to air pollution, whereas the mobile phone is not. Based on a random sample of 10% of the output clusters, we manually identified the main sources of errors as related to: i) false image matching due to problems with contour detection; ii) SIFT performing best for detecting different images of the same objects, but exhibiting lower performance on the more complex task of detecting similar objects; iii) we applied our image matching methods using default parameters and thresholds: further improvements could be obtained by in-domain tuning.

4 Conclusions

In this work, we presented some initial steps in developing a methodology to computationally model the challenging phenomenon of iconic images. More specifically, we focused on the task of building a repository of iconic images in a minimally supervised way by bootstrapping based on images found on Web encyclopedic resources.

As future work, we plan to better combine heterogeneous information from text and images, as well as use deeper representations for both information sources – cf. joint semantic representations such as specific LDA-based topic models and bags of visual (SIFT) features (Rasiwasia et al., 2010; Feng and Lapata, 2010). This, in turn, can be applied to a variety of different tasks such as the automatic semantification of captions, query generation and expansion. On the computer vision side, we are instead particularly interested in exploring region-growing algorithms to detect textured or homogeneous regions, and to allow for a segmentation of textured regions without contours, e.g., a cloudy sky or a view of a forest landscape.

Downloads The dataset presented in this paper is freely available for research purposes at `https://madata.bib.uni-mannheim.de/87/`.

References

Roberto Brunelli. 2009. *Template Matching Techniques in Computer Vision: Theory and Practice*. Wiley Publishing.

Navneet Dalal and Bill Triggs. 2005. Histograms of oriented gradients for human detection. In *Proc. of CVPR*, pages 886–893.

Yansong Feng and Mirella Lapata. 2010. Topic models for image annotation and text illustration. In *Proc. of HLT '10*, pages 831–839.

Ming-Kuei Hu. 1962. Visual pattern recognition by moment invariants. *IRE Transactions on Information Theory*, 8(2):179–187.

David G. Lowe. 2004. Distinctive image features from scale-invariant keypoints. *International Journal of Computer Vision*, 60(2):91–110.

S. O'Neill and Nicholas Smith. 2014. Climate change and visual imagery. *Wiley Interdisciplinary Reviews: Climate Change*, 5(1):73–87.

Nikhil Rasiwasia, Jose Costa Pereira, Emanuele Coviello, Gabriel Doyle, Gert R.G. Lanckriet, Roger Levy, and Nuno Vasconcelos. 2010. A new approach to cross-modal multimedia retrieval. In *Proc. of MM '10*, pages 251–260.

Paul Viola and Michael Jones. 2001. Rapid object detection using a boosted cascade of simple features. In *Proc. of CVPR*, pages 511–518.

Figure 2: Sample iconic image clusters. Above a poor cluster on wildfire, below two good clusters on pollution and deforestation.

Cross-media Cross-genre Information Ranking Multi-media Information Networks

Tongtao Zhang
Rensselaer Polytechnic Institute
zhangt13@rpi.edu

Haibo Li
Nuance
lihaibo.c@gmail.com

Hongzhao Huang
R.P.I.
huangh9@rpi.edu

Heng Ji
R.P.I.
jih@rpi.edu

Min-Hsuan Tsai **Shen-Fu Tsai** **Thomas Huang**
University of Illinois at Urbana-Champaign
mtsai2@illinois.edu stsai8@illinois.edu huang@ifp.uiuc.edu

Abstract

Current web technology has brought us a scenario that information about a certain topic is widely dispersed in data from different domains and data modalities, such as texts and images from news and social media. Automatic extraction of the most informative and important multimedia summary (e.g. a ranked list of inter-connected texts and images) from massive amounts of cross-media and cross-genre data can significantly save users' time and effort that is consumed in browsing. In this paper, we propose a novel method to address this new task based on automatically constructed **M**ulti-media **I**nformation **Net**works (**MiNets**) by incorporating cross-genre knowledge and inferring implicit similarity across texts and images. The facts from MiNets are exploited in a novel random walk-based algorithm to iteratively propagate ranking scores across multiple data modalities. Experimental results demonstrated the effectiveness of our MiNets-based approach and the power of cross-media cross-genre inference.

1 Introduction

Recent development on web technology – especially on fast connection and large-scale storage systems – has enabled social and news media to fulfill their jobs more efficiently in time and depth. However, such development also raises some problems such as overwhelming social media information and distracting news media contents. In emergent scenarios such as facing an incoming disaster (*e.g.*, Hurricane Irene in 2011 or Sandy in 2012), tweets and news are often repeatedly spread and forwarded in certain circles and contents are often overlapped by each other. However, browsing these messages and pages is almost unpleasant and inefficient. Therefore, an automatic summarization on piles of tweets and news is always necessary and welcomed, among which ranking is the most intuitive way to inform the users about the most informative content.

A passive solution is prompting the users to add more key words when typing the search query as most search engines do. However, without prior knowledge or due to the word limit, it is never trivial for the users to establish a satisfied ranking list for topics which attract more public attention. Recent changes on some Google Search have integrated image search and adopted some heterogenous content analysis, nevertheless, the connection between image and the keywords are still arbitrarily determined by the users, thus it is still far from optimal.

Active solutions which attempt to summarize information only focused on single data modalities. For example, Zanzotto et al. (2011) provided a comprehensive comparison about summarization methods for tweets. Zhao et al. (2011) developed a context-sensitive topical PageRank (Brin and Page, 1998) method to extract topical key phrase from Twitter as a way to summarize twitter content. As a new prospective, Feng and Lapata (2010) used LDA to annotate images, but this does not firmly integrate the information across different data types. Huang et al. (2012) presented a tweet ranking approach but only focused on single data modality (i.e., text).

Other conventional solutions towards analyzing the relationship or links between the instances have long been proposed and applied, such as PageRank (Brin and Page, 1998)and VisualRank (Jing and Baluja, 2008). The former is excessively used in heterogeneous networks (i.e., webpages and resources) but they are mainly based on linkage itself. VisualRank, which is based on PageRank, is a content-based linkage method but is confined with homogeneous networks.

Above all, our goal is to integrate cross-media inference and create the linkage among the information extracted from those heterogenous data. Our novel **M**ulti-media **I**nformation **Net**works (**MiNets**) representation initializes our idea about a basic ontology of the ranking system.

The main contribution of this work is to fill in the domain gaps across different network genres and bridge them in a principled method. In this work, we manage to discover the hidden links or structures between the heterogeneous networks in different genres. We combine joint inference to resolve information conflicts across multi-genre

Proceedings of the 25th International Conference on Computational Linguistics, pages 74–81,
Dublin, Ireland, August 23-29 2014.

networks. We can also effectively measure, share and transfer complementary information and knowledge across multi-genre networks using structured correspondence.

The work is presented in sections as follows. We firstly introduce an overview of our system in Section 2. Detailed approaches in information extraction and constructing meta-information network are then followed in Section 3. Measurement across the multimedia information are proposed in Section 4 and 5. In Section 6 we demonstrate the results and performance gain.

2 Approach Overview

Within the context of an event where users generate a vast amount of multi-media messages in forms of tweets and images, we aim to provide a ranked subset of the most informative ones. Given a set of tweets $T = \{t_1, ..., t_n\}$, and a set of images $P = \{p_1, ..., p_m\}$ as input, our approach provides ordered lists of the most informative tweets or images (a.k.a objects) so that the informativeness of an object in position i is higher than or equal to that of an object in position $i + 1$. We consider the degree of informativeness of a certain object as the extent to which it provides valuable information to people who are involved in or tracking the event in question.

During emergent events, there are tight correlations between social media and web documents. Important information shared in social media tends to be posted in web documents. Therefore we also integrate information in a formal genre such as web documents to enhance the ranking quality of tweets and images. It consists of two main sub-tasks:

- ***Multimedia Information Network (MiNet) Construction***:
  Construct **MiNet** from cross-media and cross-genre information (i.e. tweets, images, sentences of web documents). Given a set of tweets and images on a specific topic as input, the formal genre web documents and images from the embedded URLs in those tweets are retrieved. Afterwards, a set of sentences and images are extracted from the web documents. Then we exploit advanced text Information Extraction and image Concept Extraction techniques to extract meta-information and construct the meta-information network. Together with three sets of heterogeneous input data, MiNet is constructed.

- ***MiNet-Based Information Ranking***: Rank the tweets and images. By extending and adapting Tri-HITS (Huang et al., 2012), we propose EN-Tri-HITs, an random walk-based propagation algorithm which iteratively propagate ranking scores for sentences, tweets, and images across **MiNet** to refine the tweet and image rankings.

3 Meta-information Network

When integrating information from different data modalities, meta-information network plays a pivotal role for representing interesting concepts and relations between them. We automatically construct the initial information networks using our state-of-the-art information extraction and image concept extraction techniques. A meta-information network is a heterogeneous network including a set of "information graphs" which is formally defined as: $G = \{G_i : G_i = (V_i, E_i)\}$, where V_i is the collection of concept nodes, and E_i is the collection of edges linking one concept to the other. An example is depicted in Figure 1. The meta-information network contains human knowledge pertaining to the target domain that could improve the performance of text process and image analysis. In this paper, we first construct meta-information networks separately from texts and images, and then fuse and enrich them through effective cross-media linking methods.

3.1 Information Extraction from Texts

Extracting salient types of facts for a meta-information network is challenging. In this paper we tackle this problem from two angles to balance the trade-off between quality and granularity/annotation cost. On one hand, to reveal deep semantics in meta-information network, we focus on achieving high-quality extraction for pre-defined fine-grained types such as those in NIST Automatic Content Extraction (ACE) [1]. For example, a "*Person/Individual*" node may include attributes such as "*Birth-Place*", and a "*Organization/Employee*" node may include attributes such as "*City-of-Headquarter*". These two nodes may be connected via a "*Employment/End-Position*" link.

We apply an Information Extraction (IE) system (Li et al., 2013) to extract entities, relations and events defined in ACE2005. There are 7 types of entities, 18 types of relations and 33 types of events. This system is based on a joint framework using structured perceptron with efficient beam-search and incorporating diverse lexical, syntactic, semantic and ontological features. We convert the IE output into the graph structured representation of meta-information network by mapping each entity as a node, and link entity nodes by semantic relations or events they are involved. For example, the relations between entities are naturally mapped to links in the meta-information network, such as the "*employment*" relation between "*Bill Read*" and "*Hurricane Center*". In addition, if an event

[1] http://www.itl.nist.gov/iad/894.01/tests/ace/

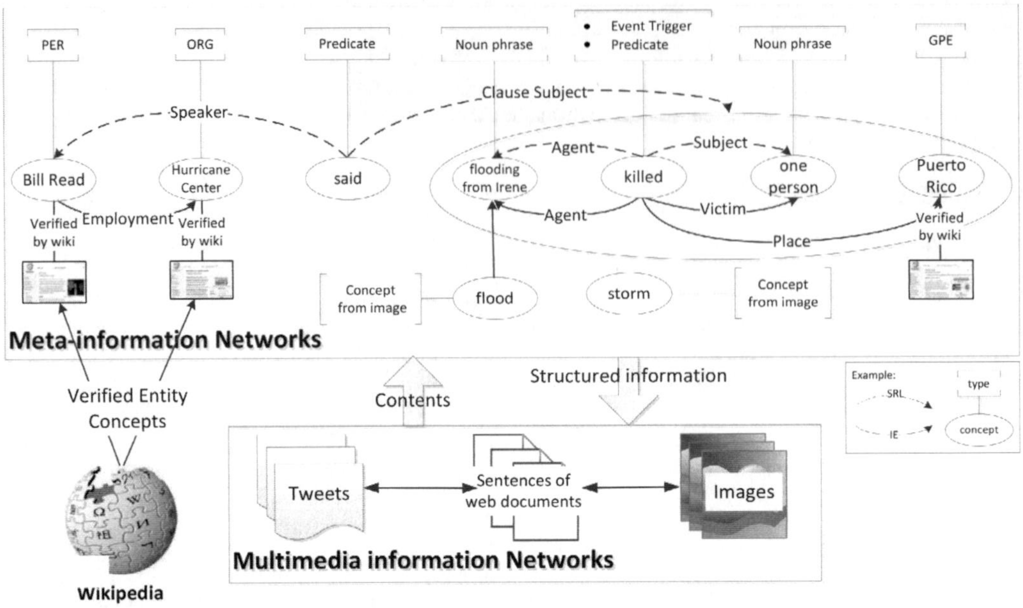

Figure 1: An example of meta-information network. Sentence: "Bill Read, Hurricane Center director, said that flooding from Irene killed at least one person in Puerto Rico"

argument is an entity, we also add an "*Event Argument*" link between the event trigger and the entity, such as the link between "*Irene*" and "*killed*".

On the other hand, in order to enrich the meta-information network, we extract more coarse-grained salient fact types based on Semantic Role Labeling (SRL) (Pradhan et al., 2008). For example, given the sentence "*In North Carolina, 10 counties are being evacuated.*", the "evacuation" event is not included in ACE. However, the SRL system can successfully detect the predicate ("evacuated") and its semantic roles ("10 counties" and "North Carolina"). These argument heads and predicates are added into the meta-information network as vertices, and edges are added between each predicate-argument pairs.

We merge entity mentions across tweets and web documents based on a cross-document entity clustering system described in (Chen and Ji, 2011). Moreover, for the same type of nodes from the SRL system, we also merge them by string matching across documents.

3.2 Concept Extraction from Images

We also developed a concept modeling approach by extending the similar framework in previous work (Tsai et al., 2012), Probabilistic Logical Tree (PLT), to extract semantic concepts from images. PLT integrates the logical and statistical inferences in a unifying framework where the existing primitive concepts are connected into a potentially unlimited vocabulary of high-level concepts by basic logical operations. In contrast, most existing image concept extraction algorithms either only learn a flat correlative concept structure, or a simple hierarchical structure without logical connections.

With an efficient statistical learning algorithm, the complex concepts in upper level of PLT are modeled upon some logically connected primitive concepts. This statistical learning approach is very flexible, where each concept in PLT can be modeled from distinctive feature spaces with the most suitable feature descriptors (e.g., visual features such as color and shape for scenery concepts).

For our case study on "Hurricane Irene" scenario, we apply this algorithm to extract the hierarchical concept trees with roots "flood" or "storm" from all the images in web documents whose URLs are contained in tweets.

The main problem is the classifications of the concepts such that it may be properly be placed onto an ontology. In order to enrich the hierarchy, we seek to classify these linkages through the use of the semi-structured and structured data that exists on Wikipedia. We use pattern matching to extract *is-a* relations from the first paragraphs of Wikipedia articles. For example, starting from our initial concept "Hurricane Irene", we can find its *is-a* relation with "Tropical Cyclone", and then climb up one more level to "Storm" where we can further mine lower concepts such as "Tornado" and "Snow Storm".

4 Multi-media Information Networks

A **M**ultimedia **In**formation **Net**work (*MINet*) is a structured collection made up of a set of multimedia documents (e.g., texts and images) and links between these documents. Each link corresponds to a specific relationship between nodes, such as hyperlinks between web documents or similarity links between tweets. In this paper, we construct our MINet based on two forms of contents from different domains: tweets, web documents (plain texts) and images.

4.1 Within-media Linking

4.1.1 Text-Text Similarity

Taking web document for example, we construct the meta-information network $G = \{G_i : G_i = (V_i, E_i)\}$ for all web documents D, in which each web document $d_i \in D$ corresponds to G_i. Given the meta-information network G, we compute the weight of each vertex $v_j \in V_i$ as $weight_{v_j} = \frac{nf(v_j,d)}{AVE(D)}$,

where $nf(v_j, d)$ is the mention number of node v_j appearing in a document d and $AVE(D)$ is the average number of mentions in a document d, which is defined as $AVE(D) = \frac{\sum_{d \in D} \text{concept mentions in } d}{|D|}$.

Similarly, we define the weight of each link $e_k \in E_i$ as $weight_{e_k} = \frac{nf(e_k,d)}{AVE(D)}$, where $nf(e_k, d)$ is the mention number of the node e_k in a document d and $AVE(D)$ is the average number of mentions in a document d, which is defined as $AVE(D) = \frac{\sum_{d \in D} \text{relation mentions in } d}{|D|}$.

If two edges share the same type and link nodes corresponding to the same tokens, we consider them as two mentions involved in a relation. Based on the weight of each concept mention and relation mention, we count their frequencies and transform them into vectors. Finally, we compute cosine similarity between every two vectors.

4.1.2 Image-Image Similarity

We extract Histogram of Oriented Gradients (HOG) features (Dalal and Triggs, 2005) from patches in images and apply Hierarchical Gaussianization (Zhou et al., 2009) to those HOG feature vectors. We learn a Gaussian mixture model (GMM) to obtain the statistics of the patches of an image by adapting the distribution of the extracted HOG features from these image patches and each image is represented by a super-vector. Based on the obtained image representation, the image-image similarity is simply a cosine similarity between two HG super-vectors.

4.2 Cross-media Linking

In order to obtain cross-media similarity, we propose a method based on transfer learning technique (Qi et al., 2012). Given a set of m points $[p_1, p_2, \ldots, p_m]$ in the source (image) domain $\mathcal{P}$, a set of n points $[t_1, t_2, \ldots, t_n]$ in the target (text) domain $\mathcal{T}$, and a set of N corresponding pairs $\mathcal{C} = \{(p_{a_i}, t_{b_i}\}_{i=1}^{N}$ in these two domains, we aim to find a cross-media similarity function:

$$G(p,t) = \ell((Up)^T(Vt)) = \ell(p^T St)), \tag{1}$$

where U and V are the linear embedding of $\mathcal{P}$ and $\mathcal{T}$, respectively. $S = U^T V$ is the *cross-domain similarity matrix* and $\ell(\theta) = \frac{1}{1+e^{-\theta}}$ is the logistic sigmoid function.

The key to S in Equation 1 is to solve the optimization problem blow:

$$\min_{S} \bar{\mathcal{L}}_s(S) + \lambda \bar{\mathcal{L}}_d(S) + \gamma \bar{\Omega}(S), \tag{2}$$

where $\bar{\mathcal{L}}_s(S) = \sum_{(x,y)\in\mathcal{C}} \log(1 + \exp(-p^T St))$, and $\bar{\Omega}(S) = \|S\|_*$ is the nuclear norm that is the surrogate of the matrix rank. Also, we have

$$\bar{\mathcal{L}}_d(S) = \frac{1}{2}\sum K_{\mathcal{P}}(p,p')d_{\mathcal{T}}(p,p') + \frac{1}{2}\sum K_{\mathcal{T}}(t,t')d_{\mathcal{P}}(t,t'),$$

where $K(\cdot,\cdot)$ is the similarity matrix among the points in a single domain and $d(\cdot,\cdot)$ defines the distance between two points due to the transfer.

Taking one step further, we have

$$\bar{\mathcal{L}}_d(S) = \text{tr}(L_{\mathcal{T}} Q_{\mathcal{T}}(S)^T K_{\mathcal{P}} Q_{\mathcal{P}}(S)) + \text{tr}(L_{\mathcal{X}} Q_{\mathcal{P}}(S)^T K_{\mathcal{T}} Q_{\mathcal{T}}(S)),$$

where $L_{\mathcal{P}}$ and $L_{\mathcal{T}}$ are the Laplacian matrices for $K_{\mathcal{P}}$ and $K_{\mathcal{T}}$, respectively.

To solve the optimization problem (2) with nuclear norm regularization we follow the proximal gradient method (Toh and Yun, 2010) with the following gradients:

$$\triangledown \bar{\mathcal{L}}_s(S) = P(J_{\mathcal{C}} \circ H)P^T, \triangledown \bar{\mathcal{L}}_d(S) = P((K_{\mathcal{P}} Q_{\mathcal{P}} L_{\mathcal{T}} + L_{\mathcal{P}} Q_{\mathcal{T}} K_{\mathcal{T}}) \circ H)P^T \tag{3}$$

$J_{\mathcal{C}}$ is an $m \times n$ matrix with its (i,j)-th entry 1 if $(p_i, t_j) \in \mathcal{C}$, otherwise 0. H is also an $m \times n$ matrix whose (i,j)-th entry where $H_{ij} = \ell'(p_i^T S t_j)$.

Hence we have

$$\nabla \bar{\mathcal{L}}(S) = P(\mathcal{G} \circ H)T^T, \tag{4}$$

where $\mathcal{G} = J_{\mathcal{C}} + \lambda K_{\mathcal{P}} Q_{\mathcal{P}} L_{\mathcal{T}} + \lambda L_{\mathcal{P}} Q_{\mathcal{T}} K_{\mathcal{T}}$. With the gradient in (4), one can solve the problem (2) using the proximal gradient method.

5 MiNet-Based Information Ranking: EN-Tri-HITs

5.1 Initializing Ranking Scores

Input: A set of tweets (T), and images (P) and web documents (W) on a given topic.
Output: Ranking scores (S_t) for T and (S_p) for P.

Use TextRank to compute initial ranking scores S_p^0 for P, S_t^0 for T and S_w^0 for W;
Construct multimedia information networks across P, T and W;
$k \leftarrow 0$, *diff* $\leftarrow 10e6$;
while $k <$ MaxIteration and *diff* $>$ MinThreshold **do**
  Use Eq. (5) (6) and (7) to compute S_p^{k+1}, S_t^{k+1} and S_w^{k+1};
  Normalize S_p^{k+1}, S_t^{k+1} and S_w^{k+1};
  diff $\leftarrow \max(\sum(|S_t^{k+1} - S_t^k|), \sum(|S_p^{k+1} - S_p^k|))$;
  $k \leftarrow k + 1$
end while

Algorithm 1: EN-Tri-HITS: Random walk on multimedia information networks

Graph-based ranking algorithms have been widely used to analyze relations between vertices in graphs. In this paper, we adapted PageRank (Brin and Page, 1998; Mihalcea and Tarau, 2004; Jing and Baluja, 2008) to compute initial ranking scores in tweet-only and image-only networks where edges between tweets or images are determined by their cosine similarity.

The ranking score is computed as follows:

$$S(V_i) = (1-d) + d * \sum_{V_j \in In(V_i)} \frac{w_{ji}}{\sum_{V_k \in Out(V_j)} w_{jk}} S(V_j),$$

where V_i is a vertex with $S(V_i)$ as its ranking score; $In(V_i)$ and $Out(V_i)$ are the incoming edge set and outgoing edge set of V_i, respectively; w_{ij} is the weight for the edge between two vertices V_i and V_j. An edge links two vertices that represent text units when their cosine similarity of shared content exceeds or equals to a predefined threshold δ_t.

5.2 Random Walk on Multimedia Information Networks

We introduce a novel algorithm to incorporate both initial ranking scores and global evidence from multimedia information networks. It propagates ranking scores across MiNets iteratively. Our algorithm is a natural extension of Tri-HITS (Huang et al., 2012) based on the mutual reinforcement to boost linked objects.

By extending Tri-HITS, we develop enhanced Tri-HITS (EN-Tri-HITs) to handle multimedia information networks with three types of objects: Tweets (T), sentences of web documents (W) and images (P). EN-Tri-HITs is able to handle more complicated network structure with more links. Given the similarity matrices M^{tw} (between tweets and sentences of web documents), M^{wp} (between sentences of web documents and images) and M^{tp} (between tweets and images), and initial ranking scores of $S^0(p)$, $S^0(t)$ and $S^0(w)$, we aim to refine the initial ranking scores and obtain the final ranking scores $S(w)$, $S(t)$ and $S(p)$. Starting from images $S(p)$, the update process considers both the initial score $S^0(p)$ and the propagation from connected tweets $S(t)$ and web documents $S(w)$, which can be expressed as:

$$\hat{S}_w(p_j) = \sum_{i \in W} m_{ij}^{wp} S(w_i), \hat{S}_t(p_j) = \sum_{k \in T} m_{kj}^{tp} S(t_k),$$

$$S(p_j) = (1 - \lambda_{wp} - \lambda_{tp}) S^0(p_j) + \lambda_{wp} \frac{\hat{S}_w(p_j)}{\sum_j \hat{S}_w(p_j)} + \lambda_{tp} \frac{\hat{S}_t(p_j)}{\sum_j \hat{S}_t(p_j)}, \tag{5}$$

Set ID	Tweets	Web Doc (Sentences)	Images
1	1171	41(1272)	183
2	1116	47(1634)	265
3	1184	69(1639)	346
All	3471	157(4545)	794

Table 1: Data Statistics: Numbers of each item in the dataset.

	word	word +IE	word +SRL	word +IE+SRL
I+W	0.545	0.539	0.521	0.583
I+T	0.422	0.436	0.407	0.489
I+W+T	0.526	0.513	0.492	0.541

Table 2: NDCG@5 of Images. The image ranking baseline performance is 0.421. **I** stands for Image; **W** Web Documents; **T** Tweets

where $\lambda_{wp}, \lambda_{tp} \in [0, 1]$ $(\lambda_{wp} + \lambda_{tp} \leq 1)$ are the parameters to balance between initial and propagated ranking scores. Similar to Tri-HITS, EN-Tri-HITS normalizes the propagated ranking scores $\hat{S}_w(p_i)$ and $\hat{S}_t(p_i)$.

Similarly, we define the propagations from images and web documents to tweets as follows:

$$\hat{S}_p(t_k) = \sum_{i \in P} m_{ik}^{pt} S(p_i), \hat{S}_w(t_k) = \sum_{j \in W} m_{jk}^{wt} S(w_j),$$

$$S(t_k) = (1 - \lambda_{wt} - \lambda_{pt}) S^0(t_k) + \lambda_{wt} \frac{\hat{S}_p(t_k)}{\sum_k \hat{S}_p(t_k)} + \lambda_{pt} \frac{\hat{S}_w(t_k)}{\sum_k \hat{S}_w(t_k)}, \tag{6}$$

where M^{pt} is the transpose of M^{tp}, λ_{pt} and λ_{wt} are parameters to balance between initial and propagated ranking scores.

Each sentence of web documents $S(w_j)$ may be influenced by the propagation from both tweets and images:

$$\hat{S}_t(w_i) = \sum_{k \in T} m_{ki}^{tw} S(t_k), \hat{S}_p(w_i) = \sum_{i \in P} m_{ji}^{pw} S(p_j),$$

$$S(w_i) = (1 - \lambda_{tw} - \lambda_{pw}) S^0(w_i) + \lambda_{tw} \frac{\hat{S}_t(w_i)}{\sum_i \hat{S}_t(w_i)} + \lambda_{pw} \frac{\hat{S}_p(w_i)}{\sum_i \hat{S}_p(w_i)}, \tag{7}$$

where M^{pw} is the transpose of M^{wp}, λ_{tw} and λ_{pw} are parameters to balance between initial and propagated ranking scores.

Algorithm 1 summarizes En-Tri-HITS.

6 Experiments

6.1 Data and Scoring Metric

Currently there are no information ranking related benchmark data sets publicly available, therefore we build our own data set and network ontology.

We crawled 3471 tweets during a three-hour period and extracted key phrases from these tweets, then we use the key phrases as image search queries. The image search queries are submitted to Bing Image Search API and we take the top 10 images for each query. We extract a 512-d GIST feature from each image for meta information training. For image similarity metrics, we resize images to a maximum of 240×240 and segmented into patches with three different sizes (16, 25 and 31) by a 6-pixel step size. A 128-d Histogram of Oriented Gradients (HOG) feature is extracted from each patch and followed by a PCA dimension reduction to 80-d. The size of dimension of the final feature vector for each image is 42,496.

We create the ground truth based on human assessment of informativeness on a 5-star likert scale, with grade 5 as the most informative and 1 as the least informative. Table 1 presents an overview on our data sets. We conduct 3-fold cross-validation for our experiments.

To evaluate tweet ranking, we use *nDCG* as our evaluation metric (Järvelin and Kekäläinen, 2002), which considers both the informativeness and the position of a tweet:

$$nDCG(\Phi, k) = \frac{1}{|\Phi|} \sum_{i=1}^{|\Phi|} \frac{DCG_{ik}}{IDCG_{ik}}, DCG_{ik} = \sum_{j=1}^{k} \frac{2^{rel_{ij}} - 1}{\log(1 + j)},$$

where Φ is the set of documents in the test set, with each document corresponding to an hour of tweets in our case, rel_{ij} is the human-annotated label for the tweet j in the document i, and $IDCG_{ik}$ is the DCG score of the ideal ranking. The average *nDCG* score for the top k tweets is: $Avg@k = \sum_{i=1}^{k} nDCG(\Phi, i)/k$. To favor diversity of top ranked tweets, redundant tweets are penalized to lower down the final score.

6.2 Impact of Cross-media Inference

Table 2 and Figure 2 present the image ranking results. The results indicate that methods integrating heterogeneous networks outperform the baseline of image ranking (0.421). When web documents are aligned with images (row 1), the ranking quality improves significantly, proving that web documents can help detect informative images by adding support from text media of formal genre. However, the text media of informal genre, such as tweets, almost cannot help improve the ranking performance.

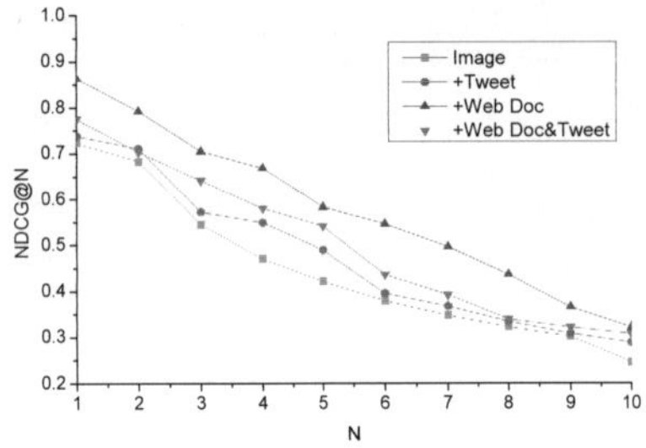

Figure 2: NDCG@n score of Images with Various n

	word	word +IE	word +SRL	word +IE+SRL
T	0.675	0.691	0.697	0.700
T+W	0.766	0.771	0.757	0.809
T+I	0.675	0.691	0.667	0.700
T+W+I	0.722	0.771	0.757	0.809

Table 3: NDCG@5 of Tweets

6.3 Impact of Cross-genre Inference

Methods that integrate heterogeneous networks after filtering, outperform the baseline TextRank, as shown in Table 3. When tweets are aligned with web documents, the ranking quality improves significantly, proving that web documents can help infer informative tweets by adding support from a formal genre. The fact that tweets with low initial ranking scores are aligned with web documents helps promote their ranking positions. For example, the ranking of the tweet "*Hurricane Irene: City by City Forecasts http://t.co/x1t122A*" is improved compared to TextRank, benefitting from the fact that 10 retrieved web documents are about this topic.

6.4 Remaining Error Analysis

Enhanced Tri-HITS shows encouraging improvements in ranking quality with respect to a state-of-the-art model such as TextRank. However, there are still some issues to be addressed for further improvements.

(i) Long tweets preferred. We tracked tweets containing the keywords "Hurricane" and "Irene". Using such a query might also return tweets that are not related to the event being followed. This may occur either because the terms are ambiguous, or because of spam being injected into trending conversations to make it visible. For example, the tweet "*Hurricane Kitty: http://t.co/cdIexE3*" is an advertisement, which is not topically related to Irene.

(ii) Deep semantic analysis of the content, especially for images. We rely on distinct terms to refer to the same concept. More extensive semantic analyses of text can help identify those terms, possibly enhancing the propagation process. For example, we can explore existing text dictionaries such as WordNet (Miller, 1995) to mine synonym/hypernym/hyponym relations, and Brown clusters (Brown et al., 1992) to mine other types of relations in order to enrich the concepts extracted from images.

7 Conclusion and Future Work

In this paper, we propose a comprehensive information ranking approach which facilitates measurement on cross-media/cross-genre informativeness based on a novel multi-media information network representation **MiNet**. We establish links via information extraction method from text and images and verification with Wikipedia. In addition, we propose similarity measurement on intra-media and cross-media using transfer learning techniques. We also introduce a novel En-Tri-Hits algorithm to evaluate the ranking scores across **MiNet**. Experiments have demonstrated that our cross-media/cross-genre ranking method is able to significantly boost the performance of multi-media tweet ranking. In the future, we aim to focus on enhancing the quality of concept extraction by exploiting cross-media inference that goes beyond simple fusion.

Acknowledgement

This work was supported by the U.S. Army Research Laboratory under Cooperative Agreement No. W911NF-09-2-0053 (NS-CTA), U.S. NSF CAREER Award under Grant IIS-0953149, U.S. DARPA Award No. FA8750-13-2-0041 in the ?Deep Exploration and Filtering of Text? (DEFT) Program, IBM Faculty award and RPI faculty start-up grant. The views and conclusions contained in this document are those of the authors and should not be interpreted as representing the official policies, either expressed or implied, of the U.S. Government. The

U.S. Government is authorized to reproduce and distribute reprints for Government purposes notwithstanding any copyright notation here on.

References

Sergey Brin and Lawrence Page. 1998. The anatomy of a large-scale hypertextual web search engine. *Computer Networks*, 30(1-7):107–117.

Peter F. Brown, Peter V. deSouza, Robert L. Mercer, Vincent J. Della Pietra, and Jenifer C. Lai. 1992. Class-based n-gram models of natural language. *Computational Linguistics*, 18:467–479.

Zheng Chen and Heng Ji. 2011. Collaborative ranking: A case study on entity linking. In *Proc. EMNLP2011*.

Navneet Dalal and Bill Triggs. 2005. Histograms of oriented gradients for human detection. In *In CVPR*, pages 886–893.

Yansong Feng and Mirella Lapata. 2010. Topic models for image annotation and text illustration. In *Human Language Technologies: The 2010 Annual Conference of the North American Chapter of the Association for Computational Linguistics*, HLT '10, pages 831–839, Stroudsburg, PA, USA. Association for Computational Linguistics.

Hongzhao Huang, Arkaitz Zubiaga, Heng Ji, Hongbo Deng, Dong Wang, Hieu Le, Tarek Abdelzaher, Jiawei Han, Alice Leung, John Hancock, and Clare Voss. 2012. Tweet ranking based on heterogeneous networks. In *Proc. COLING 2012*, pages 1239–1256, Mumbai, India. The COLING 2012 Organizing Committee.

Kalervo Järvelin and Jaana Kekäläinen. 2002. Cumulated gain-based evaluation of ir techniques. *ACM Trans. Inf. Syst.*, 20(4):422–446, October.

Yushi Jing and Shumeet Baluja. 2008. Visualrank: Applying pagerank to large-scale image search. *IEEE Trans. Pattern Anal. Mach. Intell.*, 30(11):1877–1890.

Qi Li, Heng Ji, and Liang Huang. 2013. Joint event extraction via structured prediction with global features. In *Proc. ACL2013*, pages 73–82.

R. Mihalcea and P. Tarau. 2004. Textrank: Bringing order into texts. In *Proceedings of EMNLP*, volume 4. Barcelona: ACL.

George A. Miller. 1995. Wordnet: A lexical database for english. *COMMUNICATIONS OF THE ACM*, 38:39–41.

Sameer Pradhan, Wayne Ward, and James H. Martin. 2008. Towards robust semantic role labeling. In *Computational Linguistics Special Issue on Semantic Role Labeling*, volume 34, pages 289–310.

Guo-Jun Qi, Charu C. Aggarwal, and Thomas S. Huang. 2012. Transfer learning of distance metrics by cross-domain metric sampling across heterogeneous spaces. In *SDM*, pages 528–539.

Kim-Chuan Toh and Sangwoon Yun. 2010. An accelerated proximal gradient algorithm for nuclear norm regularized linear least squares problems. *Pacific Journal of Optimization*.

Shen-Fu Tsai, Henry Hao Tang, Feng Tang, and Thomas S. Huang. 2012. Ontological inference framework with joint ontology construction and learning for image understanding. In *IEEE International Conference on Multimedia and Expo (ICME) 2012*.

Fabio Massimo Zanzotto, Marco Pennacchiotti, and Kostas Tsioutsiouliklis. 2011. Linguistic redundancy in twitter. In *Proceedings of the Conference on Empirical Methods in Natural Language Processing*, EMNLP '11, pages 659–669, Stroudsburg, PA, USA. Association for Computational Linguistics.

Wayne X. Zhao, Jing Jiang, Jing He, Yang Song, Palakorn Achananuparp, Ee P. Lim, and Xiaoming Li. 2011. Topical keyphrase extraction from Twitter. In *Proceedings of the 49th Annual Meeting of the Association for Computational Linguistics: Human Language Technologies - Volume 1*, HLT '11, pages 379–388, Stroudsburg, PA, USA. Association for Computational Linguistics.

Xi Zhou, Na Cui, Zhen Li, Feng Liang, and Thomas S. Huang. 2009. Hierarchical gaussianization for image classification. In *ICCV*, pages 1971–1977.

Speech-accompanying gestures in Russian: functions and verbal context

Yulia Nikolaeva
Moscow State University
julianikk@gmail.com

Abstract

The study of the relationships between speech and gesture promises a lot of insights into speech production and comprehension processes. In this work we explore syntactic and semantic characteristics of verbal correlates of speech-accompanying gestures. The results of the corpora studies show, that we can reveal the statistical probability for certain types of gestures to appear in given context. For example, semantic correlates of deictic gestures are mostly noun phrases, and only in few cases these gestures correspond to adverbs, although they may coincide with any part of a clause. Single beats differ from other gesture types in their tendency to accompany speech disfluencies, discourse markers, and unimportant parts of a clause. Looking from the perspective if the meaning of words, accompanied by gestures, we can see, that new or re-activated referents might be presented with deictic gestures, uncertainty or direct speech are a domain of beat gestures.

1 Introduction

Gesticulation or speech-accompanying gestures perform the same functions, serve the same goals and relate to the same information as do the words, as showed in (McNeill, 1992). At the same time the interplay of speech and gesticulation, especially distribution of pragmatic, semantic and referential meanings still stays unclear. Maha Salem and her colleagues point out that synchronization of different modalities for conversational agents or robotic platforms "is either achieved only approximately or by solely adapting one modality to the other, e.g. by adjusting gesture speed to the timing of running speech" (Salem et al. 2011). Our work is aimed to describe statistical probability for different types of gestures to appear in certain verbal contexts. These contexts were described depending on their morphological and syntactical characteristics, as shown in part 3.1. To achieve this goal we created two 20-minutes corpora consisting of TV talk-show fragments and retellings of "The pear stories" (Chafe, 1980).

2 Data analysis

2.1 Corpus description

We formed two different corpora to compare gesture properties in different types of discourse, namely dialogue and narration. The first one included seven fragments of TV interviews and panel discussion of some common social issues and was supposed to include various types and styles of conversation. The aim of this corpus was to register as many examples of gestures with diverse functions in different contexts, as possible. The second corpus consisted of eight retelling of "The pear stories" made by university students with very little or no interventions by a listener, thus it was more homogeneous from the viewpoint of genre, topic and discourse structure, so it allowed comparing gesture features, concerning global discourse structure. The results show, that most gesture functions are common for different genres.

Proceedings of the 25th International Conference on Computational Linguistics, pages 82–86,
Dublin, Ireland, August 23-29 2014.

2.2 Transcribing and coding

2.2.1 Gesture types

Coding concentrated on movements of the hands. Gestures were divided into five groups, using modified D. McNeill's classification (1992). Besides deictics, we distinguish descriptive, meta-discursive, beat and rhythmic gestures. Considering the fact that distinctions between iconic and metaphoric gestures are not always obvious (see e.g. Gullberg, 1995), we reviewed these classes as descriptive and meta-discursive, relying on the form of the gesture and its relation to speech. Meta-discursive gestures treat simultaneous words as if from the outside, regarding speech as an object that can be transferred to an addressee, or manipulated in a different way (e.g. a whole that can be divided into parts, or a process that can be accelerated or slowed down). Descriptive gestures concern to the storyline and reflect the content of the illustrated words. Also we distinguish single beats and rhythmic gestures (named in Ekman, Friesen, 1969). So, the main ground for this classification was the form of the gesture, also taking into account its meaning and relation to the corresponding words. The future analysis proved the validity of this division.

2.2.2 Characteristics of speech segments accompanied by gestures

We examined the following types of gesture correlates:

1. full clauses, which can describe the line of the story or else can be
    a. meta-discursive (*We are talking about...)*;
    b. citations (*He asked: "How do you do it?"*);
    c. repetition of the previous clause;
    d. reformulation or elaboration of the previous clause;
    e. false-start.
2. noun phrases, divided into groups relying on their accessibility and syntactical role;
3. adverbs, considering their semantics;
4. verbs and verbal phrases, taking into account their syntactical form and meaning
5. discourse markers, also divided into groups, following Schiffrin (1987).

We labeled all the items in the corpora according to this list and compared the probability to be accompanied of every type of gesture (or to appear without any gesture). For referential gestures we counted the speech segments with the same meaning, for beats and rhythmics only the temporal correspondence was possible.

3 Results

The first corpus contains 545 gestures, the second one – 338 gestures. It seems worth to mention, that proportions of gesture types were similar to those in D. McNeill's study (1992), taking into account the difference in classification (Table 1).

Table 1. Frequency of gesture types in three corpora.

	The pear stories		Talk-shows		D. McNeill's corpus	
Deictic	36	11%	45	8%	28	5%
Descriptive (iconic)	193	57%	195	36%	261	44%
Meta-discursive (metaphoric)	57	17%	87	16%	42	7%
Beat	47	14%	134	25%	268	45%
Rhythmic	3	1%	83	15%		
Emblems	2	1%	1	0%	-	-
Total	338		545		599	100%

Table 2. Verbal correlates with each type of gestures.

	Noun phrase	Verb phrase	Adverb	Clause	Unfinished clause	Discourse markers	Total
Deictic	19%	-	12%	(5%)	-	-	9%
Descriptive	33%	48%	40%	35%	-	27%	45%
Meta-discursive	19%	11%	10%	16%	32%	24%	16%
Beat	24%	30%	36%	-	68%	49%	20%
Rhythmic	5%	11%	2%	44%	-	-	10%
Total	100%	100%	100%	100%	100%	100%	100%

Table 2 shows comparative frequency of each type of gestures to appear with different syntactic units. For deictics temporal correlates are shown in brackets.

Table 3. Certain types of clauses with speech-accompanying gestures.

	Meta-discursive	Citation	Repetition	Reformulation	Regulatory clause	Total for these clauses
Deictic	6%	5%	-	-	1%	4%
Descriptive	14%	17%	13%	21%	6%	18%
Meta-discursive	9%	4%	6%	4%	2%	7%
Beat	6%	16%	25%	4%	10%	11%
Rhythmic	4%	16%	-	8%	4%	8%

Table 3 summarizes percentage of some special clauses with gestures.

Analysis of the data in Tables 1-3 is presented below.

3.1 Deictic gestures correlates

Deictic gestures illustrate noun phrases (87%) and adverbs of time and place (13%), although they may appear in any part of a clause. There was even an example, where the gesture was used without an explicit verbal correlate (1) (the underlined words are accompanied by the gesture).

(1) Go!
(right palm facing the center, fingers extended toward the listener)

When used with adverbs, deictics can reveal standard metaphors, such as *past is behind us* (Lakoff, Johnson, 1980), or appeal to common knowledge in the context of discourse, see (1).

(2) Like now and here.
(right palm up, fingers towards the listener slightly curved)

Deictic gestures often mark the clauses of meta-discursive level, when the speaker points at himself or at a listener, and also these gestures accompany citations, placing a referent in the space near the speaker or illustrating adverbs.

3.2 Descriptive gestures correlates

These gestures tend to illustrate verbs and less often can be seen with noun phrases, comparing to other gesture types. Only descriptive gestures, that have complex form and can carry much information additional to words, were met with interjections.

When used with clauses, these gestures tend to appear with reformulations, what can be explained as a speaker's intention to elaborate and to force her/his idea, so that visual illustration is needed, whether in order to resolve verbalization problems, the speaker's rhetoric aim or listener's demand (when the last does not completely understand the message).

3.3 Meta-discursive gestures correlates

The most often example of this gesture type is palm up opened hand (Müller, 2004). The semantics of the gesture reveals *conduit metaphor* (Lakoff, Johnson, 1980), when a speaker passes his words or ideas to a listener.

Meta-discursive gestures more often refer not to a single word, but to a phrase or a part of a discourse. Their form is less connected to the meaning of accompanied words, than it is with two previous types. They are used to emphasize related words and often coincide with prosodic accentuation.

Meta-discursive gestures tend to appear with more static parts oa a clause, like noun phrases and discourse markers, and less often are met with verbal phrases and adverbs. It can be explained in connection with the meaning of the *conduit metaphor*, which interprets the words said by a speaker like a material object passed to a listener. Nouns are less easier to be seen as objects than verbs. So, NPs with meta-discursive gestures serve as topics or themes in the segment of a discourse. When they emphasize a whole clause, these gestures underline important links in the logic chain composed by the speaker; usually these statements contain causes, consequences, or concessions, crucial for understanding of the described facts.

Obviously, these gestures are often used with meta-discursive clauses, describing, for example, the structure of a narration or intentions of a speaker. Also they tend to accompany literal repetitions of a previous clause. This shows that meta-discursive gestures are also a rhetoric instrument, used with less graphic predicates, than descriptive gestures, and with less thought-out statements, than rhythmics.

3.4 Beat and rhythmic gestures correlates

Short simple movements, usually up and down, can have only single words as their correlates, not phrases or clauses. They are twice more often met with discourse markers, speech disfluencies, and conjunctions, than other gestures. Also they tend to mark citations and repetitions. We suggest the hypothesis that beats are oriented at a speaker and their use is motivated by cognitive tasks resolved by a speaker. Another hypothesis of high beats frequency during the least interesting parts of a discourse can be that they serve as pause-fillers, showing the listener, that the speech is not finished yet.

Rhythmic gestures label each syllable of a word or each word in a phrase and often cover the whole clause. They are never met with discourse markers, pauses, or false starts, so we can suppose, that these gestures tend to mark well-planned parts of a discourse and serve as conscious rhetoric instrument. They tend to accompany citations, which are important in the discourse or emphasized by a speaker.

4 Conclusion

Deictic gestures may appear in any part of a clause, even without explicit verbal correlate, but semantically they correspond to an adverb of time or place or to a noun phrase. Another tendency for these gestures is to illustrate meta-discursive sentences, describing the actual situation of communication.

Descriptive gestures can be met with verbs and verbal phrases more often, than other types, and they are usually used with the reformulations and other important part of the discourse, contributing to the story-line. They avoid noun phrases and especially discourse markers.

Meta-discursive gestures apparently are used with meta-discursive clauses. Yet they tend to illustrate unfinished clauses, noun phrases or discourse markers. They are not usual with verb phrases, citations and reformulations.

Beats are remarkable for their tendency to appear with citations and repetitions, and especially speech disfluencies and discourse markers.

Rhythmic gestures usually accentuate long segments of discourse, at least a clause, and they can be used to underline citations, which the speaker considers to be important in his speech.

Acknowledgements

The research is supported by Russian Foundation for Basic Research, grant 14-06-00211 "Discourse production: method of observation, experiment and modeling".

Reference

Chafe, Wallace. 1980. The pear stories: Cognitive, cultural, and linguistic aspects of narrative production. Norwood, NJ: Ablex.

Chafe, Wallace. 1994. Discourse, consciousness, and time: The flow and displacement of conscious experience in speaking and writing. Chicago: University of Chicago Press.

Ekman, Paul; Friesen, Wallace 1969. The repertoire of nonverbal behavior. Categories, origins, usage and encoding. *Semiotica,* 1(1): 49-98.

Gullberg, Marianne. 1995. Giving language a hand: gesture as a cue based communicative strategy. *Lund University, Dept. of Linguistics, Working Papers*, 44: 41-60.

Lakoff, George; Johnson, Mark. 1980. Metaphors We Live by. Chicago: University of Chicago Press.

McNeill, David. (1992). Hand and Mind: What Gestures Reveal About Thought. Chicago: University of Chicago Press.

Müller, Cornelia. 2004. Forms and uses of the Palm Up Open Hand: A case of a gesture family? In C. Müller & R. Posner (Eds.), The Semantics and Pragmatics of Everyday Gestures. Berlin: Weidler, pp. 233-256.

Salem, Maha; Kopp, Stefan; Wachsmuth, Ipke; Joublin, Frank. 2011. A Multimodal Scheduler for Synchronized Humanoid Robot Gesture and Speech. In: Book of Extended Abstracts of the 9th International Gesture Workshop, GW2011, pp. 64-67.

Schiffrin, Debora. 1987. Discourse markers. Cambridge: Cambridge University Press.

DALES: Automated Tool for Detection, Annotation, Labelling and Segmentation of Multiple Objects in Multi-Camera Video Streams

M. Bhat and J. I. Olszewska
University of Gloucestershire
School of Computing and Technology
The Park, Cheltenham, GL50 2RH, UK
jolszewska@glos.ac.uk

Abstract

In this paper, we propose a new software tool called DALES to extract semantic information from multi-view videos based on the analysis of their visual content. Our system is fully automatic and is well suited for multi-camera environment. Once the multi-view video sequences are loaded into DALES, our software performs the detection, counting, and segmentation of the visual objects evolving in the provided video streams. Then, these objects of interest are processed in order to be labelled, and the related frames are thus annotated with the corresponding semantic content. Moreover, a textual script is automatically generated with the video annotations. DALES system shows excellent performance in terms of accuracy and computational speed and is robustly designed to ensure view synchronization.

1 Introduction

With the increasing use of electronic equipments, storage devices and computational systems for applications such as video surveillance (Kumar et al., 2010) and sport event monitoring (Alsuqayhi and Olszewska, 2013), the development of automated tools to process the resulting big amount of visual data in order to extract meaningful information becomes a necessity.

In particular, the design of multi-view video annotation systems is a challenging, new task. It aims to process multi-view video streams which consist of video sequences of a dynamic scene captured simultaneously by multiple cameras. Such multi input system is dedicated to automatically analyse the visual content of the multi-camera records and to generate semantic and visual annotations, in the way to assist users in the understanding and reasoning about large amount of acquired data.

For this purpose, data should be processed through different, major stages such as object-of-interest detection and segmentation, frame labelling, and video annotation. In the literature, most of the works dealing with the analysis of multi-camera video streams are focused on the sole task of tracking multiple, moving objects and use different approaches such as background subtraction (Diaz et al., 2013), Bayesian framework (Hsu et al., 2013), particle filter (Choi and Yoo, 2013), or Cardinalized Probability Hypothesis Density (CPHD) based filter (Lamard et al., 2013). On the other hand, research on video annotation has lead to the development of several efficient systems (Town, 2004; Natarajan and Nevatia, 2005; Bai et al., 2007; Vrusias et al., 2007), but all designed for a single camera video stream input.

In this paper, we describe a full system which takes multi-camera video stream inputs and performs visual data processing to generate multi-view video annotations. Our system has been developed in context of outdoor video-surveillance and is an automatic Detection, Annotation, LabElling and Segmentation (DALES) software tool. It presents also the advantage to have an entire chain of data processing from visual to textual one, reducing thus the semantic gap.

As camera calibration is in general an expensive process (Black et al., 2002) and in real life, surveillance application measurements of camera parameters are not readily available (Guler et al., 2003), DALES system does not involve any camera calibration parameters.

Proceedings of the 25th International Conference on Computational Linguistics, pages 87–94, Dublin, Ireland, August 23-29 2014.

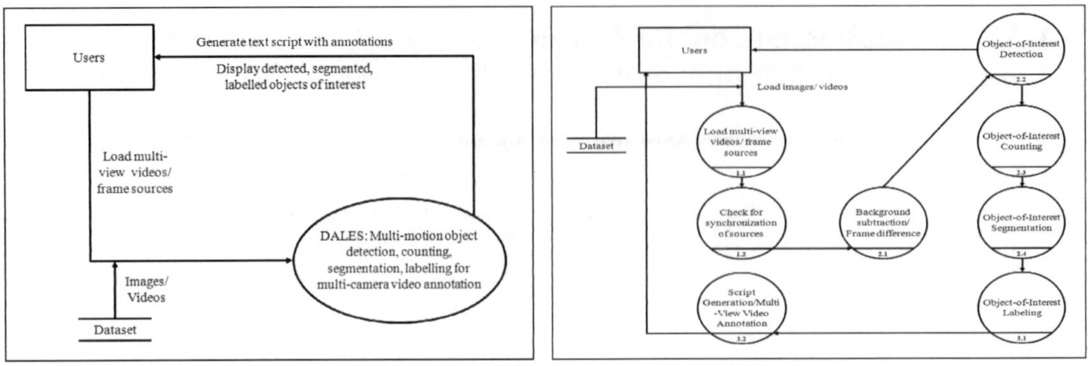

(a) (b)

Figure 1: Overview of the flow of data within DALES software: (a) Context level Data Flow Diagram; (b) Second level Data Flow Diagram.

DALES provides not only the automatic annotation of multi-view video streams, but also performs, in multi-camera environment, tasks such as multiple object-of-interest detection and segmentation, target counting and labelling, and image annotations. Our approach could cope with any dynamic scene recorded by pan-tilt-zoom (PTZ) static cameras with overlapping color views, unlike systems such as (Kettnaker and Zabih, 1999) based on non-overlapping cameras. The acquired multi-view sequences could contain complex backgrounds, moving objects or noisy foregrounds, and present illumination variations or poor resolution.

Hence, the contribution of this paper is twofold:

- the automated, textual annotation of multi-camera video streams based on visual features;
- the development of a full, automatic system covering all the phases from multiple, visual multi-motion target detection to multi-view video annotation and text-script generation.

The paper is structured as follows. In Section 2, we describe our DALES system for fast, multiple video-object detection, segmentation, labeling and effective multi-view video annotation. Our tool has been successfully tested on standard, real-world video-surveillance dataset as reported and discussed in Section 3. Conclusions are presented in Section 4.

2 DALES System

DALES system architecture is presented in Section 2.1, while its two main computational stages, one at the object-of-interest level, the second one at the frame/video levels are described in Sections 2.2-2.3 and Section 2.4, respectively.

2.1 System Architecture

DALES software tool has been prototyped according to the Rapid Application Development (RAD) methodology and using object-oriented approach (C++, 2011). The data flow diagrams (DFDs) shown in Figs. 1 (a)-(b) display the flow of data within different stages of the system. DFDs give an account of the type of data input, the processing involved with these data as well as the final data we get, each higher level of DFDs elaborating the system further.

In order to start the computation of multi-view, multiple object-of-interest detection and counting, target segmentation and labelling, multi-stream video annotations and script generation, DALES system requires multi-view camera synchronization. This is achieved in the multiple views by checking the correspondence of the file names of the files in all the views during the loading phase (Figs. 2(a), 3(a)).

On the other hand, DALES could be used as a viewer of annotated, multi-view videos by loading the generated text script (Fig. 2(b)).

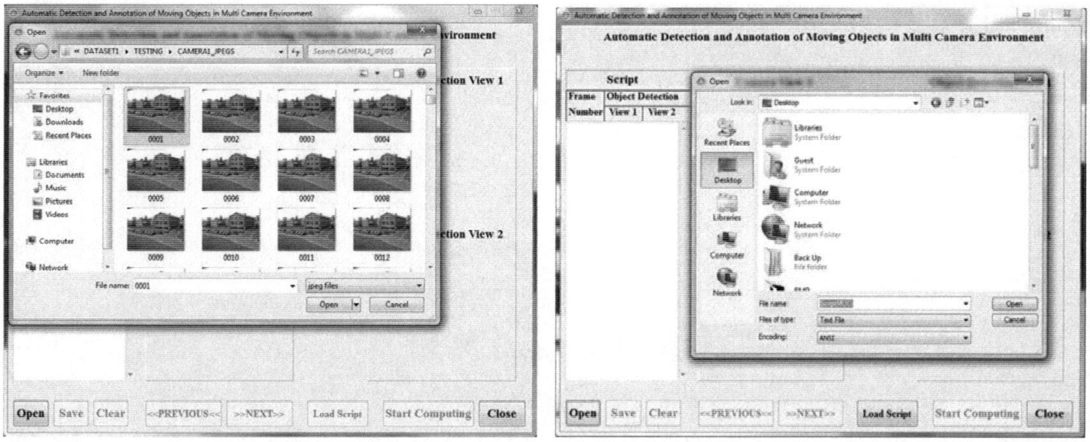

(a) (b)

Figure 2: The initialisation of DALES software could be done either by providing (a) the video sequence folder name, in order to use the software to process the multi-view video; or by providing (b) a text script with video annotation, in order to run the software to visualize the frames and corresponding annotations.

2.2 Multiple-Object Detection, Segmentation, and Counting

A number of solutions exists for detecting multiple objects of interest in video scenes (Olszewska and McCluskey, 2011; Olszewska, 2011; Olszewska, 2012b). In particular, background subtraction has long been used in the literature as it provides a useful approach to both detect and segment objects of interest. This method could be computed by difference between two consecutive frames (Archetti et al., 2006), by subtracting the current frame from the background (Toyama et al., 1995; Haritaoglu et al., 2000), or combining both frame difference and background subtraction techniques (Huang et al., 2007, Yao et al., 2009).

In our scenario, images $I(x,y)$ we consider may be taken from very different cameras, different lighting, etc. For that, we compute blobs separately in each of the views. The blobs are defined by labeled connected regions, which are obtained by background subtraction. The latter technique consists in computing the difference between the current image intensity $I(x,y)$ and a background model, and afterwards, in extracting the foreground.

To model the background, we adopt the running Gaussian average (RGA) (Wren et al., 1997), characterized by the mean μ_b and the variance σ_b^2, rather than, for example, the Gaussian mixture model (GMM) (Stauffer and Grimson, 1999; Friedman and Russell, 1997; Zivkovic and van der Heijden, 2004), since the RGA method is much more suitable for real-time tracking.

Next, the foreground is determined by

$$F(x,y) = \begin{cases} 1 & \text{if } |I(x,y) - \mu_b| > n \cdot \sigma_b, \text{ with } n \in \mathbb{N}_0, \\ 0 & \text{otherwise.} \end{cases} \quad (1)$$

Finally, morphological operations (Haralick, 1988) are applied to the extracted foreground F, in order to exploit the existing information on the neighboring pixels,

$$f(x,y) = Morph(F(x,y)). \quad (2)$$

2.3 Object Labeling

In this work, the detected and segmented object from a frame is automatically labelled by comparing it with a given example object based on the Scale Invariant Feature Transform (SIFT) descriptors (Olszewska, 2012a).

Algorithm 1 Matching Algorithm

Given $A' = A, B' = B, M = \varnothing$,
for all $a_i \in A'$ **do**
  for all $b_j \in B'$ **do**
    repeat
      if

$$\begin{aligned} & d_P(a_i, b_j) && = \min_{b \in B'} d_P(a_i, b) \\ \wedge \ & d_P(b_j, a_i) && = \min_{a \in A'} d_P(b_j, a) \\ \wedge \ & d_P(a_i, b_j) && \leq d_H(A, B) \\ \wedge \ & d_P(b_j, a_i) && \leq d_H(A, B) \end{aligned}$$

      then

$$\begin{aligned} & (a_i, b_j) \subset M \\ \wedge \ & A' = A \backslash \{a_i\} \wedge B' = B \backslash \{b_j\} \end{aligned}$$

      end if
    until $A' \neq \varnothing \vee B' \neq \varnothing$
  end for
end for
return M

The main steps of our labelling process are (i) the detection of object's SIFT features which are robust to rotation, translation, scale changes as well as some viewpoint variations, (ii) their matching by means of the Embedded Double Matching Algorithm (Algorithm 1) and (iii) the label inheritance. Moreover, our approach does not require any training and thus is online compatible.

The comparison between the query object and the candidate one is performed in the feature space in order to be more computationally effective and to be more robust towards noise and affine transformation, and is followed by the computation of an associated similarity measure $d_S(A, B)$, which is computed as follows

$$d_S(A, B) = \frac{\#M}{\frac{\#A + \#B}{2}}, \tag{3}$$

with A and B, the sets of SIFT features of the query and the candidate objects, respectively, and M, the set of the double-matched ones (Alqaisi et al., 2012).

The decision that a candidate object contains similar content to the query one is taken based on the fact that the similarity measure $d_S(A, B)$ is above a given threshold. In the case when the similarity measure $d_S(A, B)$ is below the given threshold, the candidate is rejected.

Finally, once the decision that a candidate object contains similar content to the query one has been taken, the label of the candidate object is automatically mapped with the predefined label of the example object.

2.4 Multi-View Annotations

Hence, by using different objects' examples, all the frames from the video dataset are indexed with the relevant semantic labels based on their visual content similarity, while the objects of interest are automatically labeled and localized within these frames (Olszewska, 2012a).

Unlike (Evans et al., 2013), which uses an early fusion, where all the cameras are used to make a decision about detection and tracking of the objects of interest, DALES system performs a late fusion. Indeed, in our system, objects of interest are detected and labelled in individual cameras independently. Next, the results are combined on the majority voting principle based on the semantic consistency of

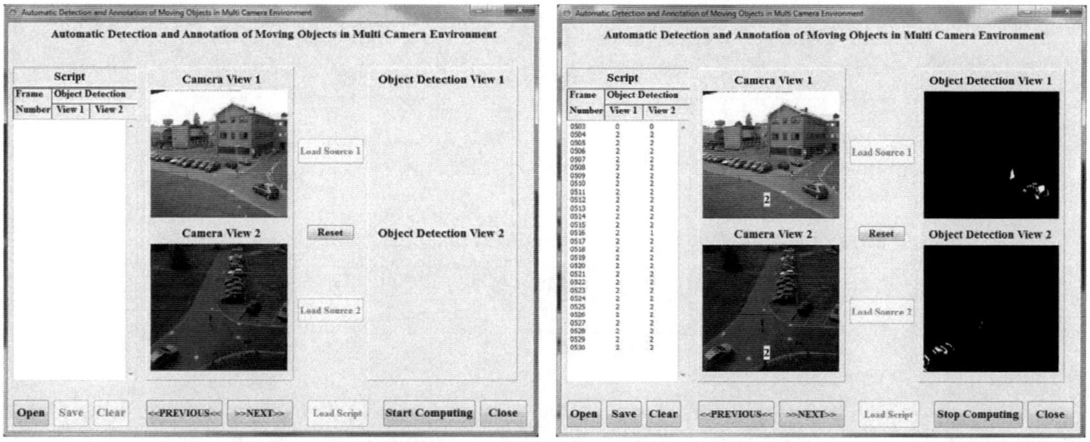

(a) (b)

Figure 3: Snapshots of DALES software windows, in the phase of: (a) loaded multi views; (b) detected moving objects.

the labels in sequential frames and across multiple camera views, rather than exploring geometrical correspondences of objects as in (Dai and Payandeh, 2013).

3 Experiments and Discussion

To validate the DALES tool, we have applied our system on the standard dataset (PETS, 2001) consisting of video-surveillance dynamic scene recorded by two PTZ cameras. This produces two videos. Each contains 2688 frames, whose average resolution is of 576x768 pixels and which were captured in outdoor environment. This database owns challenges of multi-view video stream, as well as quantity, pose, motion, size, appearance and scale variations of the objects of interest, i.e. people and cars.

All the experiments have been run on a computer with Intel Core 2 Duo Pentium T9300, 2.5 GHz, 2Gb RAM, and using our DALES software implemented with C++ (C++, 2011).

Some examples of the results of our DALES system are presented in Fig. 3(b). These frames present difficult situations such as poor foreground/background contrast or light reflection.

To assess the detection accuracy of DALES system, we adopt the standard criteria (Izadi and Saeedi, 2008) as follows:

$$detection\ rate\ (DR) = \frac{TP}{TP+FN}, \tag{4}$$

$$false\ detection\ rate\ (FAR) = \frac{FP}{FP+TP}, \tag{5}$$

with TP, true positive, FP, false positive, and FN, false negative.

The labelling accuracy of DALES system could be assessed using the following standard criterion:

$$accuracy = \frac{TP+TN}{TP+TN+FP+FN}, \tag{6}$$

with TN, true negative.

In Table 1, we have reported the average detection and false alarm rates of our DALES method against the rates achieved by (Izadi and Saeedi, 2008), while in Table 2, we have displayed the average accuracy of object-of-interest labelling of our DALES method against the rate obtained by (Athanasiadis et al., 2007).

Table 1: Average detection rates of object-of-interests in video frames.

	(Izadi and Saeedi, 2008)	DALES
average detection rate (DR)	91.3%	91.6%
average false alarm rate (FAR)	9.5%	4.9%

Table 2: Average accuracy of object-of-interest labelling in video frames.

	(Athanasiadis et al., 2007)	DALES
average accuracy	85%	95%

From Tables 1-2, we can conclude that our DALES system provides reliable detection and counting of objects of interest in multi-camera environment, and that the multiple-object labelling is very accurate as well, outperforming state-of-the art techniques. DALES total precision to annotate multi-view videos is therefore very high.

For all the dataset, the average computational speed of our DALES software is in the range of few seconds, whereas the viewer function of DALES software takes only few milliseconds to process. Hence, our developed system could be used in context of online scene analysis.

4 Conclusions

Reliable, multi-view annotation of large amount of real-time visual data, such as surveillance videos or sport event broadcasts, is a challenging topic we have copped with. For this purpose, we have developed a new software tool called DALES which processes, in multi-camera environment, (i) multiple object-of-interest detection and (ii) counting, (iii) target segmentation and (iv) labelling, (v) image annotations, (vi) multi-stream video annotations and script generation. Moreover, our DALES software suits well as a viewer to display a loaded script with the text annotations of the multi-camera video sequence and the corresponding labelled multi-view images.

Our system shows excellent performance compared to the ones found in the literature, on one hand, for multiple-target detection and segmentation and, on the other hand, for object labeling. Multi-stream annotations with DALES are thus computationally efficient and accurate.

References

T. Alqaisi, D. Gledhill, and J. I. Olszewska. 2012. Embedded double matching of local descriptors for a fast automatic recognition of real-world objects. In *Proceedings of the IEEE International Conference on Image Processing (ICIP'12)*, pages 2385–2388.

A. Alsuqayhi and J. I. Olszewska. 2013. Efficient optical character recognition system for automatic soccer player's identification. In *Proceedings of the IAPR International Conference on Computer Analysis of Images and Patterns Workshop (CAIP'13)*, pages 139–150.

F. Archetti, C. Manfredotti, V. Messina, and D. Sorrenti. 2006. Foreground-to-ghost discrimination in single-difference pre-processing. In *Proceedings of the International Conference on Advanced Concepts for Intelligent Vision Systems*, pages 23–30.

T. Athanasiadis, P. Mylonas, Y. Avrithis, and S. Kollias. 2007. Semantic image segmentation and object labeling. *IEEE Transactions on Circuits and Systems for Video Technology*, 17(3):298–312.

L. Bai, S. Lao, G. J. F. Jones, and A. F. Smeaton. 2007. Video semantic content analysis based on ontology. In *Proceedings of the IEEE International Machine Vision and Image Processing Conference*, pages 117–124.

J. Black, T. Ellis, and P. Rosin. 2002. Multi View Image Surveillance and Tracking. In *Proceedings of the IEEE Workshop on Motion and Video Computing*, pages 169–174.

C++. 2011. C++ builder. Available online at: `https://downloads.embarcadero.com/free/c_builder`.

J.-W. Choi and J.-H. Yoo. 2013. Real-time multi-person tracking in fixed surveillance camera environment. In *Proceedings of the IEEE International Conference on Consumer Electronics*.

X. Dai and S. Payandeh. 2013. Geometry-based object association and consistent labeling in multi-camera surveillance. *IEEE Journal on Emerging and Selected Topics in Circuits and Systems*, 3(2):175–184.

R. Diaz, S. Hallman, and C. C. Fowlkes. 2013. Detecting dynamic objects with multi-view background subtraction. In *Proceedings of the IEEE International Conference on Computer Vision*, pages 273–280.

M. Evans, C. J. Osborne, and J. Ferryman. 2013. Multicamera object detection and tracking with object size estimation. In *Proceedings of the IEEE International Conference on Advanced Video and Signal Based Surveillance*, pages 177–182.

N. Friedman and S. Russell. 1997. Image segmentation in video sequences: A probabilistic approach. In *Proceedings of the 13th Conference on Uncertainty in AI*.

S. Guler, J. M. Griffith, and I. A. Pushee. 2003. Tracking and handoff between multiple perspective camera views. In *Proceedings of the 32nd IEEE Workshop on Applied Imaginary Pattern Recognition*, pages 275–281.

R. M. Haralick. 1988. Mathematical morphology and computer vision. In *Proceedings of the IEEE Asilomar Conference on Signals, Systems and Computers*, volume 1, pages 468–479.

I. Haritaoglu, D. Harwood, and L. Davis. 2000. Real-time surveillance of people and their activities. *IEEE Transactions on Pattern Analysis and Machine Intelligence*, 77(8):809–830.

H.-H. Hsu, W.-M. Yang, and T. K. Shih. 2013. Multicamera object detection and tracking with object size estimation. In *Proceedings of the IEEE Conference Anthology*, pages 1–4.

W. Huang, Z. Liu, and W. Pan. 2007. The precise recognition of moving object in complex background. In *Proceedings of 3rd IEEE International Conference on Natural Computation*, volume 2, pages 246–252.

M. Izadi and P. Saeedi. 2008. Robust region-based background subtraction and shadow removing using colour and gradient information. In *Proceedings of the 19th IEEE International Conference on Pattern Recognition*, pages 1–5.

V. Kettnaker and R. Zabih. 1999. Bayesian multi-camera surveillance. In *Proceedings of the IEEE Conference on Computer Vision and Pattern Recognition*, volume 2, pages 1–5.

K. S. Kumar, S. Prasad, P. K. Saroj, and R. C. Tripathi. 2010. Multiple cameras using real-time object tracking for surveillance and security system. In *Proceedings of the IEEE International Conference on Emerging Trends in Engineering and Technology*, pages 213–218.

L. Lamard, R. Chapuis, and J.-P. Boyer. 2013. CPHD Filter addressing occlusions with pedestrians and vehicles tracking. In *Proceedings of the IEEE International Intelligent Vehicles Symposium*, pages 1125–1130.

P. Natarajan and R. Nevatia. 2005. EDF: A framework for semantic annotation of video. In *Proceedings of the IEEE International Conference on Computer Vision Workshops*, page 1876.

J. I. Olszewska and T. L. McCluskey. 2011. Ontology-coupled active contours for dynamic video scene understanding. In *Proceedings of the IEEE International Conference on Intelligent Engineering Systems*, pages 369–374.

J. I. Olszewska. 2011. Spatio-temporal visual ontology. In *Proceedings of the 1st EPSRC Workshop on Vision and Language (VL'2011)*.

J. I. Olszewska. 2012a. A new approach for automatic object labeling. In *Proceedings of the 2nd EPSRC Workshop on Vision and Language (VL'2012)*.

J. I. Olszewska. 2012b. Multi-target parametric active contours to support ontological domain representation. In *Proceedings of the RFIA Conference*, pages 779–784.

PETS. 2001. PETS Dataset. Available online at: `ftp://ftp.pets.rdg.ac.uk/pub/PETS2001`.

C. Stauffer and W. Grimson. 1999. Adaptive background mixture model for real-time tracking. In *Proceedings of the IEEE Conference on Computer Vision and Pattern Recognition*.

C. Town. 2004. Ontology-driven Bayesian networks for dynamic scene understanding. In *Proceedings of the IEEE International Conference on Computer Vision and Pattern Recognition Workshops*, page 116.

K. Toyama, J. Krumm, B. Brumitt, and B. Meyers. 1995. Wallflower: Principles and practice of background maintenance. In *Proceedings of the IEEE International Conference on Computer Vision*, volume 1, pages 255–261.

B. Vrusias, D. Makris, J.-P. Renno, N. Newbold, K. Ahmad, and G. Jones. 2007. A framework for ontology enriched semantic annotation of CCTV video. In *Proceedings of the IEEE International Workshop on Image Analysis for Multimedia Interactive Services*, page 5.

C. R. Wren, A. Azarbayejani, T. Darrell, and A. P. Pentland. 1997. Real-time tracking of the human body. *IEEE Transactions on Pattern Analysis and Machine Intelligence*, 19(7):780–785.

C. Yao, W. Li, and L. Gao. 2009. An efficient moving object detection algorithm using multi-mask. In *Proceedings of 6th IEEE International Conference on Fuzzy Systems and Knowledge Discovery*, volume 5, pages 354–358.

Z. Zivkovic and F. van der Heijden. 2004. Recursive unsupervised learning of finite mixture models. *IEEE Transactions on Pattern Analysis and Machine Intelligence*, 26(5):651–656.

A Hybrid Segmentation of Web Pages for Vibro-Tactile Access on Touch-Screen Devices

Waseem Safi[1] **Fabrice Maurel**[1] **Jean-Marc Routoure**[1, 2] **Pierre Beust**[1] **Gaël Dias**[1]

[1] University of Caen Basse-Normandie - UNICAEN

[2] National Superior Engineering School of Caen - ENSICAEN

14032 Caen - France

firstName.lastName@unicaen.fr

Abstract

Navigating the Web is one of important missions in the field of computer accessibility. Many specialized techniques for Visually Impaired People (VIP) succeed to extract the visual and textual information displayed on digital screens and transform it in a linear way: either through a written format on special Braille devices or a vocal output using text-to-speech synthesizers. However, many researches confirm that perception of the layout of web pages enhances web navigation and memorization. But, most existing screen readers still fail to transform the 2-dimension structures of web pages into higher orders. In this paper, we propose a new framework to enhance VIP web accessibility by affording a "first glance" web page overview, and by suggesting a hybrid segmentation algorithm to afford nested and easy navigation of web pages. In particular, the web page layout is transformed into a coarse grain structure, which is then converted into vibrating pages using a graphical vibro-tactile language. First experiments with blind users show interesting issues on touch-screen devices.

1 Introduction

In October 2013, the world health organization estimated that the number of Visually Impaired People (VIP) in the world is 285 million: 39 million of them are blind and 246 million have low vision. In particular, the organization defined four levels of visual functions depending on the international classification of diseases: normal vision, moderate visual impairment, severe visual impairment and blindness.

VIP depend on screen readers in order to deal with computer operating systems and computational programs. One of most important and desired targets by VIP is navigating the Web, considering the increased importance and expansion of web-based computational programs. Screen readers present some solutions to navigate the textual and graphical contents of web pages, either by transforming a web page into a written Braille, or into a vocal output. In addition to these solutions, some screen readers installed on touch devices transform a web page into a vocal-tactile output.

But, there are some drawbacks for these proposed solutions. On the one hand, Braille techniques are costly and only few number of VIP have learned Braille (in France in 2011, there were about 77,000 visually impaired people and only 15,000 of them had learned Braille). On the other hand, transforming the information of a web page into a vocal format might not be suitable in public and noisy environments. Finally most of Braille solutions are not suitable for mobile devices [Maurel et al, 2012].

In addition to these drawbacks, the most important one is the failure to transform the 2-dimension web page structure. Indeed, as reported by many authors, perceiving the 2D structure of web documents greatly improves navigation efficiency and memorization as it allows high level text reading strategies such as: rapid or cursory reading, finding or locating information, to name but a few [Maurel et al, 2003].

Our work focuses on developing and evaluating a sensory substitution system based on a vibro-tactile solution, which may solve the mentioned drawbacks. In particular, we study how to increase the VIP perception of a 2D web page structure and how to enhance their techniques to navigate the contents of

Proceedings of the 25th International Conference on Computational Linguistics, pages 95–102, Dublin, Ireland, August 23-29 2014.

web pages on touch-screen devices. The suggested solution is very cheap compared to Braille devices and may be efficient in noisy and public environments compared to vocal-tactile solutions.
Our contribution is three-fold: (1) designing a Tactile Vision Sensory System (TVSS) represented by an electronic circuit and an Android program in order to transform light contrasts of touch-screen devices into low-frequencies tactile vibrations; (2) designing an algorithm for segmenting web pages in order to support the visually impaired persons by a way which may enhance their ability to navigate the textual and graphical contents of web pages and (3) analyzing the effects of the suggested segmentation method on navigation models and tactics of blind persons, and its effect on enhancing their strategies for text reading and looking for textual information.

The paper is organized as follows. First, in section 2, we review most advanced VIP targeted technologies. Then, in section 3, we describe the new proposed framework. In section 4, we view the state of the art for web pages segmentation methods. In the fifth section, our hybrid segmentation method is presented and how this method could be integrated in our framework. In section 6, we enumerate the desired effects of the proposed segmentation method on navigation models and tactics of blind persons, and how it may enhance their strategies for text reading and searching of textual information. Finally, in the seventh section, perspectives and conclusions are presented.

2 VIP targeted technologies

Current products for VIP such as screen readers mainly depend on speech synthesis or Braille solutions, e.g. ChromeVox [3], Windows-Eyes [4], or JAWS (Job Access With Speech) [5]. Braille displays are complex and expensive electromechanical devices that connect to a computer and display Braille characters. Speech synthesis engines convert texts into artificial speech, where the text is analyzed and transformed into phonemes. These phonemes are then processed using signal processing techniques.

Some screen readers can also support tactile feedback when working on touch-screen devices, such as Mobile Accessibility [6] and Talkback [7] for Android, or VoiceOver [8] for IPad. Many of these products propose shortcuts for blind users to display a menu of HTML elements existing in the web page, for example headers, links and images. But, the main drawback of all these products is the fact that they transfer the information of web pages into a linear way i.e. without any indication of the 2-dimension global structure.
Many researches tried to enhance the way by which VIP interact with web pages, such as [Alaeldin et al, 2011], who proposed a tactile web navigator to enable blind people access the Web. This navigator extracts texts from web pages and sends them to a microcontroller responsible of displaying the text in Braille language using an array of solenoids. A tactile web browser for hypertext documents has been proposed by [Rotard et al, 2005]. This browser renders texts and graphics for VIP on a tactile graphics display and supports also a voice output to read textual paragraphs and to provide a vocal feedback. The authors implemented two exploration modes, one for bitmap graphics and another one for scalable vector graphics. A pin matrix device is then used to produce the output signal for blind users. The main drawback of these two proposed systems is that they need specific devices (solenoids and pin matrix), which are expensive and cannot be integrated to handled devices such as PDAs or Tablet PCs. Another interesting model called MAP-RDF (Model of Architecture of Web Pages) has been proposed by [BouIssa et al, 2011]. This model allows representing the structure of a web page and provides blind users with an overview of the web page layout and the document structure semantics. Tactos is a perceptual interaction system, which has been suggested by [Lenay et al, 2003] and consists of three elements: (1) tactile simulators (two Braille cells with 8 pins) represent a tactile feedback system, (2) a graphics tablet with a stylus represents an input device and (3) the computer. More than 30 prototypes of Tactos have been released to serve a lot of users in many domains. Tactos has been successfully used to recognize simple and complex shapes. The device has been also used in geometry teaching domain in an institution for visually impaired and blind children. Tactos also allowed psychology researchers to propose and develop new paradigms for studying perceptions and mediated communication of blind persons [Tixier et al, 2013]. However, it shows the same drawback as the previous systems, which are expensive and need specific devices. Moreover, the blind user can only explore the web page with a stylus and both hands are occupied by the system. Moreover, it is unemployable for a large set of environments, for example in public.

3 Proposed Framework

The "first glance" can be defined as the ability to understand the document layout and its structural semantics in a blink of an eye [Maurel et al, 2012]. In this work, we aim to increase the ability of visually impaired persons to understand the 2-dimension web page layout in order to enhance their tactics to navigate the Web with a vibro-tactile feedback.
The first phase in our model is to extract visual structures in the navigated web page and convert these "visual" blocks into zones (or segments) to facilitate the navigation in later phases. We achieve this phase depending on a hybrid segmentation method. Then the system represents the extracted visual elements as symbols using a graphical language. The third phase is to browse these graphical symbols depending on the size of the used touched-screen device; and in the fourth phase, our system provides a vibro-tactile feedback when the blind user touches the tablet by giving the user a vibro-tactile feedback by transforming light contrasts of touch-screen devices into low-frequencies tactile vibrations. A tablet (Asus Model TF101 with Android operating system) has being used for our tests.

To achieve the desired system, we have designed an electronic circuit, which controls two micro-vibrators placed on two fingers. A Bluetooth connection with an android tablet allows controlling the vibration intensity (i.e. amplitude) of vibrators. An Android dedicated program on the tablet views an image on the screen and detects where the user touches the tablet screen (the viewed image represents the result of web page segmentation). The intensity of the light emitted by the tablet at touched points is then transmitted to the embedded device in order to control the vibration intensity. In this paper, we focus only on the first phase (extracting visual structures in the navigated web page, and convert them into zones), with considering that detailed description of hardware components of the system, and results of pre-tests are described in [Maurel et al, 2012] and [Maurel et al, 2013].

4 Related Works

Segmenting a web page is a fundamental phase for understanding its global structure. Extracting the global structure of web pages is useful in many domains such as information retrieval, data extraction, and similarity of web pages.

Many approaches have been suggested for segmenting web pages, such as:
-1) DOM-based segmentation: it depends on analyzing the DOM tree (Document Object Model), and extracting the main structure of web pages depending on HTML tags. An example of this approach is the work of [Sanoja et al, 2013], which determines firstly the layout template of a web page, and then it divides the page into minimum blocks, and finally collects these minimum blocks into content blocks.
-2) Vision-based segmentation: this method divides the web page depending on the visual view of web page contents on a web browser. The most famous tool depends on this approach is VIPS (VIsion based Page Segmentation) [Deng et al, 2003].
-3) Image processing based segmentation: this approach captures an image for the visual view of a web page, and then depends on image processing techniques to divide the captured image into sub blocks [Cai et al, 2004] [Cao et al, 2010].
-4) Text-based Segmentation: this approach focuses on extracting only information about texts existed in a web page. After dividing the web page into blocks of texts, it could be possible to find the semantic relations between these textual blocks. This method is useful in many information retrieval domains such as question answering applications [Foucault e al, 2013].
-5) Fixed-length segmentation: this approach divides the web pages into fixed length blocks (passages), after removing all HTML tags, where each passage contains a fixed number of words [Callan, 1994].
-6) Densitometric analysis based segmentation: this approach depends on methods applied in quantitative linguistics, where text-density refers to a measure for identifying important textual segments of a web page [Kohlschütter et al, 2008].
-7) Graph-based segmentation: This approach depends on transforming the visual segments of a web page into graph nodes, then applying many common graph methods on these nodes for combining

them into blocks, or for making a clustering for these nodes. Some common works which depend on this approach are [Chakrabarti et al, 2008] [Liu et al, 2011].
-8) and Hybrid-based segmentation: This approach combines many approaches indicated previously.

5 Suggested Hybrid Segmentation Algorithm

Most of segmentation algorithms render firstly the web page using a web browser, and then segments the HTML elements into many blocks depending on the visual layout. The constructed hybrid segmentation algorithm has been tested on 154 pages collected manually from many newspaper and e-commerce sites (www.leparisien.fr, www.lefigaro.fr, www.liberation.fr, www.amazon.fr, www.materiel.net), and the results have been integrated with our under-development Android program. The obtained results are promised because the segmentation algorithm can extract well the web page blocks depending on the visual structure, and the algorithm can also convert correctly these blocks into zones (clustering the blocks). Our algorithm blends three segmentation approaches, DOM-based segmentation, vision-based segmentation, and graph-based segmentation.

Proposed Corpora

To achieve the previous mentioned model, we construct two corpora, one for training, and another for testing. We selected many criteria for crawling web pages, such as, the type of crawled pages (information web sites, and e-commerce web sites), the size (about 10,000 pages), the language (French), the version of web site (Classic, Mobile), and the technology used to build the crawled web site (framework JavaScript: JQuery, mootools, ... / CMS: Prestashop, Drupal, Joomla...).

5.1 Vision-Based Approach

In this phase, we render the web page using Mozilla FireFox browser, and getting its visual structure by injection Java-script code inside the HTML source code of the rendered web page. The obtained visual structure indicates a global hierarchy of the rendered web page, and assigns a bounding box for each HTML element. Figure 1.a represents a part of a web page, and the result of its vision-based segmentation is presented in figure 1.b.

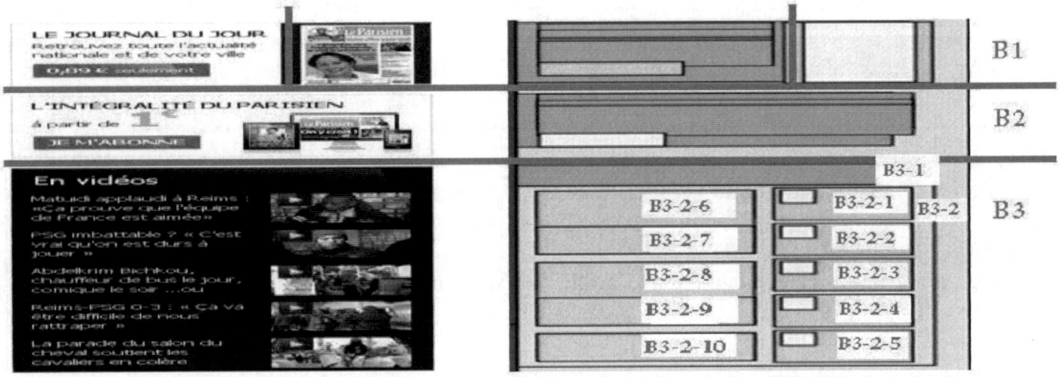

(a) A part of a web page (b) Vision-based segmentation
Figure 1. A part of a web page (leparisien.fr) and its vision-based segmentation

The input of this phase is a web page HTML source code, and its output is injected information about bounding boxes for each HTML element. In next sections, we refer to bounding boxes by blocks (i.e. each bounding box represents an HTML element, and may contain other bounding boxes.).

5.2 DOM-Based Approach

After segmenting a web page depending on its visual structure, we analyze its DOM structure by applying filters and re-organization rules for enhancing results of next phases. Dead-Nodes filter is an example of these filters: it deletes all HTML nodes that do not affect on the appearance, for example nodes with height or width equals to "0px" (zero pixel); or nodes with style properties ("display :

none" or "visibility:hidden"). An example of re-organization rules is Paragraph-Reorganization rule, where this rule re-constructs all paragraph child-nodes in one node contains the extracted text; we made this rule after analyzing many DOM structures, and observing that some paragraph nodes contain child-nodes which affect negatively on extracting the text, such as <i>, <span>, etc.., and these child-nodes contain important texts. We made many filters and re-organization rules, and integrated them with our framework, and then we tested applying these rules and filters on the vision-based segmented web pages (154 pages mentioned previously). As a result of applying the two approaches (vision-based and DOM-based), we succeeded to get the first glance visual structure for many pages.

The result of this phase is a filtered DOM-tree, each of its nodes is visible and contains a bounding box information. Figure 1.b represents a hierarchy of some HTML nodes, the first level contains 3 main blocks (B1, B2, and B3), and each one contains many sub blocks, for example B3 contains B3-1 and B3-2.

To illustrate results of applying previous two mentioned approaches, we represented an obtained filtered DOM-tree on the used tablet. Figure 2 views a graphical representation for a page web, since each rectangle represents a block in the analyzed web page. Red rectangles represent images (<img> tags), green rectangles represent links (<a> tags), blue rectangles represent list of items (<ul> or <ol> tags), and finally, black rectangles represent paragraphs (<p> tags).

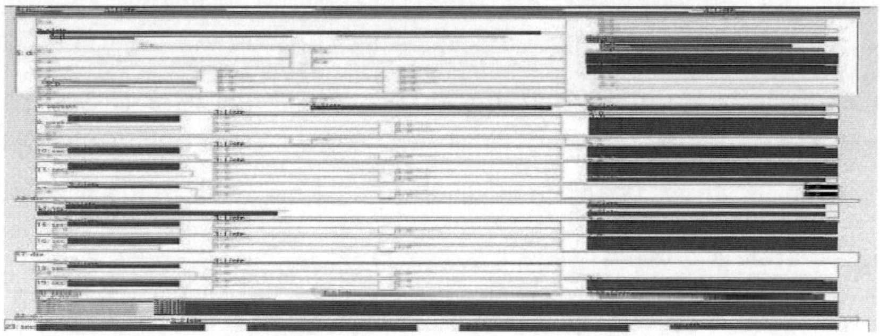

Figure 2. A graphical representation for a page web (leparisien.fr)

5.3 Graph-Based Approach

After segmenting the web page depending on its visual structures and analyzing its DOM-structure, we apply a new graph-based segmentation algorithm which called "Blocks2Zones Clustering" in order to group many similar blocks together in one zone. Clustering many blocks together is necessary in order to decrease the number of viewed blocks in some interfaces (instead of viewing many blocks, we view one zone represents these blocks and then the user can navigate intra-elements inside the zone by double clicking on the graphical element of the chosen zone.), and to group closed blocks in one zone (here, closeness depends on distances between blocks, this will be described next sections in details). The pseudo-code of the proposed algorithm is:

Blocks2Zones Clustering Algorithm
Input (Blocks, N° of desired Zones)
Output: Graph of N nodes (N Zones)
1- Transform the blocks into a graph (Non-Directed graph)
1.1. Blocks → Nodes,
1.2. Make relations between the nodes, and assign weights for these relations.
2- If number of zones >= number of blocks
end the algorithm,
Else
3- Find the node with the smallest size (node A) (Figure 3.a (6 zones), Figure 3.b (5 zones))
4- For node A, find the relation which has the largest weight (node B). (Figure 3.a (6 zones), Figure 3.b (5 zones))
5- Group the nodes A, and B (A+B). (Figure 3.a (5 zones), Figure 3.b (4 zones))
6- Repeat steps 3-4-5 till number of blocks == number of zones

Figure 3 represents some examples of applying this algorithm, where each rectangle represents a zone (a block or a collection of blocks), and the center of each ellipse represents the zone center.

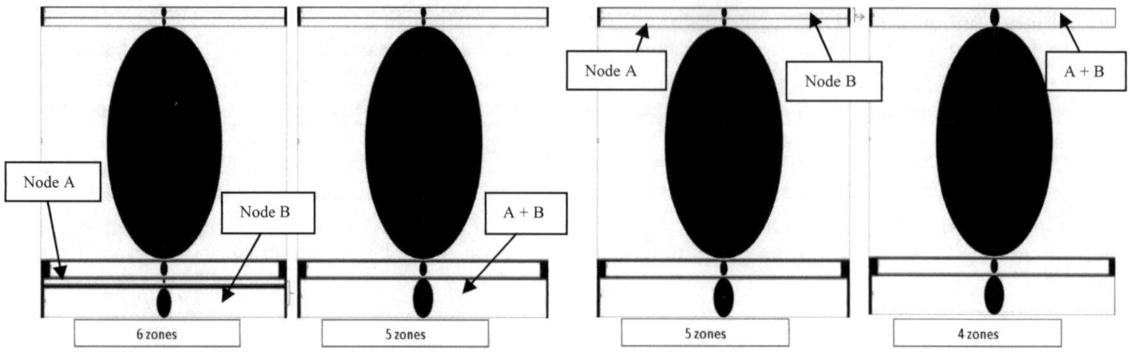

(a) Converting 6 zones to 5 zones (b) Converting 5 zones to 4 zones

Figure 3. Examples of applying Blocks2Zones clustering Algorithm

To calculate weights between nodes, we tested 2 relations of distances: the first one is Minkowski Manhattan distance ($d(p,q) = d(q,p) = \|p - q\| = \sum_{i=1}^{n} |p_i - q_i|$), and the second is Minkowski Euclidian distance ($d(p,q) = d(q,p) = \sqrt{(p_1 - q_{1)}{}^2 + (p_2 - q_{2)}{}^2 + \dots + (p_n - q_{n)}{}^2}$). To ensure which distance should be used, we applied an internal quality criterion for the two used distances; the applied criterion is Sum of Squared Error (SSE) ($SSE = \sum_{K=1}^{n} \sum_{\forall x_i \in C_K}^{n} \|x_i - \alpha_i\|^2$ Where Ck is the set of instances in cluster K, and $\alpha_{k,j} = \frac{1}{N_k} \sum_{\forall x_i \in C_K}^{n} x_{i,j}$).

Results of applying SSE measure on the two distances (Minkowski Manhattan, and Minkowski Euclidian) were the same; which means that using either Minkowski Manhattan distance or Minkowski Euclidian distance is equal in our algorithm to calculate weights between nodes.

Applying this hybrid segmentation algorithm on a filtered DOM-tree (obtained from applying Vision-based approach then Dom-based approach) converts a web page to a set of zones, each zone contains many other zones or blocks, and each block represents a visual structure and may contain many other blocks. The purpose of the proposed vibro-tactile access protocol is then to transform the semantic of symbols in these zones, or blocks, or HTML elements into vibrations with different frequencies and amplitudes.

6 Desired Effects of Suggested Algorithm on Web Navigation Models of VIP

We had finished designing the suggested algorithm, and integrated it with our framework. However, practical experiments with VIP are the most important criteria to select success or failing this algorithm in enhancing VIP web navigation models, and this is our next step to be achieved. But, depending on our previous experiments in dealing with VIP targeted techniques, we can expect some desired effects of the proposed segmentation method on navigation models and tactics of blind persons, and how it may enhance their strategies for text reading and searching of textual information.

Firstly, this segmentation model can give VIP an impression of the layout of navigated web page (first glance layout), and (as indicated previously) perceiving the 2D structure of web documents greatly improves navigation efficiency and memorization.

Secondly, this suggested segmentation method can group together many closed blocks in one zone, and in this way the user can select easily if these zone contents are important for him/her or not, for example collecting all header blocks in one zone, or collecting all footer blocks in one zone.

Thirdly, this model can allow high level text reading strategies such as rapid or cursory reading or locating information, this can be achieved by ignoring navigating any zone does not contain textual information. By the way if one zone contains textual information, the user can navigate it and decide if it contains important information for him/her or not.

7 CONCLUSION AND PERSPECTIVES

In this paper, we summarized our current work which aims to design an approach for non-visual access to web pages on touch-screen devices, and we focused on the suggested hybrid segmentation algorithm. We expect that integrating this method of segmentation with the designed vibro-tactile protocol can give VIP an impression of the first glance layout of web pages.

In the same way that the environment enables a blind person to move in space with sidewalks and textures which will be explored by his/her white cane, we hope giving the blind user an ability to navigate documents depending on "textual sidewalks" and "graphical paths" which will be discovered by his/her finger.

Next steps in this research will be 1) making real experiments to study effects of suggested segmentation algorithm on VIP web navigation models, 2) adding advances techniques in text summarization to facilitate navigating textual information, 3) adding elements to the graphical vibro-tactile language in order to represent more HTML elements such links, buttons, input fields, and other elements, 4) we plan also to add thermic actuators for translating the notion of colors. This may be very useful and hopeful for blind users to transfer information about colors.

8 References

[1] Maurel, F., Dias, G., Routoure, J-M., Vautier, M., Beust, P., Molina, M., Sann, C., « *Haptic Perception of Document Structure for Visually Impaired People on Handled Devices* », Procedia Computer Science, Volume 14, Pages 319-329, ISSN : 1877-0509, 2012.
DOI=http://dx.doi.org/10.1016/j.procs.2012.10.036

[2] Maurel, F., Vigouroux, N., Raynal, M., Oriola, B., « *Contribution of the Transmodality Concept to Improve Web Accessibility* ». In Assistive Technology Research Series, Volume 12, 2003, Pages 186-193. International conference; 1st, Smart homes and health telematics; Independent living for persons with disabilities and elderly people. ISSN : 1383-813X. 2003.

[3] http://www.chromevox.com/ [Access 24/5/2014]

[4] http://www.synapseadaptive.com/gw/wineyes.htm [Access 24/5/2014]

[5] http://www.freedomscientific.com/ [Access 24/5/2014]

[6]https://play.google.com/store/apps/details?id=es.codefactory.android.app.ma.vocalizerfrfdemo&hl=fr [Access 24/5/2014]

[7] https://play.google.com/store/apps/details?id=com.google.android.marvin.talkback&hl=fr [Access 24/5/2014]

[8] http://www.apple.com/fr/accessibility/ [Access 24/5/2014]

[9] Alaeldin, A., Mustafa , Y., Sharief, B., 2012. « *Tactile WebNavigator Device for Blind and Visually Impaired People* ». In Proceedings of the 2011 Jordan Conference on Applied Electrical Engineering and Computing Technologies, Jordan, 2011.
DOI=http://dx.doi.org/10.1109/AEECT.2011.6132519

[10] Rotard, M., Knödler, S., Ertl, T., « *A Tactile Web Browser for the Visually Disabled* ». In Proceedings of the sixteenth ACM Conference on Hypertext and Hypermedia. ACM, New York, NY, USA, 2005, pages 15-22, 2005.
DOI= http://dx.doi.org/10.1145/1083356.1083361

[11] BouIssa , Y., Mojahid, M., Oriola, B., Vigouroux, N., « *Accessibility for the Blind, an Automated Audio/Tactile Description of Pictures in Digital Documents* ». IEEE International Conference on Advances in Computational Tools for Engineering Applications, 2009, Pages: 591 – 594, 2009.
DOI=http://dx.doi.org/10.1109/ACTEA.2009.5227855

[12] Lenay, C., Gapenne, O., Hanneton, S., Marque, C., Genouëlle, C., "*Sensory Substitution, Limits and Perspectives*». In Touch for Knowing Cognitive psychology of haptic manual perception, Amsterdam, Pages: 275-292, 2003,

[13] Tixier, M., Lenay, C., Le-Bihan, G., Gapenne, O., Aubert, D., « *Designing Interactive Content with Blind Users for a Perceptual Supplementation System* », TEI 2013, 2013, in Proceedings of the 7th International Conference on Tangible, Embedded and Embodied Interaction, Barcelona, Spain, Pages 229-236, 2013.
DOI= http://dx.doi.org/10.1145/2460625.2460663

[14] Maurel, F., Safi, W., Beust, P., Routoure, J.M., « *Navigation aveugle sur dispositifs mobiles : toucher le Web... pour mieux l'entendre*», 16ème Colloque International sur le Document Électronique, CIDE16, Lille, France, Europia productions, 2013.

[15] Sanoja, A., Gançarski, S., «*Block-o-Matic: a Web Page Segmentation Tool*», BDA. Nantes, France. 2013. http://hal.archives-ouvertes.fr/hal-00881693/

[16] Deng, C., Shipeng, Y., Ji-Rong, W., Wei-Ying, M., «*VIPS: a Vision-based Page Segmentation Algorithm*», Nov. 1, 2003, Technical Report MSR-TR-2003-79, Microsoft Research. 2003. http://research.microsoft.com/pubs/70027/tr-2003-79.pdf

[17] Cai, D., He, X., Ma, W-Y., Wen, J-R., Zhang, H., 2004. « *Organizing WWW Images Based on the Analysis Of Page Layout And Web Link Structure*», Microsoft Research Asia, Beijing, China, 2004. http://research.microsoft.com/pubs/69080/25.pdf

[18] Cao, J., Mao, B., Luo, J., « *A segmentation method for web page analysis using shrinking and dividing*», International Journal of Parallel, Emergent and Distributed Systems - Network and parallel computing, Volume 25 Issue 2, April 2010. Pages: 93-104, 2010.
DOI=http://dx.doi.org/10.1080/17445760802429585

[19] Foucault, N., Rosset, S., Adda, G., « *Pré-segmentation de pages web et sélection de documents pertinent en Questions-Réponses*», TALN-RÉCITAL 2013.

[20] Callan, J.P., 1994. « *Passage- level Evidence in Document Retrieval*», the Seventeenth Annual International ACM SIGIR Conference on Research and Development in Information Retrieval, Dublin, Pages: 302-310.
Publisher: Springer-Verlag New York, Inc, 1994.
http://dl.acm.org/citation.cfm?id=188589

[21] Kohlschütter, C., Nejdl, W., « *A Densitometric Approach to Web Page Segmentation*», USA, CIKM'08, Proceedings of the 17th ACM conference on Information and knowledge management, 2008. Pages: 1173-1182.
DOI: http://dx.doi.org/10.1145/1458082.1458237

[22] Chakrabarti, D., Kumar, R., Punera, K., 2008. «*A graph-theoretic approach to webpage segmentation*». Proceedings of the 17th international conference on World Wide Web, WWW'08, ACM, USA, 2008. Pages: 377-386. Publisher: ACM New York, NY, USA, 2008.
DOI: http://dx.doi.org/10.1145/1367497.1367549

[23] Liu, X., Lin, H., Tian, Y., 2011. "*Segmenting Webpage with Gomory-Hu Tree Based Clustering*", Journal of Software, Vol 6, No 12, Pages: 2421-2425. 2011.

Expression Recognition by Using Facial And Vocal Expressions

Gholamreza Anbarjafari
IMS Lab
Institute of Technology
University of Tartu
Tartu, Estonia
sjafari@ut.ee

Alvo Aabloo
IMS Lab
Institute of Technology
University of Tartu
Tartu, Estonia
alvo.aabloo@ut.ee

Abstract

Human behaviour may be monitored by analysing facial expressions and vocal expressions. Hence an automatic technique which combines both these features will give a more accurate overall estimation of expression. In this work we propose a new method which is uses facial and vocal features to estimate the expression of the subject. Facial expressions are analysed by extracting important facial features and then clustering the movement of these features. In parallel the voice is processed by using considering sudden changes in amplitude and frequency in order to recognize the expression. Finally a weighted sum rule is used to combine the decisions obtained by facial and vocal expression recognition. The proposed technique is tested on an ongoing set of real data monitored by a psychologist.

1 Introduction

Human-computer interaction has been centre of interest of many researchers for a number of years [1-3]. In order to facilitate this interaction it is essential for the computer system, for example a robot, to understand the feelings of the user [4, 5]. Recognition of emotions has been mainly achieved by using facial expression recognition [6, 7]. Techniques using k-nearest neighbour [8], hidden Makrov model (HMM) [9], and translation of belief model [10] have been frequently used for implementation of facial expression recognition.

Vocal expression recognition has also been used separately for expression recognition [11, 12]. The combination of both facial and vocal expression is novel and many researchers are investigating an intelligent model for this fusion [13]. One of the main issues with these techniques is the application of HMM as the hidden states are usually unknown and need to be estimated based on assumed probability distributions of the data [14]. In this work we are proposing a new expression recognition tech- nique which is using both facial and vocal expressions in order to estimate the expression of the speaker. The proposed technique is benefiting from the facial and vocal features. The proposed technique is evaluated with many volunteers sitting in front of a camera under controlled illumination reading texts with expressions of happiness, sadness, disgust, surprise, anger, fear, and contempt. The initial experimental results are promising showing that the proposed technique out performs other current techniques.

2 The Proposed Expression Recognition Technique

In the proposed technique two parallel observations are made. Firstly the facial features are detected using the Viola-Jones face detector. The important features are corners of lips, upper and lower part of lips, corners and centre of eyes, nose, nose tip, corners of eyebrows, and chin. Then movements of these facial features will be used in order to recognize each of the seven basic emotions. Fig. 1 is showing the important features on the facial image which are used for expression recognition.

Proceedings of the 25th International Conference on Computational Linguistics, pages 103–105,
Dublin, Ireland, August 23-29 2014.

Fig. 1: 20 important facial features which are being used for facial expression recognition.

In addition important features of the voice of the subject are analysed. First the system will be trained by a vocal input with neutral emotion. In order to recognise expression changes in the tone of the voice will be monitored by the sudden changes in amplitude and mid and high frequencies.

The extracted features from face and voice will be combined by using weighted sum in which the weights are being assigned by experts and can be modified. In the early experimental results, the normalize weights were 3/5 and 2/5 for face and voice respectively. More imporvement is expected to achieved if supported vector machine (SVM) is employeed for fusion of the facial and vocal features. The initial experiments conducted on the different volunteers are showing the exact recognition of expressions for sadness, happiness, surprise, and anger. However expressions of contempt and fear are not being recognized properly due to their high misinterpretation with other expressions. The primarly tests are conducted on a small datasets and on the continuation of the work a standard database containing both facial and vocal senarios will be used.

3 Conclusion

In this paper we were proposing a new technique for recognition of expressions by using facial and vocal expression recognition using weighted sum. The proposed technique has been tested on a small set of group of people. The early experimental results show the high potential of the proposal as an accurate expression recognition technique.

Reference

[reference stub]

1. Z. Obrenovic and D. Starcevic, "Modeling multimodal human-computer interaction", Computer, 2004, 37(9), 65- 72.
2. S. Benbelkacem, M. Belhocine, N. Zenati-Henda, A. Bellarbi, and M. Tadjine, "Integrating human-computer interaction and business practices for mixed reality systems design: a case study", IET Software, 2014, 8(2), 86-101.
3. A. Kucukyilmaz, T. M. Sezgin, and C. Basdogan, "Intention Recognition for Dynamic Role Exchange in Haptic Collaboration", IEEE Transaction on Haptics, 2013, 6(1), 56-68.
4. Y. Tie and L. Guan, "A Deformable 3-D Facial Expression Model for Dynamic Human Emotional State Recogni- tion", IEEE Transactions on Circuits and Systems for Video Technology, 2013, 23(1), 142-157.
5. M. Pantic and L. J. M. Rothkrantz, "Toward an affect-sensitive multimodal human-computer interaction", Pro- cessing of the IEEE, 2003, 91(9), 1370-1390.
6. M. S. Bartlett, G. Littlewort, M. G. Frank, C. Lainscsek, I. R. Fasel, and J. R. Movellan, "Automatic recognition of facial actions in spontaneous expressions", Journal of Multimedia, 2006, 1(6), 22–35.
7. J. F. Cohn, L. I. Reed, Z. Ambadar, J. Xiao, T. Moriyama, and T. Moriyama, "Automatic analysis and recognition of brow actions and head motion in spontaneous facial behavior", IEEE International Conference on Systems, Man and Cybernetics, 2004, 610–616.
8. M. Yeasin, B. Bullot, and R. Sharma, "From facial expression to level of interest: A spatio-temporal approach", IEEE Coference on Computer Vision and Pattern Recognition, 2004, 922–927.

9. I. Cohen, N. Sebe, A. Garg, L. S. Chen, and T. S. Huang, "Facial expression recognition from video sequences: temporal and static modeling", Computer Vision Image Understanding, 2003, 91(1-2), 160–187.

10. Z. Hammal and M. Kunz,"Pain monitoring: A dynamic and context-sensitive system", Pattern Recognition, 2012, 45(4), 1265–1280.

11. T. L. Nwe, S. W. Foo, and L. C. D. Silva, "Speech emotion recognition using hidden markov models", Speech Communication, 2003, 41(4), 603–623.

12. A. Nogueiras, A. Moreno, A. Bonafonte, and J. B. Marino, "Speech emotion recognition using hidden markov models", proceeding of INTER-SPEECH, 2001, 2679–2682.

13. H. Meng and N. Bianchi-Berthouze, "Affective State Level Recognition in Naturalistic Facial and Vocal Expres- sions", IEEE Transaction on Cybernetics, 2014, 44(3), 315-325.

14. F. Eyben, S. Petridis, B. Schuller, G. Tzimiropoulos, and S. Zafeiriou, "Audiovisual classification of vocal out- bursts in human conversation using long-short-term memory networks", International Conference on Acoustics, Speech and Signal Processing, 2011, 5844–5847.

Formulating Queries for Collecting Training Examples in Visual Concept Classification

Rami Albatal, Kevin McGuinness, Feiyan Hu, Alan F. Smeaton
Insight Centre for Data Analytics
Dublin City University
Glasnevin, Dublin 9, Ireland.
{rami.albatal}@insight-centre.org

Abstract

Video content can be automatically analysed and indexed using trained classifiers which map low-level features to semantic concepts. Such classifiers need training data consisting of sets of images which contain such concepts and recently it has been discovered that such training data can be located using text-based search to image databases on the internet. Formulating the text queries which locate these training images is the challenge we address here. In this paper we present preliminary results on TRECVid data of concept classification using automatically crawled images as training data and we compare the results with those obtained from manually annotated training sets.

1 Introduction

Content-based access to video archives is based on learning the presence of semantic concepts in video content by mapping low-level features like colour and texture, to high-level concepts. Concept classification is typically based on training classifiers on a set of annotated ground truth images (called a training set) containing positive and negative example images of a given semantic concept. The manual creation of training sets for each concept is a time-consuming and costly task. An alternative is to automatically gather training examples using available resources on the Internet. Several recent papers have demonstrated the effectiveness of such an approach. (Griffin, 2006) used search engine results to gather material for learning the appearance of categories, (Chatfield and Zisserman, 2013) shows that effective classifiers can be trained on-the-fly at query time using examples collected from Google Image search. The AXES research search engine (McGuinness et al., 2014) uses a combination of pre-trained classifiers and on-the-fly classifiers trained using examples from Google Image search. (Kordumova et al., 2014) investigate four practices for collecting training negative and positive examples from socially tagged videos and images.

The above work exploits the visual content of the collected example images while the question of how to formulate a textual query for collecting the data is not yet considered. It is important to note here that current search engines are not use content-based image classifiers, they are based the text from the embedding pages, and that is not always accurate or scalable. This represents a unique relationship between vision (the images used to train a concept classifier) and language (the text used to find those training images). In this work, we initiate a first step to addressing the problem of formulating text queries that collect positive example images for classifier training. This first step is based on querying web resources with single-term queries and comparing the classification results with those from manually annotated training sets. The results show the potential of automatic crawling and open the way for enhancing query formulation by adding external lexical or semantic resources.

Proceedings of the 25th International Conference on Computational Linguistics, pages 106–108,
Dublin, Ireland, August 23-29 2014.

2 Automatic gathering of training examples

Our goal is to create a framework for automatic training of classifiers by gathering training examples from available resources on the Internet. The steps for formulating a query are straightforward and widely-used in information retrieval, especially query expansion. First, an initial query is pre-processed by removing stop words and applying stemming techniques; then external lexical and/or semantic bases are explored in order to enrich the query and add useful terms which help in retrieving relevant training examples and excluding false positives. The resulting query is then posted to a search engine or image databases and the retrieved images are used as positive examples for a classification algorithm. Our plan is to use the Natural Language Toolkit (Bird et al., 2009) for stemming and stop words removal, and WordNet as external lexical base (Fellbaum, 1998).

3 Experiments and results

Experiments were conducted on the TRECVid (Smeaton et al., 2006) 2014 semantic indexing development data set. Single-term queries were posted to two data sources: Google Images, and ImageNet (an image database organized according to the nouns of the WordNet hierarchy where each node is depicted by an average of +500 images). Unlike results from Google Images, examples gathered from ImageNet are classified by human annotators, and are therefore a "purer" source of training images. To ensure a high-quality training set, we first search for the concept in ImageNet; if the concept does not exist in as an ImageNet visual category, we use images retrieved using a search for the term on Google Images.

We carried out two experiments to evaluate the performance of classifiers trained on manually annotated (internal) data provided by TRECVid versus data gathered from external sources. These external sources are search engines that retrieve images using textual queries, as explained in section2. The first experiment used data from the 2013x subset of the TRECVid 2014 development data and the second used external training data gathered as discussed above in the first paragraph of this section. Accuracy in both cases was evaluated using inferred average precision (infAP) on the 2013y subset of the development data. One-vs-all linear SVM classifiers were used for both experiments, trained on visual features extracted using pre-trained deep convolutional neural networks (CNN) using the Caffe software (Jia, 2013).

Classifiers for 34 of the 60 concepts were trained using data from ImageNet and the remaining using examples from Google Images. All classifiers trained using images from Google Images demonstrated poorer infAP than those trained on internal data. Of the 34 classifiers trained on ImageNet, 7 demonstrated improved infAP (*airplane, beach, bicycling, classroom, computers, dancing, flowers, highway*). In all cases it was possible to find more positive examples on ImageNet than in the internal set. Internal out-performed ImageNet in the remaining 27 cases. There were several possible reasons for this. In many cases there were fewer examples from ImageNet than in the internal set (12/27 cases) and in some cases the ImageNet examples were incorrect. For example, in the case of the concept *"hand"*, several synsets matching the term consisted entirely of wristwatches. Finally, in other cases, the concept text (the query) was either ambiguous or insufficiently semantically rich, for example *"greeting"* (greeting cards were retrieved) and *"government leader"* (smaller subset of such leaders in internal training data).

4 Hypothesis, challenges, and future work

The experiments indicate that automatically-gathered external training data can, in some cases, outperform annotated internal training data when it is sufficiently plentiful and of high quality. Using both high-quality external data and internal examples during training has the potential to improve results overall. A more sophisticated method of gathering external training examples that takes into account the semantics of the concept and of related concepts could provide even higher-quality external data. A significant challenge is in combining such semantic query expansion with visual analysis to ensure that the additional examples collected are relevant. This could potentially be achieved by bootstrapping a classifier on internal examples and then using this to classify external examples gathered by iterative semantic query expansion, updating the classifier model with each batch of accepted training examples.

References

Steven Bird, Ewan Klein, and Edward Loper. 2009. *Natural Language Processing with Python*. O'Reilly Media, Inc., 1st edition.

Ken Chatfield and Andrew Zisserman. 2013. Visor: Towards on-the-fly large-scale object category retrieval. In *Computer Vision ACCV 2012*, volume 7725 of *Lecture Notes in Computer Science*, pages 432–446.

Christiane Fellbaum, editor. 1998. *WordNet: an electronic lexical database*. MIT Press.

Lewis D Griffin. 2006. Optimality of the basic colour categories for classification. *Multimedia Tools and Applications*, 3.6:71–85.

Yangqing Jia. 2013. Caffe: An open source convolutional architecture for fast feature embedding. `http://caffe.berkeleyvision.org/`.

S. Kordumova, X. Li, and C. G. M. Snoek. 2014. Best practices for learning video concept detectors from social media examples. *Multimedia Tools and Applications*, pages 1–25, May.

Kevin McGuinness, Robin Aly, Ken Chatfield, Omkar Parkhi, Relja Arandjelovic, Matthijs Douze, Max Kemman, Martijn Kleppe, Peggy Van Der Kreeft, Kay Macquarrie, et al. 2014. The AXES research video search system. In *IEEE International Conference on Acoustics, Speech, and Signal Processing*.

Alan F Smeaton, Paul Over, and Wessel Kraaij. 2006. Evaluation campaigns and TRECVid. In *Proceedings of the 8th ACM international workshop on Multimedia information retrieval*, pages 321–330. ACM.

Towards Succinct and Relevant Image Descriptions

Desmond Elliott
Institute of Language, Communication, and Computation
School of Informatics
University of Edinburgh
d.elliott@ed.ac.uk

What does it mean to produce a *good* description of an image? Is a description good because it correctly identifies all of the objects in the image, because it describes the interesting attributes of the objects, or because it is short, yet informative? Grice's Cooperative Principle, stated as "Make your contribution such as is required, at the stage at which it occurs, by the accepted purpose or direction of the talk exchange in which you are engaged" (Grice, 1975), alongside other ideas of pragmatics in communication, have proven useful in thinking about language generation (Hovy, 1987; McKeown et al., 1995). The Cooperative Principle provides one possible framework for thinking about the generation and evaluation of image descriptions.[1]

The immediate question is whether automatic image description is within the scope of the Cooperative Principle. Consider the task of searching for images using natural language, where the purpose of the exchange is for the user to quickly and accurately find images that match their information needs. In this scenario, the user formulates a complete sentence query to express their needs, e.g. *A sheepdog chasing sheep in a field*, and initiates an exchange with the system in the form of a sequence of *one-shot* conversations. In this exchange, both participants can describe images in natural language, and a successful outcome relies on each participant succinctly and correctly expressing their beliefs about the images. It follows from this that we can think of image description as facilitating communication between people and computers, and thus take advantage of the Principle's maxims of Quantity, Quality, Relevance, and Manner in guiding the development and evaluation of automatic image description models.

An overview of the image description literature from the perspective of Grice's maxims can be found in Table 1. The most apparent ommission is the lack of research devoted to generating minimally informative descriptions: the maxim of Quantity. Attending to this maxim will become increasingly important as the quality and coverage of object, attribute, and scene detectors increases. It would be undesirable to develop models that describe every detected object in an image because that would be likely to violate the maxim of Quantity (Spain and Perona, 2010). Similarly, if it is possible to associate an accurate attribute with each object in the image, it will be important to be sparing in the application of those attributes: is it relevant to describe "furry" sheep when there are no sheared sheep in an image?

How should image description models be evaluated with respect to the maxims of the Cooperative Principle? So far model evaulation has focused on automatic text-based measures, such as Unigram BLEU and human judgements of *semantic correctness* (see Hodosh et al. (2013) for discussion of framing image description as a ranking task, and Elliott and Keller (2014) for a correlation analysis of text-based measures against human judgements). The semantic correctness judgements task typically present a variant of "Rate the relevance of the description for this image", which only evaluates the description vis-à-vis the maxim of Relevance. One exception is the study of Mitchell et al. (2012), in which judgements about the ordering of noun phrases (the maxim of Manner) were also collected. The importance of being able to evaluate according to multiple maxims becomes clearer as computer vision becomes more accurate. It seems intuitive that a model that describes and relates every object in the image could be characterised as generating Relevant and Quality descriptions, but not necessarily descriptions of

[1]This discussion primarily applies to image *descriptions*, and not to image *captions*. See (Hodosh et al., 2013) and (Panofsky, 1939) for a discussion of the differences between descriptions and captions.

Proceedings of the 25th International Conference on Computational Linguistics, pages 109–111,
Dublin, Ireland, August 23-29 2014.

Category	Maxim	Attention in the literature
Quantity	Be as informative as required	???
	Do not be more informative than required	???
Quality	Do not say what you believe is false Do not say that for which you lack evidence	All models exploit some kind of corpus data to construct descriptions that are maximally probable (Yang et al., 2011; Li et al., 2011; Kuznetsova et al., 2012; Le et al., 2013). These approaches typically use language modelling to construct hypotheses based on the available evidence, but may eventually be false.
Relevance	Be relevant	No models try to generate irrelevant descriptions. Dodge et al. (2012) explored the separation between what can be seen/not seen in an image/caption pair.
Manner	Avoid obscure expressions	No model has been deliberately obscure.
	Avoid ambiguity	Kulkarni et al. (2011) introduced visual attributes to describe and distinguish objects.
	Be brief	???
	Be orderly	Mitchell et al. (2012) and Elliott and Keller (2013) explicitly try to predict the best ordering of objects in the final description.

Table 1: An overview of Grice's maxims and the relevant image description models. ??? means that we are unaware of any models that implicitly or explicitly claim to address this type of maxim.

adequate Quantity. It is not clear that current human judgements capture this distinction, yet the gold-standard crowdsourced descriptions almost certainly do conform to the maxim of sufficient Quantity. A further important consideration is how to obtain human judgements for multiple maxims without making the studies prohibitively expensive.

Using Grice's maxims to think about image description from the perspective of enabling effective communication helps us reconsider the state of the art of automatic image description and directions for future research. In particular, we identified the open problems of determining the minimum and most relevant aspects of an image, and the challenges of conducting human evaluations along alternative dimensions to semantic correctness.

Acknowledgments

S. Frank, D. Frassinelli, and the anonymous reviewers provided valuable feedback on this paper. The research is funded by ERC Starting Grant SYNPROC No. 203427.

References

Jesse Dodge, Amit Goyal, Xufeng Han, Alyssa Mensch, Margaret Mitchell, Karl Stratos, Kota Yamaguchi, Yejin Choi, Hal Daumé III, Alex Berg, and Tamara Berg. 2012. Detecting visual text. In *Proceedings of the 2012 Conference of the North American Chapter of the Association for Computational Linguistics: Human Language Technologies*, pages 762–772, Montréal, Canada.

Desmond Elliott and Frank Keller. 2013. Image Description using Visual Dependency Representations. In *Proceedings of the 2013 Conference on Empirical Methods in Natural Language Processing*, pages 1292–1302, Seattle, Washington, U.S.A.

Desmond Elliott and Frank Keller. 2014. Comparing Automatic Evaluation Measures for Image Description. In *Proceedings of the 52nd Annual Meeting of the Association for Computational Linguistics*, pages 452–457, Baltimore, Maryland, U.S.A.

H. Paul Grice. 1975. Logic and Conversation. In P. Cole and J. L. Morgan, editors, *Syntax and Semantics 3: Speech Arts*, pages 41–58. Academic Press, Inc.

Micah Hodosh, Peter Young, and Julia Hockenmaier. 2013. Framing Image Description as a Ranking Task: Data, Models and Evaluation Metrics. *Journal of Artificial Intelligence Research*, 47:853–899.

E Hovy. 1987. Generating natural language under pragmatic constraints. *Journal of Pragmatics*, 11(6):689–719.

Girish Kulkarni, Visruth Premraj, Sagnik Dhar, Siming Li, Yejin Choi, Alexander C. Berg, and Tamara L. Berg. 2011. Baby talk: Understanding and generating simple image descriptions. In *2011 IEEE Conference on Computer Vision and Pattern Recognition*, pages 1601–1608, Colorado Springs, Colorado, U.S.A.

Polina Kuznetsova, Vicente Ordonez, Alexander C. Berg, Tamara L. Berg, and Yejin Choi. 2012. Collective Generation of Natural Image Descriptions. In *Proceedings of the 50th Annual Meeting of the Association for Computational Linguistics*, pages 359–368, Jeju Island, South Korea.

Dieu Thu Le, Jasper Uijlings, and Raffaella Bernardi. 2013. Exploiting language models for visual recognition. In *Proceedings of the 2013 Conference on Empirical Methods in Natural Language Processing*, pages 769–779, Seattle, Washington, U.S.A.

Siming Li, Girish Kulkarni, Tamara L. Berg, Alexander C. Berg, and Yejin Choi. 2011. Composing simple image descriptions using web-scale n-grams. In *Proceedings of the Fifteenth Conference on Computational Natural Language Learning*, pages 220–228, Portland, Oregon, U.S.A.

K McKeown, J Robin, and K Kukich. 1995. Generating concise natural language summaries. *Information Processing & Management*, 31(5):703–733.

Margaret Mitchell, Jesse Dodge, Amit Goyal, Kota Yamaguchi, Karl Stratos, Alyssa Mensch, Alex Berg, Tamara Berg, and Hal Daum. 2012. Midge : Generating Image Descriptions From Computer Vision Detections. In *Proceedings of the 13th Conference of the European Chapter of the Association for Computational Linguistics*, pages 747–756, Avignon, France.

Erwin Panofsky. 1939. *Studies in Iconology*. Oxford University Press.

Merrielle Spain and Pietro Perona. 2010. Measuring and Predicting Object Importance. *International Journal of Computer Vision*, 91(1):59–76.

Yezhou Yang, Ching Lik Teo, Hal Daumé III, and Yiannis Aloimonos. 2011. Corpus-Guided Sentence Generation of Natural Images. In *Proceedings of the Conference on Empirical Methods in Natural Language Processing*, pages 444–454, Edinburgh, Scotland, UK.

Coloring Objects: Adjective-Noun Visual Semantic Compositionality

Dat Tien Nguyen[1,2] **Angeliki Lazaridou**[2] **Raffaella Bernardi**[2]
[1]EM LCT, [2]University of Trento/ Italy
name.surname@unitn.it

Abstract

This paper reports preliminary experiments aiming at verifying the conjecture that semantic compositionality is a general process irrespective of the underlying modality. In particular, we model compositionality of an attribute with an object in the visual modality as done in the case of an adjective with a noun in the linguistic modality. Our experiments show that the concept topologies in the two modalities share similarities, results that strengthen our conjecture.

1 Language and Vision

Recently, fields like computational linguistics and computer vision have converged to a common way of capturing and representing the linguistic and visual information of atomic concepts, through vector space models. At the same time, advances in computational semantics have lead to effective and linguistically inspired approaches of extending such methods from single concepts to arbitrary linguistic units (e.g. phrases), through means of vector-based semantic composition (Mitchell and Lapata, 2010).

Compositionality is not to be considered only an important component from a linguistic perspective, but also from a cognitive perspective and there has been efforts to validate it as a general cognitive process. However, in computer vision so far compositionality has received limited attention. Thus, in this work, we study the phenomenon of *visual compositionality* and we complement limited previous literature that has focused on event compositionality (Stöttinger et al., 2012) or general image structure (Socher et al., 2011), by studying models of attribute-object semantic composition.

In a nutshell, our work consists of learning vector representations of attribute-object (e.g., "red car", "cute dog" etc.) and objects (e.g., "car", "dog", "truck", "cat" etc.) and by using those compute the representation of new objects having similar attributes ("red truck", "cute cat" etc.). This question has both theoretical and applied impact. The possibility of developing a visual compositional model of attribute-object, on the one hand, could shed light on the acquisition of such ability in humans; how we learn attribute representation and compose them with different objects is still an open question within the cognitive science community (Mintz and Gleitman, 2002). On the other hand, computer vision systems could become generative and be able to recognize unseen attribute-object combinations, a component especially useful for object recognition and image retrieval.

2 Visual Compositional Model

As our source of inspiration regarding the type of compositionality, we use the *Lexical Functional* model (LF) (Baroni and Zamparelli, 2010), under which adjectives, in linguistic compositionality, are represented as linear functions (i.e., matrix of weights). Concretely, each adjective function f^W_{adj} is induced from corpus-observed vectors of adjective-noun phrases $w_i \in W_{phrase}$ and noun $w_j \in W_{noun}$, e.g., $\langle (w_{red\ car}, w_{car}), (w_{red\ flag}, w_{flag}), \ldots \rangle$, by solving the least-squares regression problem:

$$\arg\min_{f^W_{adj} \in \mathbb{R}^{d \times d}} ||W_{phrase} - f^W_{adj} W_{noun}||$$

Proceedings of the 25th International Conference on Computational Linguistics, pages 112–114,
Dublin, Ireland, August 23-29 2014.

In this work, we propose to import the LF method in the visual modality, aiming at developing a *Visual Compositional Model*. Similarly to the case of linguistic compositionality, each attribute function f^V_{attr} is induced from image-harvested vector representations of attribute-object $v_i \in V_{phrase}$ and object $v_j \in V_{object}$, e.g. for training the function f^V_{red} the following data can be used $\langle(v_{red\ car}, v_{car}), (v_{red\ flag}, v_{flag}), \ldots\rangle$.

3 Experiments

The visual representations of attribute-objects and objects are created with the PHOW-color features (Bosch et al., 2007) and SIFT color-agnostic features (Lowe, 2004) respectively. The linguistic representations for the adjective-noun W_{phrase} and noun W_{noun} are built with the word2vec toolkit[1] using a corpus of 3 billion tokens.[2] Both visual and linguistic representations consist of 300 dimensions.

In this work, we focus on attributes related to 10 colors (Russakovsky and Fei-Fei, 2012) for a total number of 9699 images depicting 202 unique objects/nouns and 886 unique phrases (attribute-object/adjective-noun). Our experiments are conducted with *aggregated attribute-object* representations obtained by summing the visual vectors extracted from images representing the same attribute-object, The same pipeline is followed for the objects to obtain *aggregated object* vectors.

This work aims at comparing the behavior of the semantically-driven compositionality process across the two modalities. For this reason, we report results on the intersection of V_{phrase} and W_{phrase}, a process that results in 266 attribute-object/adjective-noun items. Furthermore, although the training data for the two modalities are different, the size of the training data is identical, i.e., the f^V_{attr} is trained using the remaining 620 attribute-object items, whereas for the f^W_{adj}, we randomly sample 620 adjective-noun items from the language space.

3.1 Analysis of Language and Visual Semantic Spaces

This experiment aims at assessing the degree to which language and vision share commonalities. To this end, we compute the cosine similarities between all possible combination of objects (resp., nouns) and perform a correlation analysis of the similarity of the corresponding pairs in the two lists resulting in **0.45** Spearman correlation – e.g., we correlate the similarity between v_{cat} and v_{dog} with that between w_{cat} and w_{dog}. For instance, "goat" and "sheep" are highly similar in both spaces, whereas "whale" and "bird" are similar only linguistically, whereas "blackboard" and "chair" are similar only visually. The same experiment is performed between all possible combinations of attribute-object/adjective-noun items, e.g. we correlate the similarity between $v_{white\ cat}$ and $v_{black\ dog}$ with that between $w_{white\ cat}$ and $w_{black\ dog}$, resulting in **0.33** Spearman correlation (see Table 1).

Overall, our results suggest that the topologies of the semantic spaces are similar in the two modalities. Furthermore, since this phenomenon is also apparent in the cases of attribute-object and adjective-noun pairs, this alludes to the possibility of transferring approaches of semantic compositionality from the linguistic to the visual modality.

	High Visual	**Low Visual**
High Linguistic	goat-sheep, jaguar- lion black bag - brown bag, brown bear - yellow dog	baboon-transporter, bird-whale blue grass - blue van, gray whale - white deer
Low Linguistic	ball-horse, blackboard-chair red strawberry - white ball, white bear - yellow dog	baboon-sofa, backboard-panda black bag - green bridge, green table - yellow stick

Table 1: Similar and dissimilar concepts in the language and vision space.

3.2 Semantically-driven composition for attribute-object representations

The findings of the previous experiment suggest a high correlation between the visual attribute-attribute representations and the corpus-harvested adjective-noun representations. An interesting question that arises is whether we could approximate such visual representations of complex visual units, similarly to

[1] https://code.google.com/p/word2vec/

[2] http://wacky.sslmit.unibo.it, http://www.natcorp.ox.ac.uk

how is done in Computational Linguistics for approximating the text-based representations of adjective-noun phrases. Thus, this experiment is designed in order to assess the validity of the semantically-driven compositionality approach in the visual domain. Results are reported in Table 2. Since we expect that the quality of the aggregated vectors depends on the numbers of available images, we report results for subsets of the original data set that differ on the number of images per phrase.

By means of the LF composition method sketched in Section 2, we obtain the compositional representations of attribute-object (V^{comp}_{phrase}) and adjective-noun (W^{comp}_{phrase}) items. We then perform the correlation analyses between the similarities obtained in the composed visual space V^{comp}_{phrase} with: 1) the equivalent image-harvested representations V_{phrase}, 2) the equivalent corpus-derived linguistic representations W_{phrase}, 3) the equivalent compositionally-derived linguistic representations W^{comp}_{phrase}.

Overall, the correlation between V^{comp}_{space} and V_{space} suggests that the visual compositionality of attribute-object can account, to some extend, for the visual semantics of the respective image, and it further improves with the number of images we consider for obtaining the *aggregated vectors* of the visual phrases. Finally, as expected, the correlations between V^{comp}_{space} although lower than the ones reported in Section 3.1, i.e., 0.22 vs 0.32, are still non negligible.

	all phrases	$>$ 10 images	$>$ 20 images	$>$ 30 images
V^{comp}_{phrase} - V_{phrase}	0.24	0.40	0.53	**0.58**
V^{comp}_{phrase} - W_{phrase}	0.10	0.22	0.19	**0.23**
V^{comp}_{phrase} - W^{comp}_{phrase}	0.04	0.05	**0.18**	0.10

Table 2: Spearman correlations between the similarities in the V^{comp}_{phrase} and other semantic spaces.

4 Conclusions

In this work, we have experimented with semantically-driven compositionality of attributes with objects in the visual modality, by adopting an out-of-the-box composition method from the computational semantics literature. Our preliminary results have shown that the visual representations of attribute-objects when obtained compositionally reflect properties similar not only to the ones found in representations harvested automatically from images, but also from those extracted from text corpora. These results show that semantic compositionality might be a general process irrespective of the underlying modality. We have just scratched the surface on this topic and in the future we plan to experiment with a larger variety of attributes and use and design alternative visual compositional models.

Acknowledgements

The second and third author acknowledge ERC 2011 Starting Independent Research Grant n. 283554 (COMPOSES). We thank the 3 anonymous reviewers for their comments, Marco Baroni and Elia Bruni for their constant and useful feedback.

References

[Baroni and Zamparelli2010] Marco Baroni and Roberto Zamparelli. 2010. Nouns are vectors, adjectives are matrices: Representing adjective-noun constructions in semantic space. In *Proceedings of EMNLP*, 1183–1193.

[Bosch et al.2007] Anna Bosch, Andrew Zisserman, and Xavier Munoz. 2007. Image classification using random forests and ferns. In *Proceedings of ICCV*, 1–8.

[Lowe2004] David G Lowe. 2004. Distinctive image features from scale-invariant keypoints. *International Journal of Computer Vision*, 60:91–110.

[Mintz and Gleitman2002] Toben H. Mintz and Lila R. Gleitman. 2002. Adjectives really do modify nouns: the incremental and restricted nature of early adjective acquisition. *Cognition*, 84:267–293.

[Mitchell and Lapata2010] Jeff Mitchell and Mirella Lapata. 2010. Composition in distributional models of semantics. *Cognitive Science*, 34(8):1388–1429.

[Russakovsky and Fei-Fei2012] Olga Russakovsky and Li Fei-Fei. 2012. Attribute learning in large-scale datasets. In *Trends and Topics in Computer Vision*, 1–14. Springer.

[Socher et al.2011] Richard Socher, Cliff C Lin, Chris Manning, and Andrew Y Ng. 2011. Parsing natural scenes and natural language with recursive neural networks. In *Proceedings of ICML*, 129–136.

[Stöttinger et al.2012] J. Stöttinger, J.R.R. Uijlings, A.K. Pandey, N. Sebe, and F. Giunchiglia. 2012. (unseen) event recognition via semantic compositionality. In *CVPR*.

Multi-layered Image Representation for Image Interpretation

Marina Ivasic-Kos, Miran Pobar, Ivo Ipsic
Department of Informatics
University of Rijeka
R. Matejcic 2, Rijeka, Croatia
{marina, mpobar, ivoi}@uniri.hr

Abstract

In order to bridge the semantic gap between the visual context of an image and semantic concepts people would use to interpret it, we propose a multi-layered image representation model considering different amounts of knowledge needed for the interpretation of the image at each layer. Interpretation results on different semantic layers of Corel images related to outdoor scenes are presented and compared. Obtained results show positive correlation of precision and recall with the abstract level of classes used for image annotation, i.e. more generalized classes have achieved better results.

1 Introduction

Image captions and surrounding text can facilitate the retrieval of images if they exist, but the vast majority of images are not annotated with words. A number of methods have been developed in recent years to automatically annotate images with words that users might intuitively use when searching for them. This problem is challenging because different people will most likely interpret the same image with different words on different levels of abstraction. Used words reflect their knowledge about the context of the image, experience, cultural background, etc.

On the other hand, annotation methods deal with visual features such as color, texture and shape that can be extracted from raw image data, so the major goal is to bridge the semantic gap between the available features and the interpretation of the images in the way humans do. The idea is to define an image representation model that will reflect the semantic levels of words used in image interpretation.

2 Multi-layered Image Representation

Among the oldest models of image interpretation is Shatford's (1986) model that suggests image content classification into general, specific and abstract. Eakins and Graham (2000) have defined three semantic layers of image interpretation considering the context of image search. The first layer corresponds to the presence of certain combinations of low-level features, the second to the types of objects and the third to descriptions of events, activities, locations or emotions that one can associate with the image.

We propose an image representation model that follows the simplified hierarchical model of (Hare et al,. 2006) that captures the layers between the two extremes, the "raw" data of the image and its full semantics. Such image representation includes the visual content of an image and the concepts used to interpret it on different layers of image representation, Fig.1. The initial layer of representation of an image is the layer V_0, representing the raw image. The image is usually segmented (layer V_1) using methods for automatic image segmentation or into a grid. The low-level features are then extracted from the image segments (layer V_2).

The next four layers, MI_1 to MI_4, are related to different levels of semantic interpretation. The semantics includes elementary classes - EC into which image segments are classified, classes that describe the scene - SC, generalization classes - GC and derived classes – DC, organized in a hierarchy as shown in Fig 1.

Proceedings of the 25th International Conference on Computational Linguistics, pages 115–117,
Dublin, Ireland, August 23-29 2014.

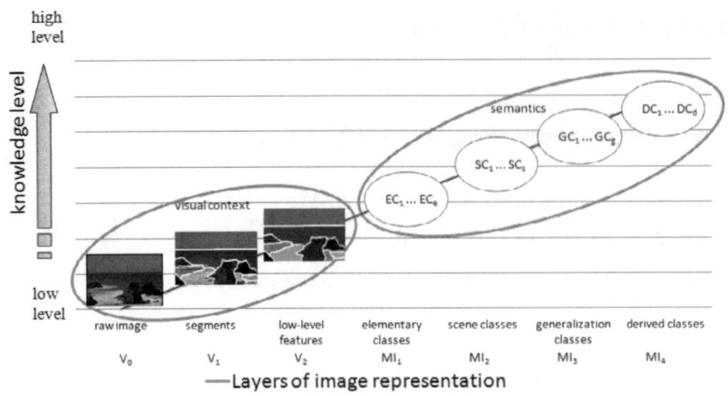

Fig. 1. Layers of image representation in relation to the knowledge level

Elementary classes correspond to objects that can be recognised in an image, like sky, water and rock for image in Fig. 1. Scene classes represent the context of the whole image, like seaside, and can be either directly obtained as a result of global classification of image features or inferred from the elementary classes. Generalization classes are defined as a generalization of scene classes, like scenery, natural scene and outdoor scene. Between generalisation classes the aggregation or generalization relation is defined. Derived classes include abstract concepts that can be associated with an image, like specific place such as the island of Cres, or emotion e.g. solitude.

The amount of knowledge required for segmentation and extraction of features in layers V_1 and V_2 is low, while the amount of knowledge required for interpreting the image in the semantic layers MI_1 to MI_4 increases. Most automatic image annotation methods are generative or discriminative models (Zhang, et al., 2012) and work with image interpretation at layers MI_1 and MI_2. For image interpretation at layers MI_3 and MI_4 knowledge representation models and a reasoning engine are needed.

3 Experiment

Our goal was to compare image interpretation results on different semantic layers. We have used a part of the Corel image database related to outdoor scenes. The data set consisted of 500 images segmented with the n-cuts algorithm. For each image segment a 16D feature vector $\boldsymbol{x}$ was computed based on CIE L*a*b* colour model and geometric properties (size, position, height, width and shape of the area) of image segments (Duygulu et al., 2002). The segments were labeled with one of the 28 keywords related to natural and artificial objects such as 'airplane', 'bird', 'lion', 'train' etc. and background objects like 'ground', 'sky', 'water' etc. The keywords correspond to the elementary classes. Some image segments were too small and couldn't be labeled manually and were excluded from data.

The final data set used for the experiment consists of 3960 segments. The data was divided into training (3160) and testing (800) subsets by a 10-fold cross validation with 20% of the observations for the holdout cross-validation.

For image classification into elementary classes Bayesian classifier was used according to the maximum posterior probability (c_{MAP}):

$$c_{MAP} = \underset{EC_i \in EC}{argmax} \frac{P(\boldsymbol{x}|EC_i)\, P(EC_i)}{P(\boldsymbol{x})}. \quad (1)$$

The conditional probability $P(\boldsymbol{x}|EC_i)$ of a feature vector $\boldsymbol{x}$ for the given elementary classes $EC_i \in EC$ and the prior probability $P(EC_i), \forall EC_i \in EC$ are estimated according to data in the training set. It is taken into account that the evidence factor is a scale factor that does not influence the classification results and is not calculated.

The results of the image-segments classification are compared with the ground truth and the precision and recall measures are calculated. The achieved average precision for classification of elementary classes is 32.6% and average recall is 27.5%.

To predict concepts on layers MI_2 and higher we have used the knowledge representation scheme based on fuzzy Petri nets with an integrated fuzzy inference engine (Ribaric and Pavesic, 2009). The fuzzy knowledge base contains the following main components: fuzzy spatial and co-occurrence relationships between elementary classes, fuzzy aggregation relationships between elementary classes and scene classes, and fuzzy generalization relationships between scene classes and generalization classes. The knowledge chunks considering spatial and co-occurrence relationships as well as aggregation relationships are computed from the training set. The training set is also used to estimated the truth of these relationships. The hierarchical and generalization relationships are defined according to expert knowledge and so is their truth. There were 15 scene classes defined in the knowledge base such as Scene Lion, Scene Shuttle and Seaside and 13 generalization classes on different levels of abstraction, such as Wild Cats, Wildlife, Natural Scene, and Man-Made Objects.

The obtained results show positive correlation of precision and recall with the abstract level of semantic concepts used for image interpretation. For scene classes achieved results are little bit higher than for elementary classes, with precision of 37% and 31% for recall. For generalised classes the obtained results are significantly better, with precision of 52% and recall of 42%.

In Table 1, some positive examples of a multilayered image interpretation following the proposed model are shown.

Image example:		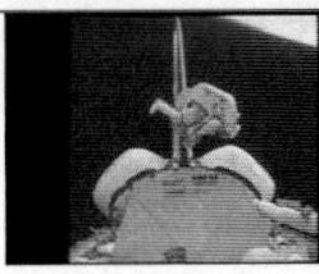			
Multi-layered image interpretation	MI_1	'shuttle'	'train', 'tracks ', 'sky' -	'grass', 'tiger'	'water', 'sand', 'sky', 'road'
	MI_2	'Scene Shuttle',	'Scene Train',	'Scene Tiger',	'Seaside',
	MI_3	'Vehicle', 'Man-Made Object', 'Outdoor'	'Vehicle', 'Man-Made Object', 'Outdoor'	'Wildcat', 'Wildlife', 'Natural Scenes', 'Outdoor Scene'	'Natural Scenes', 'Outdoor Scene'
	MI_4	'Space'	'Transport'	-	'Vacation'

Table 1. Examples of multilayered image interpretation

4 Conclusion

The suggested model of image representation corresponds to the interpretation of images that are inherent to humans. It involves image interpretation at different semantic levels. For each semantic level we tested interpretation accuracy on outdoor scenes and positive correlations of precision and recall with respect to the abstract level of semantic concepts were obtained.

Reference

P. Duygulu, K. Barnard, J. F. G. de Freitas, and D. A. Forsyth. 2002. *Object recognition as machine translation: Learning a lexicon for a fixed image vocabulary*, ECCV 2002, UK, pp. 97–112.

J. Eakins and M. Graham. 2000. *Content-based image retrieval.* Technical Report JTAP-039, JISC, Institute for Image Data Research, University of Northumbria, Newcastle.

J. S. Hare, P. H. Lewis, P. G. B. Enser and C. J. Sandom. 2006. Mind the Gap: *Another look at the problem of the semantic gap in image retrieval.* Multimedia Content Analysis, Management and Retrieval, USA.

S. Ribaric and N. Pavesic. 2009. Inference Procedures for Fuzzy Knowledge Representation Scheme, Applied Artificial Intelligence, vol. 23, 2009, pp. 16-43.

D. Zhang, M. M. Islam and G. Lu. 2012. *A review on automatic image annotation techniques*. Pattern Recognition, 45(1), 346-362.

The Last 10 Metres: Using Visual Analysis and Verbal Communication in Guiding Visually Impaired Smartphone Users to Entrances

Anja Belz
Computing, Engineering and Maths
University of Brighton
Lewes Road, Brighton BN2 4GJ, UK
a.s.belz@brighton.ac.uk

Anil Bharath
Department of Bioengineering
Imperial College London
Prince Consort Road, London SW7 2BP, UK
a.bharath@imperial.ac.uk

1 Introduction

Blindness and partial sight are increasing, due to changing demographics and greater incidence of diseases such as diabetes, at vast financial and human cost (WHO, 2013). Organisations for the visually impaired stress the importance of independent living, of which safe and independent travel is an integral part. While existing smartphone facilities such as Apple's Siri are encouraging, the supporting localisation services are not sufficiently accurate or precise to enable navigation between e.g. a bus stop or taxi rank and the entrance to a public space such as a hospital, supermarket or train station.

In this paper, we report plans and progress to date of research addressing 'the problem of the Last 10 Metres.' We are developing methods for safely guiding users not just to the general vicinity of a target destination (as done by GPS-based services), but right up to the main entrance of the target destination, by a combination of semantically and visually enriched maps, visual analysis, and language generation.

2 Overview

The core task is to help users navigate approach paths to building entrances. Navigation guidance is delivered via a smartphone app with voice and haptic output. The app uses detailed, semantically tagged maps in which public buildings (museums, schools, hospitals, etc.) and the pavements, landmarks and other visual cues found in the approaches to their entrances (See Figure 2) are annotated. The maps differ from existing resources in that they have (i) more detailed information on pedestrian-relevant features, including obstructions and hazards, and (ii) computational descriptions of 'visual paths,' i.e. information about approach paths to entrances including image sequencess taken along the path (visual cues).

The navigation app provides guidance from the point where a GPS-based system drops the user: theoretically within 10m of a destination building, but in reality, anything up to a few hundred metres away from the actual building entrance. Our research is focused on developing a novel pedestrian guidance system that uses semantically and visually enriched maps, visual cues from user-generated live-feed video, and verbal and haptic communication to guide visually impaired pedestrians during the last few metres to the entrance of their destination, dropping them not just somewhere near, say, the British Museum, but more precisely and much more challengingly, right in front of the museum's main entrance.

3 Usage Scenario

The user employs their usual GPS-based app to get near a target destination, then our Last 10m app takes over: (1) User requests guidance to an entrance to their target building; (2) System retrieves relevant local map from server; (3) System converts guidance request to a specific target entrance T annotated on map; (4) Given location of T on map, system determines location U of user on map; (5) System computes approach path P from U to T; (6) System starts guiding user along P; at the same time system carries out continuous monitoring of user behaviour and surroundings, interacting with user as necessary: (a) System monitors that user stays on track; (b) System monitors path ahead to identify any obstacles; (c) System issues warnings and update information as necessary, and deals with user requests, e.g. information about an object detected by the user, location updates or output modality changes.

Proceedings of the 25th International Conference on Computational Linguistics, pages 118–120,
Dublin, Ireland, August 23-29 2014.

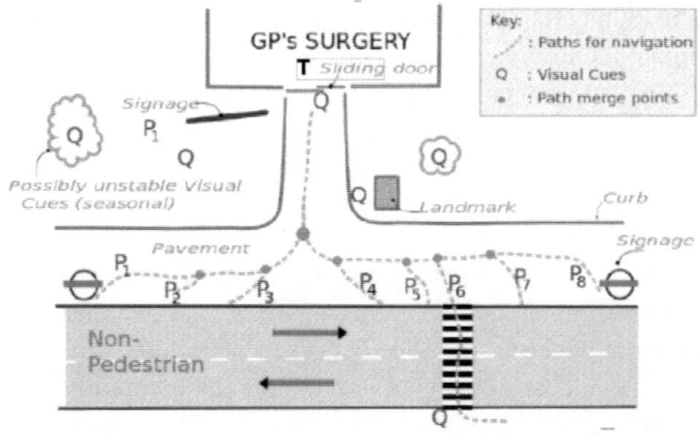

Figure 1: Illustration of the navigational context that we are addressing.

4 Key Challenges

4.1 Mapping Challenges

Semantically enriched local maps: Using OpenStreetMap,[1] which already includes many different kinds of relevant 'urban' tags such as 'tree', 'bus_stop', 'post_box', 'traffic_signals', etc., as a starting point, we are investigating ways of involving some of the 1.5 million volunteer mappers to create a new OSM layer of highly fine-grained local information and snapshots of visual cues.

Computing path from U to T: Adapting methods developed for similar purposes (Zeng et al., 2008), compute geometric paths from U to T; if necessary recompute these paths on the fly on the basis of obstacles that have been detected (see below).

4.2 Vision Challenges

Locating user on map based on visual cues: The task is to locate the user precisely on the map (within a given radius determined on the basis of GPS output) by identifying landmarks and visual cues in user-generated live feed and matching these to the tags and images in the semantically enriched local maps. In a pilot study (Rivera-Rubio et al., 2013), conducted within indoor, but highly ambiguous corridors, we have found that with relatively modest processes, paths can be distinguished with reasonable certainty using visual cues alone. In more extensive tests, verified with surveying equipment (Rivera-Rubio et al., 2014), we found that user location on a path can be inferred from hand-held and wearable cameras.

Continuous route monitoring: (a) monitoring of path ahead to identify obstacles and other danger using computer vision techniques and map information, (b) monitoring actual path against target path, updating target path and adapting instructions to user as necessary. Monitoring is based on local maps, visual information obtained on the fly (Davison et al., 2007; Alcantarilla et al., 2010; Pradeep and Medioni, 2010) from smartphone camera live feeds, as well as information from inertial sensors, etc.

4.3 Communication Challenges

While 'smart canes' are promising technological improvements for visually impaired (VI) navigation, our research has shown that the VI community sharply divides into white cane users and guide dog owners, with the latter category in particular objecting to the use of a white cane. For this reason we are focusing on smartphone apps delivering verbal and haptic output (which is suitable for both types of users). We view the main communication challenges to be the following.

Interaction Management: Managing (a) the interaction between user and system, including allowing user interrupts and system alerts, and (b) any resulting changes to system behaviour. This includes allowing the user to input navigation and configuration options for the route before or during the journey.

Communicating navigation guidance: In the absence of interrupts from the continuous route monitoring processes described above, the system communicates route guidance along the target path to the user. We will carry out detailed requirements analyses to determine what kind of instructions and what

[1] http://www.openstreetmap.org

level of detail are most useful. While the assumption is that most instructions are best communicated via brief spoken outputs, a core question is what part of the guidance can be delivered by haptic output, e.g. different types/locations of vibration indicating different direction/speed of movement.

Communicating warnings: The properties required of warnings differ from navigation guidance, in that the nature of the danger and the required user reaction need to be conveyed as quickly and as efficiently as possible, with information ordered in terms of urgency. It is likely that a larger proportion of warnings (than of navigation instructions) are best conveyed by haptic and simple audio output.

Communicating uncertainty: If the system detects a hazard in the path ahead, identification of the type of hazard and appropriate user action will come with a confidence measure < 1. The degree of uncertainty in what the system has identified must be conveyed to the user. E.g. if a postbox is tagged in the map, and the continuous monitoring component has detected an object ahead that it has recognised with high confidence as a postbox, then it may be enough to simply steer the user around it. However, if the system detects an obstruction at head height which is not annotated in the map and which it classifies with similar confidence levels as several things, then this uncertainty has to be expressed in the verbal output, and the user may have to further investigate.

Communicating varying levels of detail: Similarly, when describing a hazard or verbalising route guidance, not all the detail about objects and routes available to the system needs to be conveyed to the user in every situation. For this purpose the system design incorporates a content selection component (CSC) which decides the appropriate level of detail given the context.

A suitable way to generate verbal output in line with the above communication requirements is probabilistic natural language generation (NLG) technology (Belz, 2008) which offers the possibility of automatically training the verbal output generator to adapt to different user requirements and usage contexts.

5 Current Work

We are currently in the early stages of developing the various components of the Last 10m system. We have carried out preliminary experiments in indoors path recognition identification (Rivera-Rubio et al., 2013; 2014), and conducted initial consultation sessions with VI people. The next step is to design Wizard-of-Oz experiments in order to obtain sizeable corpora of example instructions (produced by humans playing the role of the system) appropriate in a variety of contexts which is then used both for training NLG components and for other aspects of system design. At the same time we are improving the path computation algorithms (which provide important input to the CSC), using, for the time being, a small number of semantically and visually enriched local maps of entrances at our universities.

References

P. F. Alcantarilla, L. M. Bergasa, and F. Dellaert. 2010. Visual odometry priors for robust EKF-SLAM. In *Proceedings of the 2010 IEEE International Conference on Robotics and Automation*, pages 3501–3506.

A. Belz. 2008. Automatic generation of weather forecast texts using comprehensive probabilistic generation-space models. *Natural Language Engineering*, 14(4):431–455.

A. Davison, I. D. Reid, N. D. Molton, and O. Stasse. 2007. MonoSLAM: Real-time single camera SLAM. *IEEE Transactions on Pattern Analysis and Machine Intelligence*, 29(6):1052–1067.

V. Pradeep and G. Medioni. 2010. Robot vision for the visually impaired. In *Proceedings of the 2010 Computer Vision and Pattern Recognition Workshop (CVPR)*, pages 15–22.

J. Rivera-Rubio, S. Idrees, I. Alexiou, L. Hadjilucas, and A.A. Bharath. 2013. Mobile visual assistive apps: Benchmarks of vision algorithm performance. In *New Trends in Image Analysis and Processing (ICIAP 2013)*, volume 8158 of *Lecture Notes in Computer Science*, pages 30–40.

J. Rivera-Rubio, I. Alexiou, A.A. Bharath, R. Secoli, Dickens, and E. Lupu. 2014. Associating locations from wearable cameras. In *Proceedings of the 25th British Machine Vision Conference*. To Appear.

WHO. 2013. Visual impairment and blindness. Fact Sheet No. 282, World Health Organization.

Q. Zeng, C. L. Teo, B. Rebsamen, and E. Burdet. 2008. Collaborative path planning for a robotic wheelchair. *Disability and Rehabilitation Assistive Technology*, 3(6):315–324.

Keyphrase Extraction using Textual and Visual Features*

Yaakov HaCohen-Kerner[1], Stefanos Vrochidis[2], Dimitris Liparas[2], Anastasia Moumtzidou[2], Ioannis Kompatsiaris[2]

[1] Dept. of Computer Science, Jerusalem College of Technology – Lev Academic Center, 21 Havaad Haleumi St., P.O.B. 16031, 9116001 Jerusalem, Israel, kerner@jct.ac.il
[2] Information Techologies Institute, Centre for Research and Technology Hellas, Thermi-Thessaloniki, Greece, {stefanos, dliparas, moumtzid, ikom}@iti.gr

Abstract

Many current documents include multimedia consisting of text, images and embedded videos. This paper presents a general method that uses Random Forests to automatically extract keyphrases that can be used as very short summaries and to help in retrieval, classification and clustering processes.

1 Introduction

A keyphrase is an important concept, presented either as a single word (unigram), e.g.: 'extraction', 'keyphrase' or as a collocation, i.e., a meaningful group of two or more words, e.g.: 'keyphrase extraction'. Keyphrases can be regarded as very short summaries and can be used for representing documents in retrieval, classification and clustering problems.

Nowadays, many documents (e.g. web pages, articles) include multimedia consisting of text, images and embedded videos. In this case, the keyphrase extraction process should not be limited to the textual data but also consider the audiovisual data.

In this context, this paper proposes a novel framework for automatic keyphrase extraction from documents containing text and images based on supervised learning and textual and visual features.

2 Baseline Methods for Keyphrase Extraction

In this section, we introduce the baseline methods we use for keyphrase extraction using textual and visual information.

2.1 Textual Keyprhase Extraction

In all methods, words and terms that have a grammatical role for the language are excluded from the key words list according to Fox's stop list. This stop list contains 421 high frequency stop list words (e.g.: we, this, and, when, in, usually, also, near).

(1) **Term Frequency (TF):** This method rates a term according to the number of its occurrences in the text. Only the N terms with the highest TF in the document are selected.

(2) **Term length (TL):** TL rates a term according to the number of the words included in the term.

(3) **First N Terms (FN)**: Only the first N terms in the document are selected. The assumption is that the most important keyphrases are found at the beginning of the document because people tend to place important information at the beginning. This method is based on the baseline summarization method which chooses the first N sentences. This simple method provides a relatively strong baseline for the performance of any text-summarization method.

(4) **Last N Terms (LN)**: Only the last N terms in the document are selected. The assumption is that the most important keyphrases are found at the end of the document because people tend to place their important keyphrases in their conclusions which are usually placed near to the end.

Proceedings of the 25th International Conference on Computational Linguistics, pages 121–123, Dublin, Ireland, August 23-29 2014.

(5) **At the Beginning of its Paragraph (PB):** This method rates a term according to its relative position in its paragraph. The assumption is that the most important keyphrases are likely to be found close to the beginning of their paragraphs.
(6) **At the End of its Paragraph (PE):** This method rates a term according to its relative position in its paragraph. The assumption is that the most important keyphrases are likely to be found close to end of their paragraphs.
(7) **Resemblance to Title (RT)**: This method rates a term according to the resemblance of its sentence to the title of the article. Sentences that resemble the title will be granted a higher score.
(8) **Maximal Section Headline Importance (MSHI):** This method rates a term according to its most important presence in a section or headline of the article. It is a known that some parts of papers are more important from the viewpoint of presence of keyphrases. Such parts can be headlines and sections as: abstract, introduction and conclusions.
(9) **Accumulative Section Headline Importance (ASHI):** This method is very similar to the previous one. However, it rates a term according to all its presences in important sections or headlines of the article.
(10) **Negative Brackets (NBR):** Phrases found in brackets are not likely to be keyphrases. Therefore, they are defined as negative phrases, and will grant negative scores.

These methods were applied to extract and learn keyphrases from scientific articles (HaCohen-Kerner et al., 2005).

2.2 Visual Keyprhase Extraction

On the other hand, visual keyphrase extraction is performed for a pre-defined set of keyphrases (e.g. demonstration, moving car, etc.). The predefined keyphrases are selected in order to be relevant to the domain of interest. In the following, low level visual features (SIFT, SURF) are extracted (Markatopoulou, et al., 2013). We apply supervised machine learning using Random Forests (RF) (Breiman, 2001) to detect the presence of each concept in an image. RF have been successfully applied to several image classification problems (e.g. (Bosch et al., 2007; Xu et al., 2012)). Moreover, an important motivation for using RF was the application of late fusion based on the RF operational capabilities, which is discussed below.

In the training phase, the feature vectors from each low level feature vector are used as input for the construction of a single RF. The training set can be constructed either manually or automatically. In the automatic case, we submit a text query to a general purpose web search engine (e.g. Google, Bing) to retrieve relevant images, while irrelevant images can be selected randomly from the web. From the RFs that are constructed (one for each descriptor), we compute the weights for each modality in the following way. From the out-of-bag (OOB) error estimate of each modality's RF, the corresponding OOB accuracy values are computed. These values are computed for each concept separately. Then the values are normalized and serve as weights for the different modalities. Finally, each image is represented with a vector that includes the scores for each predefined visual keyphrase.

It should be noted that the visual concept/keyphrase detectors perform decently for specific visual concepts (e.g. news studio: 0,5 MEIAP (Mean Extended Inferred Average Precision)), while for some others (e.g. bridge: 0,02MEIAP) the performance is very low (Markatopoulou, et al., 2013). Therefore, the representation is based on visual concepts for which the trained models can perform decently.

3 The Proposed Supervised Extraction Model

Our model, in general, is composed of the following steps:

For each document:

(1) Extract all possible n-grams (n=1, 2, 3) that do not contain stop-list words.
(2) Transform these n-grams into lower case.
(3) Apply all baseline textual extraction methods on these n-grams.
(4) Apply variable selection using Random Forests on all textual features (the results of the textual baseline methods) in order to find the best combination of the textual features (Genuer, et al. 2010).

(5) Extract visual keyphrases for each image and calculate the average score for each visual keyphrase to represent the document.
(6) Apply variable selection using Random Forests on all visual features in order to find the best performing visual features (Genuer, et al. 2010).
(7) After the feature selection two fusion techniques are investigated:
    a. Early fusion: Concatenation of the textual and visual vectors in a single vector. In the case of unsupervised tasks (e.g. retrieval, clustering) the L1 distances between these vectors are considered to compute similarity measures. In supervised tasks (e.g. classification) we train a RF with the concatenated vector using as training set manually annotated documents.
    b. Weighted late fusion: In the case of unsupervised tasks similarity scores are computed independently for each modality and the results are fused. In order to calculate the weights a regression model based on Support Vector Machines is applied. In the case of supervised tasks we train two RF (i.e. one for each modality) using a manually constructed training set and finally we apply weighted late fusion based on the OOB error estimate using the approach mentioned in chapter 2.

4 Conclusions and Future Work

The proposed approach is work in progress so specific results are not yet available. However, initial results using weighted late fusion (based on OOB estimate) of textual features and visual low level features for a representative (i.e. histograms and not concepts) have shown that the results are improved when compared to the ones generated with using only textual features. The next steps of this work include application of the proposed method to retrieval, clustering and classification problems of web pages and news articles, which include multimodal information such as text and images.

Future directions for research are: (1) Developing additional baseline methods for keyphrase extraction, (2) Applying other ML methods in order to find the most effective combination between these baseline methods, (3) Conducting more experiments using additional documents from additional domains (5) Development of Methodology for predefined visual concept selection, and (6) Applying ML to extract keyphrases using both textual and low level visual features.

Concerning research on additional domains, there are many potential research directions. For instance the following research questions can be addressed: (1) Which baseline extraction methods are good for which domains? (2) Which are the specific reasons for methods to perform better or worse on different domains? (3) Which are the guidelines to choose the correct methods for a certain domain? (4) Can the appropriateness of a method for a domain be estimated automatically?

Acknowledgment: This work is supported by MULTISENSOR project (FP7-610411) partially funded by the European Commission. The authors would like to acknowledge networking support by the COST Action IC1307: The European Network on Integrating Vision and Language (iV&L Net) and the COST Action IC1002: MUMIA.

References

1. Anna Bosch., Andrew Zisserman, and Xavier Munoz. 2007. Image classification using random forests and ferns. In ICCV, pp. 1-8.
2. Leo Breiman. 2001. Random Forests. In Machine Learning, 45(1): 5-32.
3. Christopher Fox. 1990. A Stop List for General Text. ACM-SIGIR Forum, 24, pp. 19–35.
4. Yaakov HaCohen-Kerner, Zuriel Gross, and Asaf Masa. 2005. Automatic extraction and learning of keyphrases from scientific articles. In Computational Linguistics and Intelligent Text Processing, pp. 657-669, Springer Berlin Heidelberg.
5. Fotini Markatopoulou, Anastasia Moumtzidou, Christos Tzelepis, Kostas Avgerinakis, Nikolaos Gkalelis, Stefanos Vrochidis, Vasileios Mezaris, and Ioannis Kompatsiaris. 2013. "ITI-CERTH participation to TRECVID 2013," in TRECVID 2013 Workshop, Gaithersburg, MD, USA.
6. Baoxun Xu, Yunming Ye, and Lei Nie. 2012. An improved random forest classifier for image classification. In, International Conference on Information and Automation (ICIA), pp. 795-800, IEEE.
7. Robin Genuera, Jean-Michel Poggi, and Christine Tuleau-Malot. 2010. Variable Selection using Random Forests, In Pattern Recognition Letters 31(14):2225-2236.

Towards automatic annotation of communicative gesturing

Kristiina Jokinen
University of Tartu
Estonia
kristiina.jokinen@ut.ee

Graham Wilcock
University of Helsinki
Finland
graham.wilcock@helsinki.fi

Abstract

We report on-going work on automatic annotation of head and hand gestures in videos of conversational interaction. The Anvil annotation tool was extended by two plugins for automatic face and hand tracking. The results of automatic annotation are compared with the human annotations on the same data.

1 Introduction

Hand and head movements are important in human communication as they not only accompany speech to emphasize the message, but also coordinate and control the interaction. However, video analysis of human behaviour is a slow and resource-consuming procedure even by trained annotators using tools such as Anvil (Kipp 2001). There is an urgent need for more advanced tools to speed up the process by performing higher-level annotation functions automatically.

We use two Anvil plugins, a face tracker (Jongejan 2012) and a hand tracker (Saatmann 2014), that automatically create annotations for head and hand movements. Objects are recognized based on visual features such as colour and texture, and Haar-liked digital image features, using OpenCV framework. Motion trajectories are estimated by calculating the mean velocity and acceleration during the time span of a set of frames (we experimented with 7 frames as more than 10 makes the algorithm insensitive for quick, short movements). Movement annotations with respect to velocity and acceleration are marked on the appropriate Anvil track, to indicate the movement and its start and stop. The interface has controls for minimum saturation threshold and for how many frames to skip (Figure 1).

Figure 1 Anvil interface of the new hand tracker plugin.

2 Comparison of human and automatic annotations

Compared with human annotation the trackers are good at detecting some movements but prone to mis-detecting other movements. Problems occurred e.g. when the hue of the hands was similar to the background colour, or if the direction of the movement is reversed quickly, so that the time span is not long enough to detect velocity up to the thresholds (short head movements). Acceleration annotation did not recognize movements if they start and stop slowly. Changing the detection threshold can improve results, but is a trade-off as it prevents small movements being detected. However, the plugins will be of great help in multimodal analysis. Using the plugins reduces the time spent on annotating these movements, which in turn results annotations in increased productivity.

Proceedings of the 25th International Conference on Computational Linguistics, pages 124–125, Dublin, Ireland, August 23-29 2014.

Here we present a more detailed analysis of the human and automatic annotations with reference to face tracking. The annotated hand and head movements are listed in Table 1. From the collected data we used four sample videos, each about six minutes long, altogether 45 303 frames. Table 2 shows the number of elements automatically recognized using velocity and acceleration, with precision scores, i.e. manually annotated gestures correctly recognized by the automatic annotation.

Head movements		
Nod down	Backward	Waggle
Nod up	Forward	Shake
Turn sideways	Tilt	Other

Hand movements
Both
Single
Complex
Other

Table 1. Annotation features for head and hand movements.

Gesture	**Manual annotation**	**Velocity**	**Acceleration**
NodDown	149	110 (74%)	108 (72%)
NodUp	42	15 (36%)	27 (64%)
TurnSide	40	29 (73%)	27 (68%)
HeadBackward	27	18 (67%)	14 (52%)
HeadForward	21	17 (81%)	18 (86%)
Tilt	57	35 (61%)	29 (51%)
Waggle	12	11 (92%)	8 (67%)
HeadOther	3	2 (67%)	1 (33%)
Total	**351**	**237 (73%)**	**232 (66%)**

Table 2. Manual and automatic head movement annotations for 4 videos.
Precision: Velocity 73%, Acceleration 66%

Figure 2 shows two examples of the annotation results on the Anvil annotation board, one where the face tracker recognized head movements appropriately, and one where the face tracker "invented" movements which the human annotator does not recognize as communicative gestures.

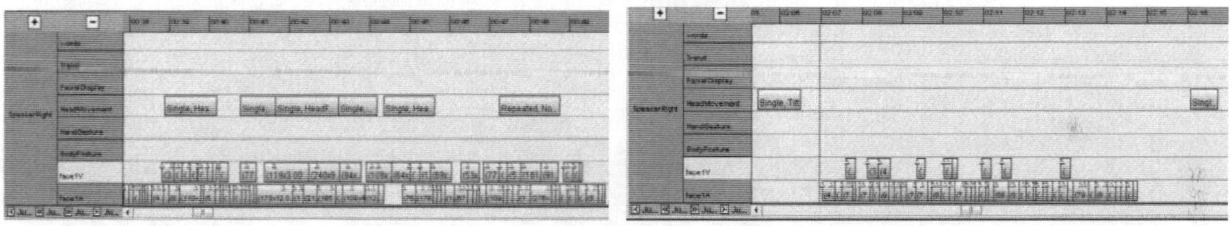

Figure 2. Face tracker detecting manual annotation categories (left) and inventing face movements (right).

3 Future work

Following the work outlined in Jokinen and Scherer (2012), we will compare the top-down linguistic-pragmatic analysis of movements with the bottom-up signal-level observations. We will also use a machine-learning approach to analyse if there are any systematics with the problematic cases. We may also explore if a recognized movement can be automatically interpreted with respect to communicative intentions. In human-robot interaction, the automatic gesture recognition model can be used to study the robot's understanding of the situation and of human control gestures, cf. Han et al. (2012).

References

Han, J., Campbell, N., Jokinen, K. and Wilcock, G. (2012). Investigating the use of non-verbal cues in human-robot interaction with a Nao robot, in *Proceedings of 3rd IEEE International Conference on Cognitive Infocommunications (CogInfoCom 2012)*, Kosice, 679-683.

Jokinen, K. and Scherer S. (2012). Embodied Communicative Activity in Cooperative Conversational Interactions - studies in Visual Interaction Management. *Acta Polytechnica Hungarica.* 9(1), pp. 19-40.

Jongejan, B. (2012) Automatic annotation of face velocity and acceleration in Anvil. *Proceedings of the Language Resources and Evaluation Conference (LREC-2012). Istanbul, Turkey.*

Kipp, M. (2001). Anvil – A generic annotation tool for multimodal dialogue. *Proceedings of the Seventh European Conference on Speech Communication and Technology, pp. 1367-1370.*

Saatmann, P. (2014). Experiments With Hand-tracking Algorithm in Video Conversations. *Proceedings of the 5th Nordic Symposium on Multimodal Communication.*

Author Index

Association for Computational Linguistics
209 N. Eighth Street
Stroudsburg, Pennsylvania 18360

CURRAN ASSOCIATES INC
proceedings.com